Walking with Birds

Walking with Birds

An Exploration of Wildlife and Landscape in a Cumbrian Valley

Colin Whittle

Brambleby Books

Walking with Birds – An exploration of wildlife
and landscape in a Cumbrian valley
Copyright © Colin Whittle 2015

The author has asserted his right
under the Copyright, Designs and Patents Act 1988
to be identified as the Author of this Work.

A CIP catalogue record for this book is available
from the British Library

ISBN 978 1908241 351

Cover and plates design by Tanya Warren – Creatix
Cover image by the author

First published in 2015 by BRAMBLEBY BOOKS
www.bramblebybooks.co.uk

Printed on FSC paper and bound by
Berforts Information Press, UK

For Audrey

We shall not cease from exploration
And the end of all our exploring
Will be to arrive where we started,
And know the place for the first time.

T.S. Eliot, *Little Gidding*

No star was ever born out of the struggling intellect.

Sir Arnold Bax

Contents

Introduction

This book is the culmination of a lifetime's fascination and involvement with wildlife, wild places and landscape, centred mainly around my home in the Cumbrian valley of Great Langdale, and described over the last fifty or so years in a series of diaries. These discontinuous jottings record not only direct observations in respect of wildlife – but also reflections on their context within season and, importantly, how the whole relates on a more personal basis. Of particular interest has been the development of a fascination with the voices of birds. This interest was first stimulated at the age of eleven by the birthday gift of Viscount Grey's *The Charm of Birds* in a beautiful 1927 edition with woodcuts by Robert Gibbins. This has been a constant companion and over the years helped to consolidate the conviction that, for me, birds would never be merely names, organised assemblages and maps of feathers, to be collected, ticked off in lists of one kind or another – year lists, country lists, life lists and so on. The other growing conviction was that the birds that mattered most to me were those of my daily life within my own landscape, although I have written about, photographed, studied and sketched wildlife in many of Britain's wild places, I remain essentially a 'home-patch' man – dedicated to the wildlife and landscape of a small enough area for a life-long involvement, but with sufficient diversity of habitat and its contained wildlife to generate a continuum of commitment. By contemporary standards I am a 'bad bird-watcher', completely unacceptable as a 'birder' as defined by today's jargon!

Most of the text consists of transcripts of spontaneously recorded observations made during walks and later transferred directly to the page in the present tense in an attempt to preserve the integrity and excitement of the now-by-now experience. Although in the original voice recordings every note heard, every sighting and bit of behaviour was noted, to reproduce so much repetitive detail within the text is undesirable and material for inclusion has been, I hope, carefully selected. It is by the continuous observation of the ordinary that the extraordinary and more interesting are revealed. I have also referred things of mythological, folk or literary relevance, whether to a flower or a bird or a particular landscape, thus enhancing the prime imaginative response. These excursions ranged over the length and breadth of the valley trying to build up an intimate personal portrait of the wildlife within a specific landscape which, although it has 'a local habitation and a name' may at the same time be regarded as a microcosm of our countryside in general, such 'explorations' meeting much the same local wildlife – and always so much to look at, so much time simply standing still, listening, and always time spent just sitting about on personally designated – almost ritual – 'sitting stones', simply being there.

I have tried to follow two major characteristics of birds as sub-themes running throughout the text – flight and song – represented by Buzzard and Blackbird respectively – the Buzzard because in its varied flight modes it is one of the most characteristic and observable inhabitants of the skies over our Cumbrian valleys; and the Blackbird as by far the most charismatic songbird of our parks and gardens nationwide. A third theme running throughout is that of the superb coast which forms the western margin of our valley systems, and it seems particularly appropriate to follow our own river to its ultimate mouth, joining other Cumbrian rivers flowing into the vast complexities of Morecambe Bay and its wide open shining spaces, where water and mud and air and sun fuse into hazed mystery, and their multitudes of birds slip back and forth between it and the now.

We live in an age of ever-increasing alienation from the natural world, a kind of desperate social sickness in which the priorities are acknowledged to be wealth, status, image, pleasure and instant gratification in almost everything. Man's development has been ever more, and more wilfully, towards the cerebral and away from the instinctive or imaginative modes which are his traditional, essential links with the natural world. I believe it is necessary to find another balance between the often unconsciously acquired corrosive influences on our consciousness by this sickness in what is loosely called the 'real' world – commerce, politics, globalisation etc. – and the reality of our evolutionary place in the real natural world by an ancient genetic right and mode of belonging, of birth and death. I believe it is this latter reality that exerts such a strong, subtle pull on the increasing numbers of people who seek some sort of – perhaps unacknowledged – relationship with landscape and wildlife, for many, probably, more deeply felt than can be given expression. It is, perhaps, better to regard this strong, subtle urge positively as a personal process of re-discovery of one's natural place, rather than the more alienated negativism by which such processes are seen as 'escapes' from the 'real world.' It is such an ongoing exploration of, and re-alignment with, the wildlife and landscape of my own little bit of the world that I have sought to communicate here.

October

1 October

Bright and cool, with early morning mist just clearing the Common and meadows. All the way down river the placid water surface dimples with dew-fall from overhanging leaves and branch ends. The local Dipper flies piping down river from under the bridge where it nests each year. Only a few weeks ago the pair was busy with their fat, grey, rather scaly-looking youngsters as they were introduced to the mysteries of underwater foraging. Now they have gone, and this bird remains the only one to be seen. All's very quiet, save for the autumn song of Robins, both sexes singing until they form pairs later in the winter, and an occasional tinkle from Goldfinches, a sound entirely appropriate to the visual chime of dewdrops pendant from grasses. A mixed group of Mallard picks about the dewy grass clumps, poking into the matted density of their bases; their beaks emerge shining as if glazed.

The river, the arterial flow of the entire valley, is quite low after a long dry late summer, the water very clear, but there's not a fish to be seen in this long pool where I love to sit in the mornings, and where fifty years ago I cast flies for the many small, sweet trout. My diary notes for September 23rd 1962 relating to this same pool read: "There was a great number of trout, somewhere in the region of 300 fish in all. They moved together, individuals within a corporate body, trout of all sizes and colours. There were hardly any further downstream, so this was possibly a gathering for the spawning run which would take them up the tiniest little runnels and gutters in the shadow of the Pikes at the head of the valley." The gradually accelerating and complicated chemistry associated with a long build-up of acidity to a lethally low Ph, the slow leaching into many of our Cumbrian rivers of noxious agricultural deposits from fertilisers to sheep dips, as well as years of acid rain have slowly worked their poison on the once teeming trout numbers in Great Langdale Beck. Mink predation has also been blamed. Despite its present lack of fish, however, the local Pied and Grey Wagtails as well as the Dippers still thrive and rear their young on the multitudinous insects which hatch from river bed larvae. The lack of fish notwithstanding, our resident Goosanders still perform their annual ritual of bringing their youngsters to this very pool to learn proficiency in snorkling for fish!

2 October

A bright, fine morning, with a breeze from the north-west and Robin song from all quarters. A skein of about 30 grey geese came over very high on a north-south heading, shape-changing as it crossed the sky – a sight and sound evocative of distant wilderness.

The 'old' meadow footpath dates from when the field entrance was straight off the road and went down the middle of the long meadow, predating the car park and the construction (about mid-1970s) of the 'permitted' riverside path. This was once one of Langdale's great meadows – cropped for the sweet hay in which in Yellow Wagtails once nested, but becoming casualties of changes in grass culture and the cropping of silage. There was, then, no fenced off river-side footpath – visitors and locals alike (save for the few local fishermen) walked down the middle of the meadow. One of the great pleasures on a warm summer's evening was to stroll

13

up the meadows with the village and Pikes forming the most perfect background, still the finest walking approach to the village. The inevitable growth in tourist numbers wrought a corresponding decline in hay yield, whilst at the same time ever more people wanted to walk by the river. When the field tenancy changed, a new 'permitted' riverside path was constructed bringing with it all the trauma to wildlife caused by increasing numbers of people invading the hitherto undisturbed buffer or comfort zones on both sides of the river. One immediate consequence was the sad loss of Curlew as a locally breeding species. There is always this question of the balance between human pleasure and convenience and environmental degradation with its inevitable negative effect on wildlife.

Other than Robins and an occasional Crow there's not a sound, but both air and ear still resonate with the passage of geese. Between this and the next field a magnificent old oak overhanging the kissing gate the posts of which bear waymark signs, for this is part of the designated Cumbria Way. We cross this narrow field, by-passing the overgrown gutter flowing down to the river – a favourite place for Mallard, Herons and, in both winter and spring, Snipe. To our left rise the glacier-scraped roches moutonnées (a very fine viewpoint for the village and the Pikes) at the base of which is a straggle of thorns from which, in season, the Yellowhammer sings. A splendid feature at the end of this little meadow is a group of a dozen or so large oaks (the Gateway Oaks) overhanging an old gateway from which another small meadow leads to the field edge stream, crossed by a little clapper bridge made from one of those old gate stoups through which holes have been bored at one time to take horizontal poles. Cross this little bridge, over the waymarked stile to the exit where it joins the riverside path now bereft of its former wild informality in the cause of 'enhancement' – a gritted, flattened and rolled 'improved' pavement providing access to all comers.

14

Our little, grey Herwick ewes and their still grizzled dark grey and black lambs graze placidly in the morning sunshine. I pause at my sitting stones by the river as I always do. Having visited the past, and commented on change and all its implications in respect of wildlife loss and the commercial pressures to please an ever increasing flow of tourists, it would be very churlish indeed not to acknowledge that this is my much cherished home-patch and I wouldn't be anywhere else!

3 October

A 'clashy' morning – scudding grey showers giving way to blue skies and bold white cumulus. Four Swallows fly high over Elterwater Hall. Next year's hazel catkins by the bridge are tightly furled, but the many nuts which earlier promised a bumper crop have already been taken. Many horse chestnuts are changing colour, strewing the ground beneath with their polished brown-leather conkers; the beeches, too, are firing up their autumn glory, yellowing rapidly towards shades of russet-brown. This characteristic beauty of the beech is best displayed against a darker background, due to the orderly disposition of its leaves, alternate along the branch ends which sweep upwards in an elegant curve as compared with, say, oak, whose leaves bunch randomly.

The track from the Hall to the cottages at Oak Bank is a relatively little-walked area where I've often come across the unexpected – Roe Deer browsing in the open meadow below the path; a Fox lying up under the bank drowsing a summer afternoon away; the local Buzzard perching on the wall; the mysterious Woodcock too, for this mossy, leaf-littered bank of birches has been favoured by Woodcock for many years. Its extremely cryptic colouring and secretive habits make it difficult to study, but it is thought (*The Breeding Birds of Cumbria, A Tetrad Atlas 1997-2001* by Stott *et al.*, hereafter referred to as 'new *Atlas*') to have declined throughout Cumbria by some 40+%. From March to July they perform their 'roding' flight, not yet fully understood but with undoubted territorial function. They're to be seen most often on fine, warm, late spring, or early summer evenings towards dusk. One of the local pairs includes the river as part of its territorial boundary, and its strange, randomly alternated croaky grunts and squeaks are audible some time before the bird itself becomes visible. A Woodcock sighting was always a red-letter evening, relatively scarce as they were even some years ago and I recall a most peculiar coincidence. A strange thing happened in 1988. I had not seen a Woodcock all spring and had particularly missed their twilight performance. On 24th May I made a quarter-sheet painting of a silhouetted Woodcock at twilight flying over the solitary pine standing then at the edge of the village bowling green, and over which a Woodcock had regularly passed each year in its roding flight – one of its territory markers. The very next evening my painted sky actually happened and a Woodcock overflew the bowling green pine! Our native population is augmented each year by birds from Europe and the sense of myth and mystery surrounding this strangest of birds is enhanced by the former belief that these migratory Woodcock spent their absent time on the moon being piloted back to their winter quarters by Goldcrests!

4 October

For the best part of nearly six months the sensation of being swamped by green becomes overpowering, mainly, perhaps, because there is no distant horizon to give a sense of space – the hills sweep up on all sides, from late spring onwards covered with dense growths of bracken. Today there's a welcome touch of autumn in the air, and without wishing my time away I look forward to the seasonal change and its revelations – the true shape and colour of things, the strength and serenity of tree trunks; and the hills, in the clearer, brighter, less humid air, displaying ever more of their detail as each colour comes to sing its own special note, from the exquisite golden ochres and silvers of the ridge top grasses (mountains surely were never meant to be clad in the same greens as the valleys!) past the variegated greys of crag and scree down to the immense, suffocating seas of bracken turning almost visibly from their exhausted greens to russets and ochres.

5 October

To Leighton Moss, the day emerging slowly from a dour start to a midafternoon of ravishing light – all golds and powdery blues. The extensive phragmytes beds are now losing their purple lustre as the downy seed heads form, and the warming sun stimulates the squadrons of small dragonflies hawking above the beds where the air is dense with small hatching insects. On the shallow lagoons Shoveller and Teal bask in the warm hazy sun. The drake Shoveller's white breast gleams in the sunshine, his scapulars sharply white-edged as if etched along the flank. How very clearly the pale nictitating membrane shows against the darkly iridescent green between the Teal's head stripes. Two Buzzards circle over the reed beds to our right, one of them a this-year's youngster, its call characteristically broken in mid-utterance. Suddenly, dark against the back-lit misty brightness of the phragmytes seed heads, a Red Deer hind and calf emerge from behind the reeds, pausing for a few moments before slowly grazing their way to some open ground on the edge of the next large reed bed until they're lost in the vegetation.

At the next pool a couple of rough branches emerging from the waterside vegetation resolve into a Red stag's head and antlers as he basks in the warm sun, the rest of him lying down, hidden. The telescope reveals each antler to consist of two 'tops', one 'tray' or 'trez' tine, one 'bay' or 'bez' tine and one brow tine, giving him ten points and making him, I suppose, about four years old. These are very strong, sturdy antlers with a heavy-looking beam, suggesting calcium-rich foraging in the local limestone woodlands. He gets up, turns momentarily into the light and suddenly the previously seen hind and calf are there with him. He roars. A second hind with calf reveal themselves – group siesta time in the dense vegetation over which large numbers of dragonflies join in mating flight zoom, their wings gauzy and golden backlit by the soft yellow sunshine.

Midafternoon at the estuary hides and the light is exquisite. The declining sun is directly ahead and the reflected blues in the lagoons glitter with pale lemon ripples, whilst the gold of the lower sky seems dusted with delicate, soft powder blues. Most of the birds are silhouettes and identification is difficult – hundreds of mixed waders, some as if drowsing in a blue-gold dream, or preening, others feeding, all silhouetted against this shimmer of powder blue and lemon, accompanied by the repeated cries of restless Redshank and the occasional Curlew from the salt marsh beyond. To either side are hundreds of birds more easy to watch – great numbers of Lapwings in various stages of plumage, at least 400 or 500 Redshank, with smaller numbers of Godwits (both species) and Dunlin scattered here and there. Small parties of Redshank emerge from the shimmering light, white underwings flashed high over backs on landing, and for a few moments the air is resonant with their rather mournful whistles. Large numbers of Wigeon move relentlessly forwards as they crop the grass on the lagoon banks. Very noticeable today is the pungent smell released by massed nettles at this time of the year, but only when warmed by the sun. But the afternoon is changing fast, the sun wades pale and watery through damp layers of drifting grey cloud and by the time we reach home there's a rising wind spinning heavy rain down the valley.

6 October

Somewhat brighter after last night's torrential rains, with showers bowling down the valley from the west, and I have come down to my favourite sitting stones. The river is higher than it's been all summer and the air is dominated by the sound of its various voices, rolling, gliding, rushing. When in full spate like this I feel I can say, as Eliot said of the river at the opening of *The Dry Salvages* (from *The Four Quartets*):

"I do not know much about gods; but I think that the river Is a strong brown god, sullen, untamed and intractable."

I have spent hundreds of early morning hours on these sitting stones, by the long pool at the end of the first meadow, watched and admired many wonderful and fascinating things – little parties of winter Long-tailed Tits like, as someone once said, 'animated musical notes' among the alders; a pair of Crows at their nest on the far bank as devoted and domesticated as any Robin or Blue Tit; autumn and winter parties of zippy little Siskins; a summer dragonfly in her seemingly inexhaustible vertical dance over the shallows dipping and dipping endlessly as she laid over 300 eggs; the play of an early morning mink family; a fox trotting past in the frozen snow on his way home after a night's hunting; the delicate tread of a Roe doe testing the strength of the current 50 yards downstream before committing herself to a crossing; the fascination of trout shadows playing over dappled stones when the river is low in midsummer; the startling electric blue flash as a Kingfisher flies past; the screel of Swifts hurtling like black lightning against the blue; the always fascinating hatches of flies as they rise and fall, like myriads of golden motes in a mist, backlit against the early morning sun; the quiet, confiding pleasure of a few minutes spent in company with one of the loveliest of all our ducks, the female Mallard. Today the wonder is the water itself – that sense of power in the inexorable momentum of its vertical depth over its horizontal bed. The water surface shows a variety of more subtle movement – the interaction of swirl and ripple re-forming continuously into all manner of arabesques, curls and whirlpools, merging, changing direction, form and shape, endlessly hypnotic, complex in the extreme and apparently on the surface only. A 'strong brown god' indeed, hiding his awesome power in the surge of his unseen depths and surface shape-shifting.

7 October

Heavily overcast, mild and windless, the upper valley totally obscured in a dense grey 'atmosphere'. As I leave the house, the unmistakeable wing-flickering shape of a Kestrel, pursued by a few highly agitated Sparrows, flies over the lane. Autumn has played its usual trick with the brackens on the Common – all those along the lower part of the Common have turned a dramatic blend of orangey-yellow and russet-brown which glow against the still dark greens of the brackens higher on the fell.

By 4pm the afternoon brightens a little in the east over Loughrigg. Suddenly, up from the shadowy depths of the river this day is sparked bright and alive by the chinkling song of one of my favourite birds, the Dipper. We are so fortunate here, living with our mountain-fed beck, to know that the Dipper will sing all winter through irrespective of ice or frost, blizzard or blinding rain. Even its Latin scientific name, *Cinclus cinclus* (pronounced with a proper, hard, Latinate 'c', if you please – no degenerate softening of this vital consonant!), being onomatopoeic betrays something of the chiming quality of this song – a warbling mixture of many different, clearly enunciated notes and a bright tumble of double notes and chirrups, bounced out in a manner entirely appropriate to the glittery splash of water over rocks or as if dragged over a pebbly bed. On a brooding day such as this, it is a sound to gladden the heart. In *The Charm of Birds* Grey describes a riverside experience in Northumberland after a succession of blizzards had made huge drifts. The frost was intense, the river frozen except where the swiftest current kept open a channel of water. Wildlife was helpless; farmers were digging out sheep in life-saving operations – then:

> "…came up to us the sound of a Dipper singing its full song, undeterred by the conditions that were distressing all other life, unaffected by the cold, undismayed by the desolation."

The only other sound is the death rattle of leaf fall. Leaves of all sizes, shapes and colours drift down the long pool. Wherever one looks a leaf falls somewhere.

Great Langdale Beck leaves the largest basin of Elterwater (known always as the 'bottom tarn') as the fully fledged River Brathay which has its origins high on the watershed of Wrynose Pass. Here, at the Brathay's exit from Elterwater the phragmytes beds have already exchanged their subtle purples for winter's sere, biscuity tones. On the water are eight or nine Mallard, one dozing Goosander and a Little Grebe bouncing on the waves like a small dumpy kettle. A few years ago at this time one would have expected to see much larger numbers of Tufted Duck, Goosanders and the first of the winter-visiting Pochard, Teal and Goldeneye, but a combination of environmental change and declining bird populations have had their inevitable effect. Flotillas of upcurved swan-moult down ride the choppy surface like miniature Viking longships.

Nordic mythology is never very far away here, for further downstream, just above Skelwith Force, is a long wide pool, and on a summer-sunlit day one can see through the cool, green water to the long, dark green braids streaming in the current where the small Jack Pike hide, tiger-striped greens and blacks, lingering in ambush. But today its still blacks and sombre greens reflect the dark pillars of spruce and fir growing like great cathedral columns on the far bank, their reflections emphasising the funereal sobriety of this lovely pool where a lone Swan often swims, recalling Sibelius' *Swan of Tuonela* guarding the dark, mythic underworld of that ancient Finno-Ugrian folk myth the *Kalevala*. Dreaming, however, is shattered by the here and now sudden clamour of Jackdaws making their way down the valley to their evening roosts. 'Daw' is an ancient name, onomatopoeic of its various cawing utterances, and the word 'Jack', meaning small, was added simply to distinguish it from its much larger corvid relatives, Rook and Crow, as the winter-visiting Jack Snipe is distinguished from the larger Common Snipe. Although assemblies of Jackdaws seem to us quite casual, there is nothing random in the life of such a colony. These are among the most fascinating of birds, each with its own place within the very rigidly organised social structure of a colony. The individual notes within such a clamour vary much in pitch as if each bird had its own particular, identifiable voice within the flock, uttering a remarkably wide vocabulary of calls and, despite the appearance of chaos and if watched diligently, the birds will be seen to fly in pairs within the mêlée, sometimes drifting apart but always returning to their mates. In *King Solomon's Ring* Konrad Lorenz, the father of modern bird behaviour studies, showed that each of these calls related to some social function within a very highly organised society and that the success or otherwise of a colony of Jackdaws depends absolutely on the maintenance of all the social rules within the hierarchy – one cannot be downcast on a dull day when the Dipper sings and Jackdaws fling themselves exuberantly into the wind!

8 October

4.00pm – A bright afternoon with a brisk wind straight out of the north, and I set out for the high watershed between Great and Little Langdale up the bridle way known locally as Hullet's Nest. Upstream of the bridge a young Heron peers into one of the rocky pools left by the swirling river rapids. He's a bit clumsy in his passage upstream as if he'd not yet found his 'boulder-legs'. He trips, stumbles, teeters, eventually resorting to a series of undignified flaps to regain his balance. Suddenly he turns and flies downstream under the bridge.

The high watershed bridle-way of Hullet's Nest, named for the 'hullets'– Tawny Owls – living in the adjacent woods, is a steep short-cut to Little Langdale. The woods here stand deep in peace, and the sense of security generated by their still, breathing depths derives as if from inhaling their exhaled ancient silence and strength. After the steepest section, the woods drop away to the left revealing Fletcher's Wood (fletcher as in arrow-maker) across the intervening amphitheatre of Andrew's Field. Its brushy skyline is punctuated by spires of large Douglas Firs on which the local Buzzards love to high perch, surveying their territory in spring. Higher up the path there comes a point where everything opens out and one can look down over the three linked basins or tarns of Elterwater and thence all the way down the valley to the wooded hills above Windermere – one of those sudden, surprise views which seem almost inevitable in such an intimately organised landscape. A gate at the top of the climb separates the woods from the high windy plateau of the watershed. To my right the wet flush where the Bog Asphodel grows, above which the slopes of Howe Banks form the easternmost bastion of Lingmoor Fell. To my left the rough marshy pastures where Fletcher's Red Deer used to emerge to bask in the warmth of the then hay-sweet summer evenings.

At the summit is one of the most aesthetically pleasing views in the area. Bulky Wetherlam's rounded summit plunges into the shadowy bowl of Greenburn, lit by the play of slanting silvery sun shafts, behind which, silhouetted, are the perfect sweeping curves in the dip and rise of the ridge from Swirl Howe to Great Carrs, and thence along to the top of Wrynose Pass. The eye is so preoccupied by the immensity of this mountain view that for a short while it forgets the foreground which sets it to perfection – the eye gently led by the curve of the track, shining here and there with puddles reflecting the sky; the shelterbelt of trees about the unseen farm and beyond, in quite absurdly picturesque perfection, perched on a spur coming down from Lingmoor, the small white farm cottage of The Brow. Here I have one of my favourite sitting stones! In the wind it is particularly exhilarating and the rain can lash horizontally across obliterating everything, but the evenings are magic because the illumination and radiance in the sky to the west, generated by the unseen sunset and the sea, tell you surely that Valhalla is out there somewhere!

I never cease to be astounded at the 'emergency' reserves within wild creatures, a latency of power for sudden action above and beyond the normal demands of everyday life. About 100 Jackdaws rise noisily from Howe Banks crags for their evening fling in the brisk wind, swirling high over Little Langdale in spiralling circles, like so many black bits gathered by the wind from a fire burning paper. They totally envelop a solitary wind-hanging Buzzard, an obviously intolerable situation to which he responds by shooting vertically up through the black muddle of Jackdaws until he's well above them and can resume his undisturbed sail and hang over Lingmoor. This spectacle was astonishing for its speed and total effectiveness and it's probably seldom he's called upon to perform such a feat, but the ability to do it remains all the time! Remnant sprigs of ling and heather are still in flower, the heather with its tiny burned-out holes drilled by bumble bees at the base of the flower in order to harvest the pollen within. Save for a few sheep on the hillside and the occasional croak of a Crow from the crags above, all is quiet now, but one cannot help but anticipate to when the air will be ringing with Tree Pipits in late spring and circled by Buzzards from their nest on Bield Crag; when the local Peregrine will foray over the crest of Lingmoor and cause a rumpus among the Jackdaws nesting in the old quarry where both badger and fox live; to when the Curlew will leave his long, linked bubbles of sound along the windy watershed and the Snipe will drum at dawn and dusk over the rushy meadows. Meanwhile, the now of real time and the walk back home in the gathering evening.

There's the faintest sound of a Robin's subsong from the depths of a bramble bush. This whisping gossamer of sound is so unlike the Robin's normal song you'd think the same bird incapable of uttering both. Subsong, lacking the full-blooded territorial imperative of full song, is distinguished from it by being much quieter and, in the case of the Robin and the Blackbird, of rather lower pitch (to my ears), although Carrion Crows have a curious subsong higher in pitch and bearing no relationship whatsoever to its normal grating utterances. It is a fascinating aspect of bird vocalisation and is perhaps best regarded as a way a bird has of 'talking' or singing to himself alone, learning to become comfortable with the sound of his own voice, gaining self confidence before committing himself to a final utterance which will have a profound meaning for territory, nest, mate and young throughout the breeding season. It is the sound of a bird learning to communicate with the very essence of his being.

12 October

After two and a half days of torrential rain, the day begins to lighten as the rising breeze shunts rags of cloud about the misty fellsides, occasionally revealing a dark, brooding summit. Everywhere little waterfalls cascade down hillsides – splashes of foamy white among the changing colours on the upper slopes. A lone, low Peregrine, no doubt trying to break his recently rain-enforced fast and looking even more broad and bulky than usual, circles below the mist, dark and menacing. Other birds are beginning to move and it's always a sign that improvement is imminent when little groups of Jackdaws take to the air about the village. The local Kestrel, sweeping from one hunting hover to another over the Common, must work hard lest he stalls in the light wind. He tilts his body into whatever breeze he might catch, tail well fanned, his wings winnowing more or less constantly. Inevitably, one recalls Hopkins' glorious *Winover* "rung upon the rein of a wimpling wing". He surges up to perch on a small fellside thorn. He sits upright, constantly bobbing to adjust focus as the landscape is absorbed and analysed within the burning depths of the brown pools which are his eyes. He remains there for a long time, preening and maintaining a keen and interested watch on everything going on around him. A cock Blackbird comes and perches a mere three feet away on the same branch, remaining there a full five minutes, but other than to turn his head, acknowledging its presence, he remains majestically indifferent.

Strictly speaking, the hovering Kestrel does not maintain a static position but flies forward at exactly the same speed as the wind against him, a balance of forces equal and opposite, in which mode it is vital that the head is kept quite still, the eyesight fixed and focussed. Some idea of the Kestrel's as compared to human visual acuity may be imagined by the fact that were the human eye to head proportion identical to those of the Kestrel, the human eye would need to weigh between two and three pounds. So, whatever else moves – feather, wing, tail, alula – the head must stay still for the eye to mark the slightest sign of activity by his main prey item, the vole. Another attribute of his extraordinary eyesight that he shares with many other birds is an ultra-violet capability which means that his world is seen with a rather bluish cast, so that the complimentary colour will tend to 'sing' against it. When voles move they mark their trails with urine which the Kestrel's vision registers as a bright yellow, and it is this tell-tale evidence of prey presence on which his eyes must focus steady and still, and to which his every slightest movement during hovering contributes.

13 October

A much brighter morning in a brisk north-west wind. The first flocks of Starlings move about the Common and meadows – their wide wing base gives them a very direct, purposeful arrowy flight.

We climb up through the multi-coloured brackens on the fell to walk round Loughrigg Tarn. For the past several minutes we've been hearing that harsh-gargled 'kaa' which gives the game away to all who understand a little Crow – and, as if on cue, a disturbed crow-mobbed Buzzard sails out over the tree tops. He flies low and slow with quite rapid shallow wing beats, unwilling to show his flight silhouette against the sky. This is a Buzzard's cryptic flight, especially when trespassing over another's territory. Almost invisible over the browning brackens, he flies to a small crag to perch and preen. A Robin sings from a thorn high on the fell. His song carries loud and clear, for another replies from the edge of the wood some 200 or 300 yards away. They alternate singing and listening, but never sing together, each needing to ensure that the other receives the transmitted message.

On Loughrigg Tarn a couple of Great Crested Grebes dive together and surface at nearly opposite end of the tarn. How very different they appear in winter plumage, without their breeding season 'horns' – which define the head – and the rich chestnut-brown frill of cheek feathers. In winter the white cheeks and gleaming neck is often the only clue to their presence on the water. Today we see no less than six such gleaming columns revealing their owners' otherwise camouflaged presence on the choppy water.

Later – I've been watching two Robins on the neighbouring cottage roof overlooking my feeding table, and which one regards as his property. Robins usually respond to territorial infringements with a highly aggressive flight at the intruder, but not this time. The 'owner' faced up to the intruder, puffed himself out, drew himself up tall and raised his head to look over the other's head, thus displaying all the dimensions of his red breast as fully and dominantly as possible. He then sang loudly at the intruder, whose response, instead of the usual flight, was to shrink his red breast by becoming as thin and 'invisible' as possible and, after holding this posture for a few seconds, he fled!

"...Nightly sings the staring owl" (*Winter*, Shakespeare) – everything, however, is late this year; that also applies to hearing tonight the season's first Tawny Owls' vocal duels by which they define their territorial limits. The village surrounds and its gardens have for years been globed round within the hollow bubbles of linked owl song, but this year I have missed them from their stations under Orion. This owl was calling from Fletcher's Wood, well over half a mile away, and carried clearly through the dense ground mist. The Tawny Owl's apparent decline over recent years has caused much concern, and a national census is currently being conducted by The British Trust for Ornithology. Still given green status in the new *Atlas* it has been shown to have declined considerably in Cumbria. Of the two colour phases, the brown is much more widespread, but the less often seen, smaller grey phase also occurs in the woods of Great Langdale.

Traditionally a bird of ill omen, an owl appears among the awesome phenomena portending Caesar's death –

> "And yesterday the bird of night did sit
> Even at noon-day upon the market place,
> Hooting and shrieking."
> (*Julius Caesar*, Shakespeare, Act 1, Scene 3)

With these words William Shakespeare summarised all the centuries of superstition and disaster associated with owls. Certainly, recent ornithological history has shown, alas, that much more portentous things happen to owls than to men when men and owls meet! Those childhood mentors, Wol, Ben and Old Brown are, in hot flesh and death-soft feather,

28

weight for weight the most formidably powerful of all our birds of prey, dire and vengeful in rightful defence of self and nest, as more than one inquisitive human has found to his very physical cost. The wisdom of owls is legendary – all the way from the ancient Greeks with Athene's adoption of the Little Owl as her mascot – but quite unfounded for they are among the most lovely, pompous and brainless of all our birds – but that's another tale!

14 October

One of those wonderful mornings, after a night clear and bright with stars and a moon waxing towards full, but towards dawn developing a dense ground mist which melts up through sunrise golds into the most delicate high powdery blues. It's strange to walk through the sunlit village with Robins singing in every garden, but here, where mist still clings about the densely overhung river, everything is darker and colder. The only sounds are the rush of the river and the rattle of falling leaves. A rather forlorn-sounding call from the still invisible tarn betrays a lone Greylag, circling and calling until it materialises from the mist only to blend back a moment later. Suddenly a Robin sings from across the river as the Greylag continues to circle and call. Other Robins waken as the mist thins, and hints of warmth gradually replace the cold misty damp for now; at 9.15am, two Robins answer each other across the river. I watch one, perched on the topmost twigs of a large sycamore, facing the direction from which the other sings. He listens, then sings, turning his head from side to side as if to scatter his song in all directions, and suddenly Robins are singing everywhere, taking their lead from him.

This whole business of autumn song is full of perplexities, but some of the facts would seem to be these. The Robin's autumn song with its slightly more bitter timbre is also 'thinner' than the spring song. It begins after the post-breeding moult and continues through the winter and spring to the onset of the midsummer moult. During spring the testosterone-fuelled song becomes fuller and richer and is associated with all the challenges pertinent to the territorial imperative – nest site, mate, young etc. If the Robin makes autumn songs, why do not the majority of the other song birds? The seasonal depression of light, even for those few which do sing in autumn, tends to inhibit song and *vice versa*. Note how, on a bright autumn or winter morning the Starling will sit on the topmost of whatever perch is available pouring out an endless stream of exuberant babbling, whistling, wheezing and whatever mimicry he's picked up in his wanderings. The Wren, too, another strongly territorial bird, may sing throughout the season, though not necessarily his full song and, like the Robin, pauses only for the moulting recess before starting again. A brisk October morning may also stimulate a rapid burst of song from the Dunnock, and the Cole Tit may sing through most of the winter. The territorial instinct in some birds, including the Robin, is so strong that they choose specific perches from which to sing and to which they return to utter their challenges time and again. The Blackbird may be taken as model for most of our song birds. In spring he sings his territorial song, it weakens as his young grow, ceases with the moult, and he remains silent, save for the business of sub-song, until next spring. The Dipper may also sing throughout autumn and winter. The Dipper, however, chooses for his song 'perch' whatever stone he fancies at that moment. Simply being well-fed does not answer any of these questions, for autumn is the harvest of the year, the source of food/weight/energy to see birds through the rigours of winter. In some species flight is the prime expression of territorialism. The Buzzard is the obvious local example, defining all three dimensions of his breeding territory by his circling, soaring flight. A bright day with a brisk wind in late autumn, however, sees him resume this behaviour as he defines his winter territory, often at a lower altitude here among the hills. I

30

suppose the closest one can come to rationalising all these apparent inconsistencies is that all birds express the urgency of a spring breeding territory in one way or another – mainly song, but also flight. Some birds resume a form of territorial behaviour in autumn for whatever reason – midwinter pair-bonding among Robins, for example – and perhaps others, like the Dipper and the Starling, may sing simply because they feel good that morning whether their stream is frozen or the sky is blue!

Suddenly, from within the dense river-side foliage two Wrens sing at each other. What a mighty performance this is from such an otherwise unobtrusive scrap of feathers – the slightly curved, needle-thin beak opens, throat swells and tongue vibrates as he scatters his song from side to side, pouring out his seemingly endless stream of penetrating jingles, warbles and trills, beak continuously mouthing this incredible volume of sound, only shutting it when he's finished! Now there are four singing. It's as if, due to this sudden, even if belated change in the feel of the season, someone's pressed a button and the right response is happening at last.

16 October

8.00am – This morning, despite the mist, a feel of something keener in the air following a fairly hard frost, as if the year is returning to a sharper life after the stifling lushness of summer. The fact of survival has suddenly assumed priority and wild living will get harder from now on as the landscape and its inhabitants begin to pare down to starker, harsher realities. As if to emphasise this change, a group of about 80 Fieldfares sweeps over the frost-misted meadows, whilst overhead a large female Sparrowhawk orbits about the pull of her awful hunger.

Down past Kitty Hall the tarn meadows are thick with mist, their silence almost oppressive after the brightness of song in the village. As the mist changes density, it's like the slow unveiling of a new world – strangely imminent but concealing the mysteries of its making – sparkling with dewy birth-waters and being brought alive within some myth where the only realities are not what the senses perceive but what the imagination conjures. The head-high pale, gold-stemmed grasses are linked in a glittering reticulation, each seed-head curved over by the weight of a pendant dew-drop reflecting the world around it, and the seed heads are myriad.

But other realities intervene – Jays grate against the distant air, a disturbed Roe buck barks, staccato and gruff, the sound receding as he moves away from the little rocky outcrop in the middle of his dripping wood. Three shocking underfoot Snipe flash rasping up through a glitter of dew-spray and jink low, whirring over the meadow, long bill down-tipped as if feeling out a flight path through the mist. A group of Snipe on the ground is known as a 'walk', but the collective noun for a group of flying Snipe is a 'whisp', a word which admirably conveys the elusive character of this fine little bird. As they jink from side to side, there's a lost and found effect as they reveal first their pale underparts, their camouflaged upper parts lost against the background on the opposite tilt. Breeding Snipe have declined in the valley over recent years, but numbers still come to spend the winter in these marshy meadows.

The middle tarn has always been a very special place, surrounded by marsh, scrubby little willows and alder carr, and once attracted a very diverse wildlife, from the richly varied aquatic invertebrates at the bottom of a food chain which supported large numbers of fine perch and very large pike to all the birds which bred, fed and sheltered among its surrounding reedbeds. It was one of those rare places, within a stone's throw of a village, yet where one could always feel cherished by solitude, as if in an isolated country at the world's edge. Much of this feeling remains, of course, but ecological and other changes have depleted its wildlife, and the loss of that ongoing life-vibrancy brings a subtle sense of devaluation.

The feeling of walking within a burnished core of sunlight enveloped by the shifting mist enhances the already strong sense of myth and persists all the way via an overhung grassy bank where, fifty years ago, Yellow Wagtails regularly nested, to the little gravelled shores of Ashes Point.

The suddenness with which the rising sun illuminates the marginal vegetation is astonishing – the sun swimming hazily up the mist until it is as if a great beam was suddenly switched on in an almost theatrical, stage-set manner. By contrast, the sun has not yet penetrated the overhanging riverside foliage where it's dim, cold and silent. Two Dippers fly up towards their bridge. One pauses at a stone, white breast and richly chestnut flanks shining in the growing light, nictitating membrane palely flashing like some kind of Aldis-lamp signal. At times he dibbles just beneath the surface, a white-edged flow of water reaming over his head and shoulders. He's joined by his mate and, bobbing like corks, buoyant as day-old ducklings, they allow themselves to be floated downstream, foraging all the while, so that there is constant action, as if to be still for just a moment is intolerable, until they surface, flying back upstream to the bridge which is the focal point of their territory.

17 October

Clamped like a bracket around the south-west corner of the Furness peninsula, Walney Island is about nine miles long, less than a mile wide at its widest point and forms the western boundary to the channels which lead up to Barrow and its ship-building yards. At each end are extensive warrens, dunes, shingle beds and mudflats – important conservation sites. South Walney is particularly well known for holding the southernmost and only west coast colony of breeding Eiders in England.

The tide is nearly full and the afternoon sun sparkles on the inshore channel between Walney and its neighbouring island, Foulney. These two and the rest of the Furness peninsula form the southern centre for Cumbria's breeding population of Shelduck whose ducklings suffer heavy predation by the island's large breeding gull colonies. Many of these large, striking ducks fly in now to bob on the choppy water, a scene of continually flickering pied brightness in the hard sunshine. Bathed within the sun-dazzle of the seaward side the warren and bracken-clad dunes are studded with ragwort hosting Red Admiral and Peacock butterflies. The shore itself consists of a combination of firm, damp sand crazed with bird tracks of all sizes and shingle grading to larger sea-rounded stones at the tideline.

In the brilliant sun-glitter a party of Turnstones is almost indistinguishable from the tide-line stones. A solitary Curlew beats hard against the wind, is forced to deflect sideways before it can make further forward way. Despite the day-glory, all suggests the uneasiness of straightforward lifelines. A circular 'powder puff' of soft white gull contour feathers bears testimony to the recently satisfied hunger of the local Sparrowhawk.

Behind the lighthouse lie extensive gravel pits, a favoured place for waterfowl. Some 70 or 80 Brent Geese take off, the air clamorous with their nasal 'growling' flight calls as individual birds and small groups continually interchange places within the larger group, unlike the skein formations favoured by our other geese. These delightful little geese, no larger than a Mallard, exist in two races, a Dark-bellied race which breeds along the high Arctic coastal tundra of northern Scandinavia to Siberia and winters in north-west Europe, including Britain; and a Light-bellied race which breeds in Spitsbergen, Greenland and Franz-Joseph Land, choosing to winter mainly in Ireland, although some birds do winter here. It's not until early June that they reach their high Arctic grounds for a very short breeding season, leaving again early in September, making them among the earliest of winter migrant

34

waterfowl to reach us. The late 80s, early 90s saw the first arrivals, and their numbers have grown with the years, a most welcome addition to our wintering birds. Hundreds of birds intermingle overhead – Geese, Wigeon, Teal and Mallard – providing a fascinating non-stop spectacle of both sound and movement.

By 3.30pm the tide is fully ebbed, leaving swinging mud flats and bristly salt marsh, its vegetation now darkening into autumn decay. Lapwings stand sentinel-still at the junction of mud flat and salt marsh. Starlings gather on the telephone wires behind the old farm for their pre-roost meal, dropping down into the rough short pasture to strut and probe for insects and grubs. This old ruined farm is the home of the literally fabulous bird we now see approaching like a great white blunt-headed moth. Barn Owls are comparatively rare these days and, with an estimated Cumbrian population of only some 200 pairs, are on the Amber List. It flies low and direct as if buoyed on a moving bubble of air, its wings silent as a falling feather and working with metronomic regularity, scanning in front as it flies and causing a small panic among the Starlings. As well as this regular quartering beat, it is capable of great spontaneous manoeuverability when sensing the near presence of its prey. This buoyancy is the product of a small, light body combined with a large wing area and a feather structure enabling it to fly in complete silence – probably the most silent of all our raptors. Its other major adaptation is the ability to catch prey in complete darkness, famously demonstrated in an experiment as long ago as 1956. That heart-shaped facial disc funnels sound to the ears, with one ear placed slightly higher than the other on the sides of the head so that one ear hears a sound fractionally before the other, an interval long enough, however, to locate the source of that sound without error. This aural phenomenon has also been confirmed by the composer Steve Reich (in an interview with Alex Ross for his book *The Rest is Noise – Listening to the*

Twentieth Century who says, "It's an acoustic reality that if you hear a sound a fraction of a second after another it appears directional." We watch it until it disappears.

21 October

1.30pm – After a clashy morning of showers and torrential rain, a walk round Oak Howe beckons. The birches are very beautiful in the sun – pale gold and copper, lit against an ominously grey sky, the white bark of the upper branches gleaming, leaves flying like shreds of little illuminated copper pennies. Carrion Crows call and are answered, and it's worth noting that even with the much overlooked Crow, unloved and disparaged, there's seldom a harsh 'caw' which is not answered somewhere; call and answer – ancient as earth, limitless as life.

Baysbrown Wood was once managed under the traditional coppice with standards system in which hazel, rotationally cropped as coppice for a wide variety of woodland crafts, formed a harvestable understorey to the big standard hardwoods grown for their timber. The hazels are decaying on their stools, whereas only a few years ago they still bore viable nut crops, eagerly awaited and harvested by the local Red Squirrels right up to the very top of the wood under old Banks' Quarry where on a sunny autumn afternoon they could be found in a sort of drowsy ecstasy of carelessly spread limbs and snug tummies against the sun-warmed heaps of waste quarry slate.

The wood opens out to a most imposing landscape – Lingmoor high and dark against the light to my left, and from which a rough craggy and bracken-clad spur drops down to the valley; the broad meadows of Baysbrown Farm (once the Manor House of Langdale, its name derived from the Old Norse báss = cowshed, thus Brun's Cowshed) overlooked by the entire length of the north-flanking ridge rising to the high pimple of Sergeant Man. Behind and between these two ridges loom the dark bulk of Pavey Ark and part of Harrison Stickle, and there is something about the disposition of the various landscape elements seen from this precise place which make those peaks appear much higher, seeming almost to soar as they do not from any other viewpoint. As if to emphasise their apparent stupendous height, the contrasting squat spread of the farm buildings makes the perfect foreground. Lingmoor and the craggy expanse of Oak Howe Crags with its Needle loom so overhead that it is necessary to tilt the head back to watch the juncture of ridge and sky, always fascinating in a wind as it pours over the rim of the visible world – dense white clumpy cumulus towering and shape-shifting against a brilliant cobalt background which seems to have no anchor to the arching heavens, just fragments, chips of colour, as much at the mercy of the wind as the race of clouds.

An appropriately placed sitting stone provides the right vantage point for watching both the valley and the crag above. Some happy wanderer (whose name I can no longer recall), in a moment of inspired wisdom once wrote,

"Locomotion should be slow, the slower the better, and should be often interrupted by leisurely halts to sit on vantage points and stop at question marks."

It's quite impossible to overestimate the importance of strategically placed sitting stones where one can sit quietly, watching, listening and sooner or later be rewarded.

And there's a Raven wind-riding the crest of the crag, all ragged-arsed and feather-baggy in this big wind, his great head prominent in front of his wings. He's no "sad, presaging raven" (*The Jew of Malta*, Christopher Marlowe), but croaks the ancient geology of Cumbria with a voice like old rocks. Imagine the slow accumulation of silence within a rock over aeons, a silence and a tension so beyond endurance that utterance must be made – that is the voice of the Raven, full of myth and ancient runes.

In the sun-drenched autumn meadows – once hayfields full of wild flowers but now cropped for silage in due season –

a colony of feeding Rooks walks among the rough grasses with senatorial solemnity. Their baggy trousered legs together with the white face and more sharply angled forehead give Rooks the appearance of being the rather more sedate 'elders' of the Crow tribe – an illusion soon shattered when watching the noisy mayhem surrounding a rookery at nest-building time! The corvids are so easy to overlook – large, uninteresting black birds to most people – and I suspect that it is a case of over-familiarity breeding not necessarily contempt, but in-visibility, perhaps. They all express great presence and attitude. Arrogance characterises their walk, strutting their stuff as they move about their chosen feeding patch, probing, strutting a few steps and probing again, rolling their carpal joints forwards as if preparing to elbow their way through a crowd!

3.30pm – A Buzzard soars high above the valley, its call the clear ringing of an adult. It makes a sudden, fast, steep curving dive towards Lingmoor calling continuously. Suddenly there's another, and then another! They appear as if dropping through holes in the sky, the air ringing with calls, hard and urgent, and all three sail off up the valley gaining height until they're almost lost from sight, until two turn and begin counter-soaring, emphasising not only their continuing pair-bond but also demonstrating their territory. The third bird drops fast from very high and there's a brilliant twinkling flash, a small explosion of light like a star-birth – a shaft of sun catching the pale underwing coverts as he dives at the higher of the soaring pair, probably the male – his smaller size and resultant lesser wing loading enabling him to soar higher faster – and now they've all melted into the high mystery of pure light.

25 October

9.00am – After nearly 36 hours of rain, causing extensive field flooding and a raging torrent of a river, the sky is bright with great clogs of cumulus brilliantly illuminated against a clean, washed blue. Suddenly, overnight, there are many more leafless spaces in the trees. Along the riverbank footpath Campions, Herb Robert and Knapweed still flower, but there is neither song nor call nor movement, and the tarns look devoid of life. Ash leaves drift across the path; call and answer from a couple of Crows, one of which is perched in the bare top of an old alder committed to the fling of his challenge – raucous, belligerent, arrogant. Another perches on the most tenuous of twigs in the crown of a large ash – it barely holds his weight. He's head to wind and very alert, scanning, listening, for sight or sound of anything relevant to his here and now. I wonder briefly how he maintains his acuity of awareness because he's never still – teetering, balancing, continually re-adjusting the distribution of his body weight to the non-stop sway and swing of his precarious perch, but he doesn't even have to think about it and this gives him the freedom to maintain his total environmental awareness. Our lives are so ruthlessly homocentric it's sometimes difficult to release oneself back into a life-mode not dominated by thought.

Around the lane end cottages even the Wren is drowned out by the incessant chatter of our numerous Sparrows. What an admirable little bird is the cock Sparrow! He is habitually described as the least inspiring of our birds, drab, dull, dingy, and his mate even more so! But a spring cock Sparrow on a sunlit afternoon is a very neat fellow with his black bib smartly arranged down his chin, widening over his upper breast, the soft greys of his head and rump contrasting beautifully with the chestnut-brown, black trimmed wings and mantle. He may not be much of a songster, but he compensates for that with his indefatigable energy in whatever he does. Chaucer, in *The Parlement of Foules*, does not describe him as 'Venus sone' for nothing – he'll attempt to mate at every possible opportunity! For this reason sparrow eggs were once popular as an aphrodisiac, although the rather more censorious Aristotle called him "of all birds the most wanton". The newer estates in the nearby towns rarely see a Sparrow. Once so ubiquitous and numerous, he is now rather a celebrity on the amber list and his future is uncertain. We are fortunate to have a large colony making full and traditional use of the stone walls from which our cottages are built, and from which they commit totally to their energetic life-style – gossiping, squabbling (often), mating (often), nest making, feeding and bathing – busy-busy life-affirming little birds, a pleasure to have around!

26 October

8.45am – Another mild morning as I walk up by Elterwater Hall. Dawdling is essential along here because there is invariably something of interest, no matter how commonplace. Thoreau in his hut at Walden Pool speculated, among many other things, on the etymology of the word 'saunter' and settled happily on 'sainte-terre', literally 'holy ground', thus endowing the activity with associations of pilgrimage and meditation. The casual glance reveals little, but by standing still and silent one gradually becomes aware of a range of unseen activity for there is a constant tinkling chime all around, from the more obvious Chaffinch 'pink' to the soft, almost whispered 'ticking' of tits; or a flash of movement caught in the corner of an eye, literally the tail end of a flight as some small bird disappears into a bush. Some yards further along stands a male Blackbird. His immediate reaction to my approach is not to fly but to freeze, pretending that he's not there – a technique perfected by Tawny Owls during the day. 'If I'm quite still, you can't see me, because my life and reactions are movement (and hearing) determined' – might be a translation of his attitude. We maintain this tense *status quo* for as long as it takes him to 'realise' two things – if I'm not moving then, possibly I'm not there either, and even if I am I'm still outside the tolerance limit of his immediate personal space and, having confirmed this for himself, he resumes his search for food items among the fallen leaves. One of the great rewards of watching wildlife is to become personally involved with processes in which cerebration is bypassed in favour of some non-cerebral response reaction, many of the benefits of which we have largely forgotten.

A Robin sings; another, higher up the wood, replies faintly – to my ears – becoming inaudible in the rustling breeze. He sings again and then leans forward as if straining to catch that whisp of song from above before he sings once more. Yet another Robin sings, downhill from him now, so he turns right round and sings in that direction! For some time he alternately sings uphill then downhill, continually reversing his perching stance in order to do so. Two Wrens sing competitively against each other down by the river. One suddenly infringes the other's personal tolerance limit and a minute bundle of brown fury drives it off, the speed and directness of its flight making of itself a missile, almost. This tiny turbulent scrap of bird probably packs more restless activity into its meagre eight or nine grams, more energy and vitality, more volume, more sheer tetchiness and 'attitude' than any other bird. Weight for weight, the Wren is as much concentrated bird as even the Sparrowhawk, which lives permanently on the very screaming edge of avian consciousness.

29 October

1.15pm – Very mild. After another day of drenching showers the afternoon promises to be more settled. The meadows are sodden, saturated like a full sponge. A Meadow Pipit starts up from the dense grasses bordering the top tarn, its outer tail feathers glinting white as the rest of the bird is lost among the assorted browns, greys and tans of the dying vegetation. A male Goldeneye flies off in a brilliant flash of black and white, but the wind drowns out the whistle of his wings. A silhouetted Cormorant sits high on a protruding branch hanging its wings out to dry, giving them an occasional flap to stir some breeze through the feathers. The big problem common to all diving birds is that of maintaining a compromise between waterproofing by means of a preen-oil gland and fighting buoyancy whilst under water. In respect of Cormorants particularly, there is some dispute about the use or otherwise of such a gland and whether or not its feathers are water-proofed as an aid to maintaining body temperature, or water-permeable in order to facilitate diving. Whatever the answer, this heraldic posture has been blessed by generations of photo-graphers.

Near the old boathouse the first Water Rail of the season utters his strange repertoire of squeals and grunts known as 'sharming'. These shy handsome birds are crepuscular in habit and more often heard than seen. Amber-listed, it was once much more common than it is now due largely to water pollu-tion and lowland drainage schemes. They have been regular winter visitors to Elterwater's reed beds for many years and possibly in more numbers than might be thought. I have photographed them from hides here at Elterwater and in other places, observing and admiring the stealth with which they move – their long, widely spread toes distribute the weight, the arrowy bill and slim head and body designed to part the rushes smoothly and secretly, leaving no trace of their passage.

Making almost perfect reflections in the still, open water ripple rings betray a surfacing female Goldeneye. Over a series of timed dives the average duration for females is about nine seconds; for the males about fourteen. They swim astonishingly fast underwater and, I suspect, linearly rather than randomly changing direction, for they cover good distances during the course of each dive. Her golden eye gleams from the dark chocolate-brown head which always seems a size too big and bulbous-cheeked for the body that bears it! This characteristic is even more pronounced in the male, emphasised as it is by the large white spot between the bill and the gleaming golden eye and clearly demonstrates the origin of its generic name, *Bucephala*, literally cheek-headed, from the Latin *bucca* meaning cheek. On this glassy surface the female's wake streams silver far behind her. The twelve male Goldeneyes are variously plumaged – one in adult plumage, the others showing various stages and quantities of grey which must be moulted out over the winter – either first winter birds, or adults in the process still of moulting fully out of eclipse plumage. Yet another has just flown from Dead Sheep Bay – that whistling sibilance of wing has become one of the 'default' sounds of winter Elterwater.

The late October air is still dense with midges, but the season has been exceptionally mild, and many of the trees when viewed en masse show little change of colour. But the Fieldfares, Snipe, winter waterfowl and Water Rails have arrived, so perhaps things are moving at last. The silence here is as smooth and almost as tangibly glassy as the water, and into this a single Robin projects a thread of sound, sharp, like a fine hot wire drawn through the ear. A Heron flaps with measured wing beat towards the far side of the lake, where, when settled, he stands hunched and motionless staring into the reedly margins of the lake as if mesmerised by its emptiness. As it swung round to land it seemed not only to broaden its wing surface (an effect of perspective), the alula quite prominent, but also fanned its tail, extending it laterally so that there was only a minimal gap between its leading edge and the trailing edge of the secondaries. Other than the protruding legs and neck, it presented an almost vulturine soaring flight silhouette.

31 October

A fine afternoon for a change, cloud capping Wetherlam, but further into the centre Bowfell and the Pikes are well clear. Up on the Common a Buzzard circles low before gliding towards the fellside crag-ends, almost unseen against the uniformly dark tones of saturated bracken. Near the top of the old road a female Kestrel swings down the fell, casting up to hover about

30 feet above the bracken. As the breeze freshens, she does not have to work so hard, and for several seconds the only movements are continual adjustments to the fan and tilt of her tail and perhaps the slightest wingtip shakes. She dives steeply down to the brackens, at the last moment raising her wings to slip the wind, and uncurls her hard-clenched yellow-fisted talons. The pounce was unsuccessful. She casts up once more high over the ridge where she displaces a couple of Crows before dropping down the fellside to hover yet again. In this way she moves about the fellside from hunting pitch to hunting pitch and what all these variations in her hovering modes tell us is something we would not be aware of were it not for her to inform us – that with each tiny undulation and unseen irregularity across the outspread surface of the fellside the many changes in air movement are so imperceptible they are measurable only by the adjustment of a feather.

Meanwhile, up on the ridge, the two disturbed Crows indulge a wonderful display of synchro-flying and mock-diving, not unlike that performed by Ravens when pair-bonding. Each curve and turn made by one bird is immediately echoed by the other as if by reflex as they weave about the sky. Crows often form pairs and exhibit autumnal sexual behaviour before the establishment of territory. This exploratory pre-bonding behaviour reminds us that other species also exhibit similar tensions between fight, flight and bonding – Buzzards, for instance – and imagine with what enormous care a pair of Sparrowhawks must approach a process of bond-forming strong enough to support eventual mating. The male is at least a third smaller than his large and powerful mate, and their courtship is a tenuous and fragile borderland between aggression and acceptance, strung up to the very last nerve.

At 4.25pm it's becoming dusk now that we are restored to GMT.

November

1 November

The Feast of Samhain, one of the two great Celtic doorways of the year, their first day of winter – my favourite season, with that sense of restfulness in the slowing down of the earth's breathing into a sleep which promotes an ease and quiet of being in the observer. If the forthcoming season runs true, all that muggy humid warmth of summer with its rank growth and excess of greens will be purged, cleansed by something that smacks of the hostile, of wilderness in the offing drifted down from the north. The air will sharpen, and on the hill every crack, crag and gully will ring out clear-cut as though viewed through the cold lens of a hawk's eye and the horizons will tauten forwards. There's so much to enjoy – the stark structures of trees communicating their serene strength; the deep quietness of the lowland landscape resting; the passage of hard light on the fell with the clear songs of its individual colours – the silvers and bleached golds of ridge-top grasses, the multi-faceted, variegated greys of great and little crag ends. There's the magic of frost, the adventure of snow, the huge bowling briskness of cumulus tinged with yellow for wind, the dangerous excitement of great gales! And the birds! All those waders and waterfowl which pipe in the north, the mysteries of high latitudes and remote, lonely places with their cries and wild ways, bringing with them a most welcome touch of wilderness under bitter arctic stars to landscapes hedged, fenced and managed. There may be much inconvenience in winter, but to experience the landscape stripped bare, laid naked, is a return to essentials, even extremities perhaps, sensing in the wildlife that surrounds us the urgency of priorities – food, shelter, survival – which, in the comfort of our modern lives, belong in the almost forgotten pages of age-old storybooks.

Although it's nominally winter, however, its reality still seems remote. Among the Blackbirds foraging along the footpath edge is a young female – already predatory as a hawk with her pounce and stab routine – and a first winter male, turning leaves with a quiet fury of impatience. A Buzzard sails out of the wishing-gate oak at the bottom of the long meadow. He soars in tight circles, fast in the wind, turns against a patch of blue, and there's a brief moment in his spiral when his underparts are as if spot-lit by the low sun and that gleam, like a revelation, shows every detail of his under-wing plumage. One of Ted Hughes' poems, *Buzzard*, contains the following lines:

"Oh beggared eagle! Oh down-and-out falcon!...
Too low-born for the peregrine's trapeze, too dopey
For the sparrowhawk's jet controls –
Where's the high dream when you rode circles
Mewing near the sun...?"

Here Hughes is concerned with the Buzzard in a context more of falconry than natural history, comparing it with the dramatic hunting performances of Sparrowhawk, Peregrine and Eagle. The word 'Buzzard' came from the French into our Middle English as 'busard' – a stupid, worthless, slow-coach – purely from a 'sporting' point of view. In reality the Buzzard is a very successful raptor, taking anything from beetles and worms when following the plough, to frogs, moles, young crows, carrion even, and rabbits, and I once came across a Buzzard that took a Tawny Owl – no mean feat! Its re-markable tube-shaped eyes with their large image-size retinal

46

capacity are equipped with *circa* 5 times the human density of photoreceptors, critical for delivering maximum visual acuity. In practical terms this means a distance and resolution capability enabling it to see a moving rabbit – in colour, more-over – at about 1,500 yards, so that when a Buzzard soars, whether in hunting or territorial display mode, it maintains a constant sharp focus over a large area, getting his food where he finds it in a manner most convenient to himself – which endows him with a behavioural integrity equal to any Peregrine or Sparrowhawk! I follow my shining Buzzard's 'high dream' out of sight, content to let this image ride with the bird, not bothering the mind with thoughts of territory or display – time enough for the real world; let's make a little time for the realities of poetry!

The wind gusts stronger and cooler – suddenly the air is thick with leaves torn from the trees in ragged banners enhanced by the effects of counter-lighting – the dance of leaves flick-flickering highlights in the sun against the darkness of the shadowed fellside, but very dark against the lit sky. The gust dies as quickly as it rose, the leaves lose their wind-borne vitality and do not fall so much as subside gently, whirling and gyring to the ground, rattling against the empty branches as they fall. Several Carrion Crows feed in the sodden meadows, their beaks overlaid with wet soil; handsome birds, all their black shine and gloss shot with iridescence in the sun. Their foraging mode seems quite random; they strut, pause, probe and dig, pushing aside the mat of dead stuff in the grass, searching out a juicy grub, perhaps a beetle or a worm; then walk a step or two before trying again. These birds are obviously very fit and healthy, and this random manner of feeding, much as a wader appears to randomly sample the estuary mud, suggests that there must be ample food among the grass roots. It's now 9.45am; people are appearing on the footpath – it's time for me to disappear.

47

2 November

2.00pm, and clearing after yet another wet morning. A Grey Squirrel is busily gathering materials for a winter nest in the gable-end chimney of the empty cottage next door. It had been wired off against nesting Jackdaws, and it's a Jackdaw rather than the squirrel which is my main focus of interest. It hops along the roof following the squirrel, watching as it inserts its harvest from the gable-end vine before flying back to watch the squirrel at its leaf gathering. After following several such leaf-harvesting operations the Jackdaw flew away, returning immediately with another – presumably its mate. Perched together, they watch the whole operation with great interest until the squirrel disappears and they too fly away. The really interesting thing here is that the first Jackdaw obviously knew exactly where to find its mate, so immediate was the return of the two birds. I think most birds do know the exact whereabouts of their mates within a territory at all times – one of the functions of certain call notes is to maintain contact – Buzzards certainly do; a pair I once watched closely over a full season in their winter territory had their perches disposed in such a way as to overlook every flight path about that territory and from which all the other important perches were visible at all times. With such a system established, together with a known vocabulary of calls, each bird could and did know exactly where the other was at all times. Moreover, it was quite impossible to surprise them because the location of each regularly used perch overlooked not only flight paths but also any other possible approach into the heart of their territory. Jackdaws have a similar pair-bonding, but they also have a very varied vocabulary for various modes of communication, and this, too, is of the utmost importance in such pair awareness as was demonstrated by our squirrel-watching Jackdaw.

3 November

Midday – we have left rain deluging Langdale and come to the Leighton Moss estuary lagoons where many birds gather to sit out the high tide in and around this lagoon, sheltered by a dyke from the wind-blast over the salt marsh. The many bobbing Shovellers and Shelducks provide a bright emphasis on the dark squally water, but for the most part the colours are all muted – variegated greys of reflected sky in the scudding lagoon, groups of grey waders, cold mud. Gradually the eye moves from the general to the specific. On a small island a bunched mass of Knot stands quietly, buffeted occasionally as a corporate mass by an extra strong gust against which they all lean, quite by reflex, for a second only before recovering. In the water nearby stands a handsome Spotted Redshank – an elegant bird, slightly larger and longer-legged than a Common Redshank, its most beautiful plumage reserved for its coverts and tertials, so notched with white along their margins that when seen in good light the entire wing looks as though spangled with pale pearls. The choppy water threatens at times to wash its white belly – only the tops of its red legs are visible. It moves little, at times caught suddenly by a gust which momentarily rocks its concentration as it preens with extreme care and aristocratic delicacy.

A solitary Dunlin stands on the banks of the lagoon with a group of six or seven Snipe, restlessly probing into the muddy grass roots with 'stitching' sequences of rapid bill jabs. These highly camouflaged little birds are, paradoxically, perhaps the brightest waders here – there is very little cover even on the grassy banks, and the lines of the mantle, usually so important in shape-breaking, show clearly today in the poor light. Way beyond them, just discernible on the edge of the salt marsh countless thousands of Oystercatchers stretch in a long, long line, its profile visible through the telescope as a knobbly, irregular, slightly pied edge between sky and marsh, punctuated

49

here and there by the more emphatic vertical shapes of Cormorants.

Always, however, the eye returns to the little island where a pack of at least 500 Knot clusters so tightly bunched that the front row now stands up to the belly in the cold, grey water, as continual shufflings and reshufflings ripple through the birds behind. Behind them stands a rank of Black-tailed Godwits, the darker tip to their bills clearly visible, with one or two still retaining a slight hint of their glorious summer upper-breast plumage. The tide is now well into the ebb, and the Godwits initiate the gradual return to the estuary, their long legs trailing conspicuously in silhouetted flight. A stinging shower sweeps in from the sea, the hard drops causing the now restless Knot an involuntary flinch and a small group flies off, streaming a flicker of pales and darks, like a banner of leaves shredding from a tree. The rest – and there still appear to be just as many! – perform whatever preparations they deem necessary for action after their high-tide siesta – preening, leg- and wing-stretching – pale underwings flashing briefly, like signals throughout the group, shuffling and exchanging places; they are gearing up to go, yet seem reluctant. The water is now so wind-driven that their little island looks almost inundated. The birds stand belly deep, yet still they will not go! What induces these little birds to stand so in bitterly cold water facing continuous stinging rain and wind? They prefer the greater safety offered by being part of a flock, whether it's standing or flying, to taking all the risks attendant on individual action – survival before inconvenience! Suddenly, as if under the spell of a mighty corporate telepathic communication, all the remaining Knot take off with an audible rush of wings like a sharply exhaled sigh, hundreds as one bird wheeling away to feed before dark and another tide enforces another period of inactivity.

One cannot help but be moved by what these hardy little birds have endured over these last couple of hours. When one considers that this is their life-long mode, integral to their being, in addition to the often countless thousands of miles flown to and from breeding sites and winter quarters, one is left with the totally inexpressible in terms of the wonder they stimulate. Surprisingly it's now 1.45pm. The birds have gone, but that little island of Knots will linger long in the memory. Back in Langdale at the ebb of the afternoon the fields are flooded yet again, the river full and tumultuous; it's obviously rained here all day!

7 November

After three days of rain this afternoon is fine, crisp and clear, with a fresh south-west wind. Jackdaws fly high, singly or in small groups, enjoying the strong wind with their usual gusto and providing some exhilarating flying – I've been watching one drop almost vertically in a wind-slipping, high speed, tightly spiralled descent, as if constrained by an invisible cylinder, towards another on the ground after which both resumed flying together as if nothing out of the ordinary had happened. The very few small birds keep as closely sheltered as possible, consistent with going about their daily business in this uncertain, roaring weather, more like the raw bluster of March than November.

Here, on the exposed plateau at the top of the watershed between Great and Little Langdale the wind scours everything stark and bare. Not wild enough, however, for one of the crag-end Crows which sweeps out and over the ridge of Lingmoor. Flying into this wind, he does not need to flap as he rides the torrent of air along the flank of Lingmoor; he just lifts, tilts and varies the set of his wings in response to all the aerodynamic variations caused by wind and terrain. At Busk Crag he lifts straight up, flung out high above the valley as if he's at the mercy of the big wind, but he rides it, disciplines it, sets his course diagonally across the valley, refusing to be blown off-track, straight as an arrow, speeding across the wind without a single flap and apparently quite unperturbed. It's so easy to overlook these fine birds, with every man's hand and heart against them, but the more I watch and observe, the more my respect and admiration increase; they are what they have evolved to be, at the very top range of avian intelligence, enormously successful, and we should not measure them by human standards.

Down in an undisturbed quarter of Baysbrown wood there is an area of well-spaced, mature oaks, growing from an undulating carpet of moss which treacherously conceals ancient tree stumps, fallen branches and large well-cushioned boulders ideal for sitting quietly, watching and, above all, listening. Up on the watershed a gale blows, the trees and fells roar. Here, however, not a leaf stirs, not a bracken frond sways. Sitting on this mossy stone, surrounded by the huge stillness of great trees in winter nakedness, aware of their immense, silent strength accrued secretly, inwardly, over at least a century, each winter tree a column of solitude, knowing no neighbour, is truly awesome. The distant warble of a Robin sparks suddenly out of the dim, dense silence – when it ceases the ensuing silence becomes a great hole waiting to be filled by some response, but there's none; no need, therefore, for further utterance. A Crow calls in the wood below. Unlike the Robin, the Crow is answered and a dialogue ensues, dying away as the birds move further down the wood and then yet another deafening silence within which vibrates an accumulation of tensions warning of the imminent onset of rain, and it's as if everything has responded to its gathering inevitability and fled this open and exposed woodland before it arrives.

3.00pm – The sky's much darker now. The tiny mercurial figure of a Goldcrest bursts from the shadowy depths of a small nearby yew, restlessly foraging with a succession of rapid stabs and lunges, continually on the move. This, along with the Firecrest, is Britain's smallest bird, weighing a mere six grams!

Its problem is that of all very small birds – rapid heat loss. Some of the even smaller humming birds actually have to lower their metabolic rate and enter a temporary torpid state in order to survive cold tropical nights, but here the Goldcrest and other very small birds must maintain a continuous feeding rhythm in order to conserve body temperature at night, which is why they suffer so badly during very hard times. Its high-pitched voice is often used as a measure of hearing acuity, as with age our senses gradually lose their efficiency – W.H. Hudson called it "the smallest of small songs". It's had various names about the English countryside over the years, from 'Kinglet' (after its golden crown) to an East Anglian name referring specifically to its migratory habits, 'Tot o'er Seas'. A 'Tot' it might be, but a tot with the heart of an eagle! I remember one bitterly cold October morning, 1975, not long after sunrise on the shore near Minsmere – crunchy shingle backed by rough turf and gorse bushes. The sun, hidden behind massy dark purple-grey clouds, was shafting orange beams over the cold, grey-green North Sea, a great swell heaving and spitting curled crest foam as each wave rolled in. Over this hostile sea came large numbers of tiny Goldcrests, flying low across the waves for greater aerodynamic efficiency, so low they appeared to be wave-hopping, only just avoiding being sucked down by those hungry white tongues of foam. They kept coming and, as they made landfall, they did not sink exhausted to the ground but immediately embarked on the one activity vital to their survival after the expenditure of so much energy – feeding, thronging the gorse bushes as restlessly as if they had not just crossed the North Sea! This wonderful scene remains one of my birdwatching highlights, as vivid in the mind now as it was forty years ago.

9 November

A magnificent dawn this morning with dramatic contrasts between coloured light and much darker background shadows.

To the east everything is blue and smiling, sunlight sparkling over the wet meadows, with long transparent shadows cast slanting by the riverside trees. To the west, however, the birches on the hill above the village shine with an almost unreal orange, vivid against the looming dark mass of Lingmoor, and the brackens glow a strangely luminous rosy pink.

The early sunshine has stimulated some song rehearsal – a Goldfinch sings very quietly to himself in a sustained, quite musical, sub-song rather than a full song; and, almost inevitably, yet another Crow – sitting up in the meadows ash tree quietly practicing his 'bowing and bawling' routine, but not really seriously, and with no one movement carried right through to the end, being constantly interrupted by an apparently urgent need to preen somewhere. It's all very quiet and restrained – for a Crow! – and no doubt he too, like all the birds which must learn their voices and practice their songs, has routines and utterances to perfect before he manages to synchronise his bow with the assertive bellow it will have become by next spring.

Small parties of male Chaffinches feed among the alders, many of which still retain their leaves. A Robin sings over by the kissing gate. A male Goldeneye is visible against the dark waters of the top tarn with a little Teal-talk from its edge. From time to time pairs of crows cross the meadows; a Rook, its soft skin beak pouch bulging, flying up the meadow in a determinedly straight line as if it had some quite specific destination in mind for hiding whatever items he is carrying.

A party of Blue Tits, a Marsh Tit and a restless group of about a dozen Long-tailed Tits feed in the topmost twigs of a leafless sycamore, maintaining contact, ticking to each other constantly with tiny voices just verging on the edge of being audible. Suddenly they all explode out of their tree and into the cover of a still fully leafed alder, disturbed by the momentary overhead darkness of a passing Raven.

Every day is full of countless similar, almost unobserved events which tend to slip unnoticed through the gaps in our awareness. These, however, are the bread and butter events which dominate a bird's life, and often there's more mystery in these for the observer than in the more obvious, dramatic events which seize the attention. A small event is only a small event and often impossible to interpret until put into context with the life stream of all the other small events which constitute what we understand as a bird's behaviour. Putting it all together in such a way that we gain more understanding is a long-term process, but however much we put together there will always, always be some ultimate mystery – it is so for *Homo sapiens*; why should it be less so for *Corvus frugilegus*!

It's 10am, the first walkers appear on the footpath – time I, too, sought cover!

10 November

A very wet night, but mild this morning with a much brighter sky and a south-west breeze promising sunshine and showers.

At ground and brash level it's deceptively quiet in Low Wood; a fine mixture of hardwood – beech, oak, sycamore and birch with a still considerable understorey of hazel, unworked alas, but the setting for spectacular swathes of bluebells in the spring – and some very large conifers – Douglas and Silver Fir mainly with a few Redwoods here and there. Their thrashing crowns obscure both sight and sound of any small birds there might be, and the continual succession of detached, wind-blown leaves deceives the eye into yet another futile grab for binoculars! Suddenly, the real reason for coming here today – the flashed glimpse of a white rump as a Roe buck steps like a grey shadow that might have moved from a cluster of ash poles to behind a large holly bush for a few still seconds. W.H. Hudson refers to "that mouse-coloured coat which makes him invisible in the deep shade in which he is accustomed to pass the daylight hours in hiding." At this time of year he has no antlers, but his gender is betrayed by the white blaze of the caudal disc, heart-shaped in the doe and kidney-shaped in the buck. He makes his shadowy way along the wall – very delicately, like Agag, each hoof neatly placed as he picks his way amongst the litter of tree debris and mossy boulders – and cannot resist stopping just once to satisfy his curiosity about this human intruder with an intense, direct and curiously disturbing stare, both of us linked by this concentrated mutual gaze, before he moves on. There'll be a doe somewhere very close, for the pair is much together at this time of year, as, after the midsummer rut, she waits for the quiet of winter for her body to make a start on the development of the embryo she carries – that mysterious process called delayed implantation. Indeed, the Roe is, always has been, a creature of mystery. To many they are merely a garden pest. But there are other realities, and the sight of a Roe, deep in the secrecy of his thicket or, at dawn and dusk, wary at the meadow edge of the wood, has just that kind of mysterious presence, not really meant for our eyes, perhaps, but as if some kind of veil had been lifted and we've been privileged to see into a different plane of reality beyond. This is the heart of this Roe buck's territory and there he goes, neatly over a low wall and across a small leafy glade before disappearing into the darkness of the trees beyond.

Much later, nearer midnight, it is very cold and the sky is full of stars, the east dominated by Orion, each night striding higher towards his zenith in the winter sky.

11 November

10.00am – brisk with sharp showers from the south-west. Two cock Blackbirds face each other from walls each side of the lane; they 'tock' angrily, beaks raised and feathers fluffed up for maximum impression; one quickly withdraws from this confrontation, and the victorious bird immediately starts to preen vigorously, displacing the remnants of his stimulated adrenaline. A Buzzard sails overhead noisily mobbed by two Crows, diving and veering off abruptly but without getting too close! They're not as brave as Jays! They don't bother the Buzzard; he tilts from side to side on his broad span, shoots out a warning foot and sails on low and unhurried towards the far side of the lake where stands a hunched Heron, motionless, like a rather forlorn, furled grey umbrella.

Two male, two female Tufteds and two female Golden-eyes ride the choppy waters of the bottom tarn. They dive continuously and are easy to see so long as the water remains smooth and unruffled – find the rings and wait for the emergent bird – but once a squall comes over, creating a rougher flickering surface, they're very hard to see. A Raven circles low overhead; against the blue he looks massive this morning, and the light is so clear that his throat hackles look like a black mane.

The path on the upper side of the road climbs up through the wood to the delightful rocky outcrops which form the ridge of Little Loughrigg. There's a good understory of hazel growing beneath birch, oak and beech with quite a lot of young ash poles. The horse-chestnuts are often the first to turn, conkers and seedcases littering the ground beneath, but the beeches are the greatest glory – each leaf is variegated – a sere russet/brown towards the tip blends back into an orangey-yellow which in turn becomes yellow-green with ever more green as the leaf approaches the stem where the very last vestiges of sap run into it. This colour recession from leaf tip to stalk reflects the chemical changes taking place as the tree prepares itself for winter. The green chlorophyll, which has been both the dominant leaf pigment as well as the tree's engine for breathing and gaseous exchange, is gradually reduced as temperatures drop, allowing other chemical pigments, activated by sunlight, to dominate according to tree species – the browns, yellows and golds of these beeches, the flaming reds of maples and in plants like bramble and Herb Robert. At the moment, as many of these trees prepare for the final act of complete leaf fall, the overall impression is a tone of green-gold shading to a russet-gold according to the way it is lit.

A fox passed this way last night, his very fresh scat shining with purple-black elytra shards – the beetle wing-cases he cannot digest. The scat characteristically tails off to an elongated, attenuated end and, judging by the way it has dropped onto the path, our fox was going uphill towards a straggle of exposed, wind-blasted larches marking the crest of the ridge where now a wonderful rainbow arches across the ridge towards Loughrigg. These little rocky knolls make ideal perches for lingering over a flask of coffee and relishing one of the finest views in the area. The very highest places do not necessarily offer the finest views – there's no perspective of height or depth. From these medium heights all the elements of three-dimensional perspective combine to the very best advantage, particularly here as the eye travels westwards by Wetherlam over the Crinkle Crags and the ever magnificent summit pyramid of Bowfell, behind which Esk Pike and Great End are pushed back into their proper perspective and proportion by the much closer-looming Langdale Pikes.

Suddenly, appearing out of the bright sun to the south-east like a little black shooting star but gaining identifiable shape very rapidly, a male Sparrowhawk streams down the wind, very high, very fast, changing direction only to enter another sweeping, swinging turn. He moves about the sky at a tremendous speed, and is soon lost – true to all shooting stars.

13 November

A superb sunrise and a brilliant morning with a cloudless sky stimulating either courtship or rivalry between two Dunnocks up the lane. Piping vigorously and lit by the sun, tail-flicking and wing-waving their semaphore signals about the shrubbery, the birds were transformed – head and breast so often described as 'leaden' enlivened to soft pastel blue-greys, their eyes shining like wet beads.

High in an oak by the bridge a Great Spotted Woodpecker perches, his red under-tail coverts brilliant in the morning sun; as it flies off another follows, white underparts shining, the red under-tail flashing behind him, trailing in the eye like the tail of a comet. There's a strange intensity in the air this morning. Certainly all the birds seem very excitable, hyperactive even, but we've not had a morning like this for well over a month – and I wonder if it's simply this they're responding to, or do they know something about a possible change in the weather of which we're as yet unaware? A cock Blackbird sits in a gleaming silver birch perched in such a way that he receives the sun broadside on, his right wing dropped in order to present as big a feather surface to its warmth as possible, stimulating movement from the feather mites he will later remove as he preens – how he shines! He's quite motionless, looking drowsy in the unaccustomed sun, but not so drowsy that he doesn't see me approach along the lane, instantly alert, ready to fly.

In the long pool above the weir swim two male and one female Mallard – a pair and what looks like a hopeful hanger-on! We'll call the paired male Drake A, the hanger-on Drake B and the paired female Duck A. Drake A keeps a very wary eye on the unattached Drake B; the female, Duck A, is totally unconcerned about either. Drake A makes a significant tactical move, interposing himself between the other two. Drakes A and B now sit on the water facing each other preening with enormous gusto, not yet close enough for physical action, and the preening is therefore an aggression displacement activity. The slow current plays its part in this little drama and drifts the two rivals far enough apart for both aggression and its displacement to be deemed no longer necessary – apparently – until, quite suddenly Drake A decides he must shunt Drake B further down the pool for the current slowly brings Drake B and Duck A inexorably closer together once more. This whole sequence is repeated several times until both Drake A and Duck A swim fast, aggressively, grunting and whistling at Drake B. Enter right, Duck B – a new member of the cast! Duck A takes an instant dislike to Duck B and they face each other with much head bobbing and subdued whistling. We now have a most interesting situation: the former unattached Drake B likes the attached Duck A; the newly arrived Duck B seems to like the paired Drake A; but no-one wants the unattached Drake B who seems to be the source of most of the problems. Drake A now chases Drake B right down to the tail of the pool and he returns to the ducks – they seem to find his dominance attractive. While the two ducks join forces to drive away Drake B, Drake A (the Alpha-Drake) bathes vigorously until he decides that Duck A is the girl for him, and the happy pair flies off leaving Duck B, still unattached and quacking noisily, and Drake B, still unattached, swimming off in the opposite direction. What drama!! Who needs television!

A Green Woodpecker yaffles from the ochre-leaved, bleached-bone birches growing on the quarry spoil-heaps by the river. Folklore tells us that this almost manic laughter portends rain, and the bird is sometimes known as the 'Rainbird' – during all the rain we've had recently I haven't heard him once! Nowhere near as widespread as the Great Spotted Woodpecker, the Green has lost considerable ground in Cumbria over recent years due to a decline in the ants which form its staple diet. Whereas the Great Spotted is a 'Green List' species with an estimated 3,000 pairs through the county, the Green is on the Amber list, with an estimated 250 to 300 pairs (new *Atlas*), with their biggest concentrations in south Lakeland, although the Langdale area has always held good numbers.

A Mistle Thrush flies up into a nearby oak and sits perfectly still, his back to me, almost hunched, so that from the ground it looks exactly like one of the kneed bends in the branch. Very, very slowly it turns its head – so very gradually

60

that it almost seems not to move at all – until the gleam of a very beady eye betrays its watchful awareness, remaining quite still for as long as I remain equally motionless. Several Goldfinches flash about the riverside trees and the air chimes with their tinkling flock-contact calls. Edward Grey thought this sound rather 'trivial', but I must disagree. On a cold, grey winter afternoon it's the most cheering of sounds and on such a morning as this like small bubbles of rainbow. I've seen no-one for the last couple of hours, but now the car park is rapidly filling and the village is busy with Sunday people on this most brilliant of sun-days – time for me to go.

16 November

Newbarns, near Arnside, stands almost at the mouth of the long arm of estuary into which the rivers Gilpin, Bela and, mainly, Kent flow draining off the fells into the huge expanse of Morecambe Bay. The tides flood right up into the mouths of these rivers making this one of the most dangerous areas of coastal water in the entire north-west, with channels, hidden gullies, quicksands, surging currents, all of which may change, be relocated, from one tide to the next. At the same time this vast expanse of mud and its huge bio-content in the form of marine worms, large and small shellfish, combined with its daily tidal renewal make this bay one of the most important staging, migratory and wintering locations in Europe. At full ebb, on a fine day especially, it is a magical place and it is with enormous and serene satisfaction that the eye first rests on, then traverses the long, sweet curves made by channels and gullies which only tidal waters seem able to create, its sense of wilderness enhanced by the varied calls of many species of wader.

On the edge of the tide is a small area of salt marsh where a little row of Redshanks preen and doze. In the middle of an adjacent meadow a Heron stands motionless, the low sunlight just catching the line of very fine little tufted feathers beneath the lower mandible, making a pale transparent fringe of them. Between us and the coastal path stands one of this area's fascinating coastal woodlands, growing on limestone with many plants still green on the woodland floor – wood sage, dog's mercury, brambles, with good poles of oak and ash, along with birch, all well grown higher up the wood, but nearer the sea cliff they are more hard grown – gnarled and twisty, only six or seven feet high and bent-backed by the incessant brush of the wind.

This morning's tide is almost flat calm, washing in a gentle rhythm of wide, slow-curved, rocking wavelets suggestive of a restful breathing and which hardly break against the rocks at the base of the low limestone cliffs. A solitary Great Crested Grebe dives and re-surfaces, its literally singular presence emphasising the immensity of its surroundings, their furthest edges lost in a haze which obscures any sense of horizon. Further out into the bay even the wavelets become lost in an almost totally flat, glazed metallic calm, with only the slightest of ripples to betray the tide's breathing. The crest of each ripple catches an explosive flare of very intense light, for a split second only, winking capriciously first here, now there, like dancing Will-o'-the-whisps. Two dark looking Curlews fly up-estuary low over the water, so that the downward beat of each wing very nearly touches the upward beat of its reflection, but the two never actually touch.

The tide is on the turn, and we've dropped down from the cliffs to linger awhile on a sunlit, pebbly beach. Way out in the bay, beyond jagged inshore fragments of weedy reef, pale, elegant shapes tone the surface of the water – curves and arabesques caused by the underlying presence of gullies and channels, revealing also just how treacherous these waters are – the ever-present harmony of beauty and death. It's 12.15, and with the ebb birds are just beginning to move about, the occasional Curlew, one or two Redshank. A Curlew alights on the tip of a weed-strewn rock – facing out to sea, into the sun, its breast glows with soft, warm reflected light, its back in deep, cool shadow. With it arrive three or four Redshanks, the direct sun lighting up the red of their legs and bill bases as if fresh-painted and varnished. One flies a little closer up shore in a curved, gliding flight interrupted by a single rapid wing flick – on landing it raises its wings above its back in one of the most beautiful of wader gestures, like a brief flashed signal. They all pick about in the weeds, shining wet, revealed by the rapidly ebbing tide.

A lazy hour passes all too quickly. From the cliff tops there is a splendid vista of freshly exposed expanses of mud. Little straggles of Black-headed, Herring and Lesser Black-backed Gulls line the edge of the channel, looking immaculately laundered on the shining levels of mud where a couple of Crows dig for small shellfish and worms. The mud is intricately sculptured, an immense bas relief, ridged with regular, waved corrugations, each corrugated ridge itself wrinkled transversely – a surface that holds much water, now reflecting very blue from the sky. Many Curlews and a few Redshanks stand on the revealed mid-estuary mud, calling among themselves. Like the gulls, they are not feeding; some simply stand, others preen, always with a beak dip into a little blue pool at their feet. A party of 25 Mallards is quite happy to be swept down the formidably powerful current, but sufficiently under control to choose their landing place at a gently shelving bank. By 3.00pm the afternoon is shaping up for a frosty night and a brilliant sunset over the bay and, climbing out of Kendal at 4.15, I look back to a most wonder--ful 'Götterdämmerung' sunset over Arnside. Here is balance, poised as we are between setting sun and great round moon rising over the Howgills into a pale, indigo-hazed sky.

17 November

Last night was bitter, under a spectacular moon with a large corona. The morning is brilliant after the hard frost and it is good to tread firm ground on the Common after the mud baths of the previous month. The fells look superb – it's a long time since Great End stood out so near and well defined in every detail; down in the valley smoke from the village chimneys makes a slight blue haze; remnant whisps of early morning mist float about Park Fell and down into the meadows where the golden sunlight reacts with the frosted greens to produce a delicate pale lemon light diffused over everything. The great sweep of brackens across this fellside is full of slight variegations in both tone and colour which initially strikes me as odd since they all face the same full-frontal sun, but closer observation reveals that the slightly paler tones are where the stiff, rather woody bracken stems stand up without hindrance allowing the sun to slightly varnish their surface; the rather darker tones occur where the fronded upper parts of the brackens fall over the stems, obscuring their reflective surfaces. John Ruskin insisted that there's not a square inch of any surface in nature which is not subject to variegation, however subtle – a good test of the sensitivity of one's powers of observation. In the wet flushes where bog asphodel was so abundant this summer, their stems now stand up stiff and pale, like miniature corn stalks shining in the sunshine – real golden rods.

Much nearer Loughrigg Tarn a superb Mistle Thrush sits on a wall taking the sun full on his breast, head up, beak pointing at the sky, almost as if in a day dream. In the lower branches of an old oak a Carrion Crow basks in the sunshine and it too has a 'drowsy' eye – in so far as a crow is ever 'drowsy'! His relaxed left wing is allowed to droop, presenting a glossy, reflective surface towards the sun in order to derive maximum benefit from its rays. Sunbathing is a very important part of feather care, particularly on those rare days in late autumn or winter when it shines with just that extra degree or two of warmth. Accumulated warmth acquired in this way may stimulate feather parasite movement, making them more easily gathered whilst preening, and a thorough preen usually follows a session of sunbathing. I watch him for several minutes – he's so sundrenched he allows me a much closer approach than usual before flapping away across the field.

Up on the fell a Kestrel's penetrating call, persistent and querulous-sounding, betrays his presence on top of an old thorn, half of which breaks the hilltop horizon, so that he sits not only in the sun but against the intense blue of the sky, his back the colour of lit bracken. He turns, his breast was to the sun. He too is obviously sunbathing but, unlike the Crow, he's anything but relaxed. By the time we reach the river at Skelwith, the sun is already beyond its highest point, shining through the trees, cresting the rapids with glinting splashes of light among which a Dipper sings, the bright sparkle of his song entirely appropriate to the glimpses of water-shine so that Dipper-song and river-glint become a sort of 'son et lumière' performance.

The lake, too, is dark with reflection, and as a small group of Goldeneyes and Tufteds swim and dive they create ever-expanding, crest-lit ripples flaring the shadowy water. After a spectacularly flagrant sunset the northern sky becomes the place to rest the spirit – smoky indigo-blues washed with a soft grey, grading westwards towards the Pikes from blues to subtle golden-green blues descending into the dusk. The last Wren sang at 4.30pm; by 5.30pm it was promising to be frosty and the first Tawny Owls were calling by Kitty Hall.

18 November

8.15am – After another very cold, freezing night the sun is just rising, whilst the moon, to the west, sits high above Harrison Stickle. The river steams, unearthly almost, with mist playing in the sun shafts between branches, like the setting for some fantasy. Such mornings tend to arrive slowly, each long-drawn through a land of no horizons; in the frosty fog there is no sky, no land, no water – all mingle and float together, each a dream

65

of the other. Every leaf, every blade is white-spiked around the rim with frost. By Kitty Hall the big ash cascades a continual hushed rain, the whisper of leaves falling. The top tarn steams like a huge thermal pool – there's no visibility whatsoever. It hurts the eyes to look eastwards through the brilliance to the exquisitely jewelled grass-scape of the tarn meadows. On top of one of the oaks a Starling in full song-flow mimics a Mistle Thrush. He's predominantly spot-spangled now, but facing the sun there is just a hint of that purple-green iridescence which will become such a feature in the spring. His bill, too, wears its drab winter brown, but he's exuberant and cock-headed with his partially erectile head feathers and has obviously been listening to Buzzards as well as to Thrushes. His song is a fascinating bubbling performance of wheezes, rattles and whistles with a space here and there for a bit of mimicry. The flocking in to roost of several thousand Starlings as the light falls over lagoons and reed beds is one of the great wildlife spectacles of our countryside, and despite its bad publicity the magic of its massed flight, the sheer exuberance of its song and the pure shot-silk iridescent sheen of his breeding plumage surely entitle it to a more generous public attitude.

Down in the meadow where the soft rushes grow is where the winter Snipe feed. The size and the amount of hoar frost increases as it moves up the stem, so that the very greatest beauty is to be found towards its tip, as it is with the grasses, bent and tumbled into a multiplicity of curves and arabesques – not a sharp angle to be seen – until their seed heads in every minute detail present an extravaganza of frosted chaos, the low sunlight reflecting from all these facets and surfaces, transforming the meadow into a field of light, the real beauty is in the detail rather than in the mass. The middle tarn, too, is a basin of steaming mist. The marginal rushes and small willows undergo all kinds of shape changes as they seem to voyage through this wandering steamy mist. In the first stirrings of the slightest of breezes the grasses wave very gently, initiating a sparkle of minute lights switched on and off continuously over the whole expanse of the field as the sun strikes the frost crystals at different angles, like tiny shards of fractured glass catching the reflected light.

At 9.15am the moon is now sitting right on top of Harrison Stickle, about three inches from the topmost crag. Back at the river a gleaming Dipper has found the only sunlit stone in the dense, cold shadow of the opposite bank. He turns and twists continually as if under the influence of some predetermined, automatic physical response to all the fractured elements of his song, bobbing up and down, nictitating membranes flashing like a signal. Although his song seems unending, most of his notes are short, staccato jingles interrupted now and then by longer, rather wheezed notes. It may be a platitude, but if ever there was a song to be sung near the sunlit sparkle of cascading water, this is it! He's been singing non-stop for about four minutes, never still, continuously re-adjusting his position until he flies up on to an overhanging birch branch, still singing. Suddenly, without warning, he fly-dives off his branch into the deepest, swiftest current and is swept downstream, foraging vigorously to either side until at last he lies floating on top of three feet of quiet water from which he takes off and flies away upstream. Later I find him standing among wet shillets and still singing his broken shards of warble.

Between our back door and a wilderness of untended garden giving on to the meadow slopes the slate roof of an old uninhabited cottage. One of our adult Blackbirds has an extraordinary talent for split second timing whilst drinking from rain water trickling down this slate roof, judging the exact moment when the flow of water downwards forms a drop on a slate's lower edge, then putting his bill delicately to it, collecting it before it falls. This seems to be his preferred mode of drinking when it rains despite there always being a good provision of much more easily available fresh water.

20 November

Another bitterly cold night but a different sort of morning, the valley head dense with seething mists.

9.45am – Up Hullet's Nest: a solitary Blue Tit forages methodically along a dead hazel twig, picking off the bark in its search for insects with sustained determination. It is on its own, with neither call nor sight of others moving about nearby – perhaps flock membership stimulates a more restless as well as a much safer, anti-predator mode of feeding rapidly from tree to tree, finding rather than searching, but the compulsion to move in this way is removed when on its own.

On the watershed there is the always fascinating spectacle of atmosphere building and boiling in the bowl of Greenburn, sending almost transparent trailers of mist across the slopes of Lingmoor, subtly diffusing the sunlight on crag ends and softening the russet brackens to almost pink. Down the lonnin from Dale End to Little Langdale hazels are still in full, though now yellowing leaf, whilst beneath them in the sheltered tangle of the hedge bottom, nettles and many ferns are still green and some of the brambles are still flowering along with the Herb Robert and Red Campion. All this whilst the fields are white with hoar frost and ice is treacherous underfoot! Little Langdale Tarn sports a wind-crazed coating of ice, save for round the margins where reeds and alders are mirror-reflected. A Water Rail screeches in the distant rushes – its voice carrying far on such a still morning.

Back down at Skelwith the brief midday thaw is over – drops are clear, gravity-defying pendants from leaves and branches, waiting for that final stiffening into ice globules. Ice rims the river and all the basins of Elterwater, although rimmed with dark water, are iced over after a week of freezing conditions. The immaculate white wedge of an upended Swan points up towards the ever-thickening cloud. Up near the bridge, however, perched on his favourite boulder in the middle of the river, a Dipper makes his bright, babbled magic.

The village is very busy with people coming and going to and from the footpath, all busy with their own preoccupations and chatter – I don't think many notice the Dipper – that's their loss.

22 November

8.30am – A raw, freezing fog just lifting off the Common, crisply white with hoar frost after another very cold night. Despite these wintry conditions, however, the village is chirpy with Sparrows and Chaffinches 'pink' everywhere. A female Blackbird shifts leaves and in her totally focussed concentration she seems almost wantonly careless of her own safety. It's not merely a matter of overturning leaves, however. Sometimes she hops forward a pace and on the step back her claws scratch at the surface where she picks, finding small bits among the raked detritus – certainly enough to keep her continually picking. She's very beautiful, with her softly veiled speckled breast and pale tipped bill. An examination of where she was working reveals an area bared of leaves and grass right down to the soil in a circle of about six inches all around her – a very systematic approach to her foraging.

Down at the river bridge all is grey and ironbound after a week's hard frost. A gang of twelve Starlings sits in the top of the big meadow ash – wheezing, rattling, whistling blithely; one has incorporated bits of Mistle Thrush at intervals into his chattering song. This is the tallest tree in the area, on its own at the edge of the meadow and much favoured by Starlings which seem to prefer a quite separate group identity; such a single-standing tree serves not only as a vantage point but also isolates them satisfactorily. A Chaffinch flies into the same tree top and no sooner has it arrived than it is banished. The only other signs of life down here are a couple of Crows strutting and poking about in the frozen meadow, a few sheep grazing among the frosted grasses of the top tarn meadow on the far side of the river. Down at the sitting stones I come across two

Dippers foraging busily, bobbing and dipping into the river. One bobs up onto a stone with its prey, hammering at it, slapping it about, as a Kingfisher might, before part nibbling, part swallowing it – some aquatic larva, caddis fly, perhaps, ridding it of its casing. Upstream there's an outburst of Magpie rattle, and investigation reveals two Magpies, five Jackdaws and one Jay all shouting together in the same tree, very much in alarm mode, but there's nothing visible to warrant all this fuss – the branches are sparse, bare of leaves and there's nowhere large or concealed enough for any threat to hide. Perhaps, being corvids, they are simply drawn together by pure mutual dislike, but I do wonder what brought them to this particular tree in the first place – continuous urgent alarms of this kind tend to be specifically focussed among corvids. Eventually the two Magpies and the Jay depart the tree, leaving only seven Jackdaws showing every sign of agreement and contentment!

25 November

A night without frost, and much softer this morning here in Langdale. At Leighton Moss, however, a raw, bitter wind blows off the exposed mud flats and saltings. It's very exposed here, but the whisper of phragmytes and the wilderness calls of waders is always welcome music. However, there are very few waders at the estuary lagoons today because the tide is at full ebb and many birds will be out on the mud flats and saltings feeding before it begins to flow again. More palatable pickings are obviously to be found in the extensively flooded pastures which hold large numbers of Wigeon together with Oyster-catchers, Redshanks, Lapwings and various gulls, whilst one such flooded field holds quite large numbers of Black-tailed Godwits. These face into the wind and walk slowly forward together as if they were an organised party searching out and cleaning up the multitudinous small invertebrates left among the flooded grasses. There's a continuous soft, high-pitched babble as the Godwits 'talk' to each other. The sun suddenly appears, and now there's the wonderful spectacle of this brightly lit mass of waders all facing the same way, all probing the flooded grass, tilted forwards in uniformity like a Tunnicliffe painting almost, with a few birds here and there standing or preening, thus giving contrast to this spectacle of mass behaviour and just the right corrective balance to an otherwise ideally perfect scene. There's little shelter, though, on the wind-whipped estuary lagoons except, minimally, in the lee of small low islands.

Particularly pleasing are the many Gadwall. Identifiable by his white wing patch, the drake repays a prolonged examination. Initially he strikes the observer as just another rather drab-looking bird, grey-backed with a black rear end. A thorough look, however, reveals a most delicate beauty, the grey on the upper parts, the flanks and particularly the breast being intricately vermiculated with black and white, almost as if very finely scaled. Laid elegantly over the back lie the elongated, pointed scapulars, black centred, edged with a warm russet-buff. The diagnostic white patch of the speculum is emphasised by its position adjacent to the black rear end, overlapped by the elongated, grey tertials. It takes a much closer look to reveal the true glory of the drake Gadwall's wing, however, first drawn to our attention by Francis Willughby in his *Ornithology* of 1678 – "It hath on the wings three spots of different colour, one above the other, viz, a white, a black and a red one" – clearly demonstrated by Archibald Thorburn (1925) in the illustration in his *British Birds*. These are birds of a very unobtrusive beauty. The last century has seen the Gadwall move steadily westwards from its erstwhile strongholds across central Europe and Russia, and the new *Atlas* estimates a current British population of some 800 pairs, with an increasing but discontinuous distribution across south-east England. With its liking for weedy, nutrient-rich waters, there should be no shortage of suitable habitats for a most welcome extension of this very attractive duck's breeding range in England.

In the shallow lee of a muddy island rests a long line of Shovellers, hunched right down, their shoulders almost awash and their heads tucked right in as they sit the wind out. Four Redshanks arrive on the islet, alighting with the poetry of that momentary wing-lift and remaining for just a few seconds' rapid preen before leaving for somewhere more sheltered. A sky-high grey wall in the distance denotes the approach of a fierce squall, bringing hard horizontal rain whipping across the lagoon. It's a cold, grey landscape, the dark water hissing and pitted by the lashing force of huge raindrops. But the hunched Shovellers continue bouncing, dredging up weed, dozing, preening, and the sheep on the salt marsh simply turn their large, round, woolly bottoms to the wind and munch on, their front ends well sheltered by that ample spread. Thirty or 40 Lapwings are buffeted off course as they cross the lagoon, their broad wings catching the full brunt of the wind. They recover with a little jink and a sudden, reflexive surge forward as the gale relaxes for a second or two. Their wings seem to bounce back off the air as though it were a taut-stretched membrane returning the energy expended on it. The squall passes; the sun breaks through. A Raven calls from the distant woodland over which a Buzzard describes slow spirals, soaring up to meet the splendour of renewed glimmering molten light.

26 November

Intermittent rain out of a bitter north wind and the first snow is on the fells. More than anything else this one event signals a change in the year. The air feels cleansed; the hills seem higher, no longer familiar, benign, a casual playground smeared with safe summer sweat – they have become mountains, blessed for as long as the snow lasts with more than just a touch of wilderness and death, purged to the marrow of their honest Cumbrian rock. Below them the village huddles and chimney smokes mingle like the steamy breaths of cattle clustered in the same cold dawn. Glittering Orion prowls the cold skies, yet, so far, we have no owls about the village to celebrate this event.

1.15pm – Round Oak Howe. A Raven glides high over the quarry wood towards Lingmoor, calling its deep, grating, double-noted 'pruk...pruk!' A second Raven follows, circling above the wood before disappearing behind the hill, leaving the quarry resonant with a throaty triple call as if it were a still pool rippling after a thrown stone. In Baysbrown Wood a Tree Creeper works its way up an old oak; its colours very bright-seeming against the muted grey-greens of the creviced, lichened trunk. This attractive little bird is found wherever there are well-grown trees, but it is small and secretive, often overlooked, and its presence is probably best detected by learning to recognise its high-pitched call. Its shining, silvery white underparts reflect light into the cracks and crannies it explores whilst foraging; otherwise its plumage is a rich, complex arrangement of browns and ochres, set off by black accents on the wing feathers. The tail is long and specially stiffened, like that of woodpeckers, to be used as a support as it spirals its way up (never down) a tree trunk. In winter it often forages with parties of tits, always worth scanning for the presence of a Tree Creeper, and among which it avoids competition because its bill is long and finely curved, enabling it to pick and poke in the deep cracks and crannies unavailable to the short, stumpy bills of tits. Like many small birds, it is very vulnerable to wintry nights; the winters 1963, 1979 and 1981-2 saw dramatic drops in populations of many small birds. It has been suggested that on very cold nights Tree Creepers may benefit from the warmth accumulated in communal roosts, although they are unlikely to beat the record of over 50 Wrens found huddled together in the limited space of a tit nest box!

Out of the wood the wind is abrasive and bitter – small birds keep close and low. The shadow of Lingmoor, cast by the sinking sun, creeps steadily up towards the valley's opposite, north-bounding ridge, brilliantly, even dramatically illuminated against the dark grey cloud. The crest with its gold- and silvery-ochre grasses and pale ochre-grey rock, rubbed, scrubbed and cleansed by the abrasive action of this raw northerly wind, positively gleams against the leaden sky. It is a revelation to look at the valley bottom – it's nearly 3pm and there's still a lot of light in the valley; in fact, if I didn't know it was shadow I would accept it as perfectly good daylight, but the brilliance of the lit ridge defines the difference between mere light and illumination. Beyond the fine, sheep-grazed meadows between Oak Howe and Robin Ghyll Bowfell comes into view, massive and very alpine with, in this light, its perfect, pyramidal summit as remote and inaccessible-seeming as the transparent sky beyond.

A Raven circles over Raven crag; a Buzzard calls and rises slowly from the fields below. There's no wind and he must flap rather heavily in order to climb – in short, tight circles – out of the valley bottom. He's been spotted by two Crows sitting in an ash tree below the crag – they shout at him furiously, but, strangely, do not attempt to leave their tree. The light is fading fast now and perhaps they feel settled for the night. The Buzzard at last finds a slight updraught of air, which enables him to drift downwind for one segment of his spiral, but he has to flap to complete his up-wind turn. On he goes, slowly spiralling, drifting down the valley just above tree height until he disappears into Cylinders Wood where he'll find a roosting perch – cold, perhaps, but at least dry.

29 November

After a bitter night the morning sky promises a fine day. House Sparrows have been noisy all the way up the lane into the village. We really are very fortunate to have such a large population of these engaging, busy little birds, for when there's nothing else much going on you can almost guarantee there'll be goings-on among the Sparrows. Two Dunnocks call to each other from gardens on either side of the road, sharp little needle notes very similar to the calls noted on 13th November. They recall Gilbert White's letter of September 2nd 1774 in which he observes with regard to Dunnocks that, "…as soon as frosty mornings come they make a very piping plaintive noise", and it is interesting to note that 13th November was also a very fresh, cold morning after a prolonged period of muggy rain. House Sparrow and Dunnock have suffered much from unjust description – drab, or dull, or variations on the generally uninteresting. Many birds wear combinations of ochres, tans, browns, blacks and greys. These are the colours of marshland and sedge, winter woods, parched grasslands, brackened fellsides and their rocky outcrops – the landscapes in which animals live. It's so easy to be glibly explanatory about such colouration, however subtle, as if words like 'camouflage' were the whole story. These types of cryptic colouration, however, are the history of life on earth, of the heritage of their environments, of the ceaseless involvement in whether to eat or be eaten – all the problems of adaptation to predation or avoiding it, the origins of species, the very cusp of existence. The best animal art (as distinct from illustration) – Lars Jonnson, Bruno Liljefors and Charles Tunnicliffe, for example – shows wildlife in its multiplicity of forms within the landscape, illustrating both why animals are coloured the way they are and the processes of evolution.

The morning is deceptive – apparently mild, until one stands still and the cold begins to bite. The sun is just beginning to light up the meadows, rimed with frost along the shadow of the riverbank trees where about three dozen male Chaffinches forage, almost unseen in the accumulated leaf litter, and the air is full of the high chime of their 'pinking'. Some of these male Chaffinches are beginning to show a certain degree of mutual intolerance – two here are busily en-gaged in what would appear to be a rather unseasonal challenge, facing up to each other, rising and falling in a fluttered aerial 'dance' with much display of the double white wing bars — designed for exactly this purpose — whilst continually 'pinking'. Chaffinches do not usually pair up until early February, and this kind of display is more often associated with pair-formation and the hope of impressing females. The Chaffinch's specific name, 'coelebs' means bachelor, referring to the fact that many more females tend to migrate than males, thus leaving behind, in the northern parts of their range, numbers of males. This tendency to predominantly female migration among Chaffinches explains a couple of passages in Gilbert White which may be puzzling to the northern reader, one of which reads:

> "…witness those vast flocks of hen chaffinches that appear with us in the winter without hardly any cocks among them… "
> (*The Natural History of Selborne*, Letter VIII, Dec 20, 1770)

What the redoubtable Gilbert witnessed, in the far south of the country, was probably some of those 'vast flocks of females' en route from their breeding sites in northern Europe, to Ireland in particular.

Two Ravens fly across the ridge and into open sky towards Loughrigg, croaking very softly at each other. This flight differs from their pair-bonding synchro-flying display, for one appears to pursue the other, following every twist and turn rather than flying with it and yet, at the same time, without apparent aggression. A temporarily unidentified call down by the sitting stones is eventually revealed as from the very extensive and confusing vocabulary of the Great Tit! When young I was taught, if in doubt it's probably a Great Tit — and it is so surprisingly often! Within the last five minutes this particular bird has uttered several different calls, each, presumably, with significance and meaning to other Great Tits

– of which there are several – in the area. These represent just a small sample of this Great Tit's repertoire. Most notes are fairly clear, strident sounds, often with much repetition and including all sorts of variations on a theme. Even his regular song, which may be heard throughout winter, consists of variations on the theme of what is unsatisfactorily transcribed as 'tee-cher…tee-cher', although those who have lived and worked much in the countryside hear him more as the 'saw sharpener'. Perhaps the name which most reflects the multiplicity and diversity of his song and calls comes from Cornwall where the term 'pridden pral' means 'tree babbler'. Why the necessity for this bewildering diversity of calls and song? Perhaps, like plumage decoration – flashing wing bars (Chaffinch), erectile, decorative tails (Black Grouse), flaunted breasts (Robin), to name but three common examples – they are all to do with competition, display – the Great Tit with the broadest range of sounds at his disposal may be seen as both the fittest and the most successful in territorial holding and therefore most desirable by females seeking males.

The fairly wide margin of dark, clear water surrounding the iced-over centre of the tarn is just beginning to steam as the sun reluctantly generates a little warmth. One or two Golden-eyes dive, and there are very loud goosy noises from the middle tarn where the cob Mute is in full sail driving towards five unfortunate Greylags which have had the temerity to land on Elterwater! This Swan's display is magisterially awesome, exuding raw power, speed and a very high dramatic intensity and I've known nothing yet – including a flock of sixteen Whooper Swans! – able to withstand its formidable menace.

There's a solitary Woodpigeon – imagine – a solitary Wood-pigeon! – feeding in the sunshine now flooding the meadow. What a fine bird this is, and what a reflection on the magnificent power of female Sparrowhawks which regularly take such birds as prey! And so very handsome and powerful in flight! The sun is on its dusky-pink breast now; its white

77

wing bands exposed when in flight and neck-patch flash out flocking signals to other Woodpigeons as well acting as target-flashes for predators, as do the Wigeon's white upper wing-flashes and the white of gulls, all three among favourite prey species taken by Peregrines. Alas, this year has seen fewer Woodpigeons about the entire valley than any year I can remember, despite its rapid increase noted in BTO Garden Bird Surveys. Back in 1995 it was present in 66% of gardens, increasing to 85% in 2008, an increase accounted for, perhaps, by corresponding increases in garden bird feeders and the cereal content of commercially available bird foods? It picks away at small bits found among the decaying stuff at grass-root level; two or three pecks, a pause to look around – constant vigilance is essential if you're good to eat – then another two or three pecks, working in a semicircle around him before he moves on. I'm delighted to see it here this morning!

December

2 December

2.00pm – Yesterday was wet all day, flooding the river with snow-melt off the hills, and this morning was dark and wet; this afternoon it's fair enough for a short walk. Down at the bases of walls and fences everywhere birds are turning piles of accumulated leaves – one male Blackbird shifts every single leaf in his immediate area before moving on. On top of the wall is a completely tailless Robin, fluffed out like a densely feathered ball save for the points of his drooped wing tips and his head which don't quite blend with the rest of the round, bundled appearance. He tries to fly, but neither well nor far – much more a fluttered wall-top hopping, or a small feathered bouncing ball. He's obviously been involved in some kind of mishap, for it looks as if he may also have an injured leg which he favours as he moves.

Jays call from the Hall wood. One is visible now, moving about the tree tops with a long, springy, lollopy hop, aided at times by a flap with his short, broad wings, primaries splayed open. The Jay is not only our most secretive crow, he is also the most arboreal, and is far more likely to be heard than seen. Its harsh screeching alarm call earns it several descriptive names. In the exquisite but totally unpronounceable Gaelic it is 'schreachag coille' – 'screamer of the woods'. Its other calls include a churring sound and a rather strangled 'mew', but one

79

of its most surprising vocal features is its song – not something we associate much with crows, the two words 'song' and 'crow' being mutually exclusive. In the breeding season, however, the Jay does utter a kind of particularly mellifluous 'cackled' warble. If seen at all, it is usually merely a glimpse of flashing white rump and wing patches as it moves about the tree tops. A closer look, however, reveals an exotic quality we simply don't expect from the other rather funereally garbed British crows – a combination of dusky pinks, black wings and that brilliant blue shoulder patch which can be rivalled only by the Kingfisher. In addition to all these riches, it has a streaked erectile crown and a pronounced black moustachial stripe which not only emphasises the cold blue eye but endows it with a certain jaunty intensity of expression. Originally a bird exclusively of oak woodland – indeed, from its habit of burying acorns some have claimed for it a vital role in the establishment of such woodland and it has spread into parks and suburban gardens in many parts of England.

3 December
9.00am – A dull, damp morning at the top of the Grasmere side of Red Bank in a grand area of woodland, with many well-grown oaks, beeches and ashes, all mature standard trees, admixed with tall larches, pines and firs. Steel Fell and Seat Sandal are topped with cloud, and mist is boiling in the always atmospheric Grizedale Hause with its dark tarn at the bottom of which, according to legend, lies the golden crown of King Dunmail, last king of Cumbria, overlooked by the dark loom of Cofa and Dollywaggon Pikes.

The woodland path emerges onto the old Grasmere/Langdale packhorse trail over Hunting Stile; open fields drop down to the lake on my right, the fine, mature bracken-floored woodland rising to the fells above. It must be very obvious by now that the Nuthatch is a very major presence in our Cumbrian woods, and this might be an opportune place for a more detailed introduction to this beautiful and charismatic little bird. Although known to have nested in 'South Westmorland' in 1916, it was still recorded as a 'scarce resident' nearly forty years later (Stokoe, 1962) at the extreme northerly edge of its breeding range. By 1985 Hutcheson (1985) described it as 'slowly increasing its range', since when it has undergone a spectacular expansion until its variety of shrill calls has become one of the characteristic voices of our deciduous woodlands, parks and gardens. It is said to have a vocabulary of twelve notes – variations on a fairly limited theme – ranging from the piercing territorial trill at one extreme to rather thin, high contact calls at the other. Gilbert White called it the 'Jar Bird' because of the jarring sound of its hacking at trees as it searches for insects during the breeding season, but in autumn it takes acorns, hazelnuts, beech mast, inserting them into crevices in walls or bark to hammer out their sweet nutritious kernels which, as well as eating, it often hides in convenient crevices. Our local bird collects sunflower kernels and hazelnuts from our feeders, hiding them within the interstices of the next-door cottage roof slates. I watched one the other day carefully lift a nut-shaped pebble from the bird bath and carefully poke it into the soil of the nearest window box! Probably its greatest claim to British ornithological distinction, however, is that it is our only bird which can climb equally well down a tree as up. To watch a Nuthatch move on any surface other than a tree – or a dry-stone structure such as a wall or a sloping rock face, for example – is to be made aware of the limitations of such specialisation. I have a note describing a Nuthatch trying to 'walk' along a roughly tarmaced lane. Its legs are so short and its body so structured for specialised tree-climbing that it was obliged to 'leap' forwards in a sequence of very rapid, very short hops with its body held almost horizontal, parallel to the ground. In so far as any bird can look inappropriately, clumsily out of place this bird – like a grounded swift – expressed almost a denial of its evolution and function.

As one enters Grasmere village, there's a little meadow, scattered about which are eight female Blackbirds – consistent with the fact that the majority of winter migrant Blackbirds from the continent are indeed females. Spread fairly evenly over this small field, they succeed in finding a continuous source of food among the leaves and grass stalks. All our thrushes are very generalised feeders and with such a non-specialised bill can vary their diets according to availability and season – fruits, insects, invertebrates of all kinds, especially worms, and are particularly expert in doing exactly what I am watching them doing here – collecting all kinds of animal matter from the ground surface and piles of leaves and watching any animal, whether specialised or not, doing exactly what it was designed by its evolution to do is always a source of much satisfaction.

12.45pm – The day has brightened, the wind is cooler and I'm going down to Elterwater lake. The tree tops by Kitty Hall are favoured song perches for the many Starlings, local residents presumably, for filtered out from all the wheezings, rattlings and chatterings come the same bits of mimicked Buzzard and Mistle Thrush calls I've heard several times before.

A Heron takes off from near the old, now sadly dilapidated boathouse on the top tarn and, alarmed by its sudden flight, three male and two female Goldeneyes fly off with that exciting whistled sibilance as they climb rapidly and directly overhead in a long, rising slant – squat, dumpy-looking birds in flight, with short, broad wings and heads which always look too big for their bodies. Disturbance always produces a knock-on effect and three Cormorants take off with much splashing from the far side of the middle tarn. Some birds betray their remote ancestry much more readily than others; examined closely, both Starlings and Cormorants reveal the lizard beneath the skin. A group of the much more phlegmatic Tufted Duck swims without any sense of urgency from the reeds where they are vulnerable from the land out onto the secure dark water, reaming silver in their wake. I'm disappointed to see neither Teal nor Pochard – at one time both regular and numerous winter visitors – but this disappointment is superseded by curiosity at the strange behaviour of the entire water surface which looks alive with fish rising as gaseous bubbles wobble up to the surface leaving a tightly woven mosaic of ringed ripples where they burst.

Five Woodpigeons come clapping out of the Tanglewood. Several trees contain the scrappy see-through remains of what were initially only marginally less scrappy Woodpigeon nests, and in this chaos of fallen and windblown trees it's a wonder that these fragile structures have withstood the winter so far. On the far side of the river a Water Rail sharms among the reeds of the Nab. The male Bullfinch calls, an engaging, clear but plaintive pipe – an emphatic 'hweeb', pause, then 'hweeb-hweeb' with a distinctly trochaic emphasis, so that the last syllable of the linked pair sounds like a distant, but instant echo of the first. The alder catkins look superb at the moment, little blunt, bunched window-cord fingers, but such a bronzy-purple that from a distance the trees are a rich aubergine.

3.00pm – The afternoon begins to draw in. Back in the village the air is lively with Sparrow chirps and churrs – I hesitate to call it a 'noise' because it is so vigorous, full of life and interactive meanings for all those making it – it is the evening settling chatter of an organised social group and not to be dismissed in derogatory, merely human terms.

5 December

A foggy morning is followed by an afternoon in which landscapes continually come and go through drifting layers of mist. Up on the Common as we start the walk around Loughrigg Tarn, one or two Meadow Pipits flash their white outer tail feathers as they break from the fellside bracken cover, but it is the landscape that dominates everything. Dramatically dark up the valley, the Pikes are totally obscured within a dense indigo-grey 'atmosphere', whisps of pale grey cloud floating across the deeply shadowed face of Lingmoor. Towards the south a dense mass of white cloud cleaves to the valley, thinning slightly until only the fell tops emerge, they too lit only briefly by an irregular passage of beams. To the west now, changes in atmospheric density allow the Pikes to show themselves – very black, crouching like panthers within the indigo-grey haze, whilst in the gap between Bowfell and Esk Pike pale drooping whisps of cloud gather volume and momentum, pouring down into the scooped-out basin holding Angle Tarn where it seethes and 'boils', before being forced up once more as if out from this dark chaotic cradle of stupendous convection currents some revelation, pristine and shattering, should ultimately burst forth to challenge us with new meanings. Emphasising the apocalyptic nature of these atmospheric 'events', the speeding shape of a small falcon cuts across the eye with the precision of an arrow cleaving space, momentarily more symbol than bird until mind regains precedence over the usurping imagination, and the falcon resolves into a male Kestrel slanting down the sky and streaming low across the hill.

Within High Close Wood, however, all is still and quiet, sodden and saggy with wet, every leaf and twig-end droops with a clear, pendulous globule of reflected world. A little Roe buck stands quite still in a dense thicket of rhododendron and coppice wood, his presence revealed only by a sudden flash of his white kidney-shaped caudal disc, but the rest of him in his grey winter pelage is totally broken up by the tangle of stems behind which he stands looking at us. He remains motionless, and a merely casual glance might interpret his white caudal disc as yet another patch of sky glimpsed between branches – until we move and he edges further into the dark thicket.

Near the bottom of Foolstep a flock of Fieldfares gathers darkly in the tree tops. Fieldfares come to us from Norway and northern Europe where they breed communally; they have been gradually expanding their range south and westwards for many years. The Highland region of Scotland is the main breeding area for the small, irregular resident British population. Among a scatter of interesting Cumbrian sightings during the summer months from the 1970s on breeding has been recorded only twice. The problem for a colonial species must be for the initiating colonisers and whether or not, and for how long, they can sustain their occupancy in a non-vagrant, i.e. resident, situation until a viable population density builds up. In their native north-lands Fieldfares nest in birch woodland, parks and gardens, as much a local thrush as our thrushes, so in this respect at least Cumbria presents no habitat problem. Along the edges of the hard footpath from Skelwith a long string of fresh mole heaps show where their makers have taken advantage of the extra moisture provided by run-off from the path, creating a linear microenvironment favoured by worms and, consequently, moles. Buzzards also are quick to take advantage of such favourable micro-habitats, and I have picked up many Buzzard castings containing mole fur and bones along favoured fence-lines where the moisture-drip/worm/mole sequence is particularly strong. With regard to molehills, that troubled genius of Wiltshire's woods and downland, Richard Jefferies, wrote:

"The neighbourhood of those hillocks has an attraction for many birds, especially in winter...In a frost if you see a thrush on a molehill it is very likely to thaw shortly. Moles seem to feel the least change in the temperature of the earth; if it slackens they begin to labour, and cast up, unwittingly, food for the thrushes."

(*The Amateur Poacher*, 1879)

As we leave Skelwith the early evening meadows become enveloped in a dense ground mist within which rounded grey shapes, more like animated boulders than sheep, move slowly through an opaque, fragile world where what is real changes definition every second. Rather than rising from the water, the mist seems to have settled down onto it by the force of its own gravity and from which the trees emerge dimly, the mist thinning so that their crowns stand clear and crisp. Behind, less dense layers dwindle up towards a far, high ridge, forever unattainable, dark against a sky of almost impossibly delicate turquoise blending up into the palest gold. Blackbird alarms shatter into the darkening air. Blackbirds are uneasy in the twilight, their first tentative 'chook's expressing anxiety rather than alarm, but soon rising to a sharper, umlaut-ed and repeated 'chük…'. Some of this alarm probably reflects the fact that Blackbirds are ever quick to express intolerance of intrusion into their personal space – wherever they are – such infringements met with much noisy fuss, finally expressed by that metallic, ringing 'tingk!' and that sudden accelerating crescendo of harsh notes which I have long called its 'scatter alarm', partly because of its onomatopoeic nature, but also because it seems to express an urgency to do just that when disturbed. All the way up the meadow-side footpath and through the village Blackbirds enact their evening settling rituals, causing, if not alarm, at least a very watchful awareness, the final arbiters of when it is safe to settle for the night.

6 December

Bright, clear and fresh – just right for a couple of hours by the estuary down at Leighton Moss. A first sweeping glance over the lagoon reveals numbers of Shovellers and Shelducks, a muddy islet with about 40 Black-tailed Godwits, a few Lap-wings and Redshanks; on the far bank, a few Teal and a dozen Canada Geese which trumpet periodically – counterpoint to the whistling of the numerous grazing Wigeons. The incoming

86

tide is fast approaching high water, expected in an hour or so. The light, some would say, is impossible – low, direct, with a brilliant glare on the water making silhouettes of most of the birds – the waders on their mudbanks particularly – but within this shimmering air, that precious '*enveloppe*' so treasured by Claude Monet, both water and sky becoming interchangeable, both irradiated in a dream of gold and blue, an elemental haze in which dark statuesque birds stand, dip and preen with an easy serenity forgetful almost even of survival. A party of Godwits departs, leaving the remainder occupied with feather maintenance duties, stretching, scratching, preening and always with that fascinating beak-end dew-drop that would send us diving for a handkerchief! Some bathe, a matter of almost total immersion, head ducked under. One bathes particularly vigorously, splashing water over its back off which it runs in silvered mercury trails glinting in the light. An immature Heron arrives on the lagoon's grassy bank. His walk is slow and stately, but suddenly he stops and turns away in a gesture of submissive recognition as another Heron lands, a beautiful fully plumed adult, delicately coloured with subtle pastel suggestions of pink, almost, within the soft greys of its neck, plumes immaculately laid out fanwise over shoulders and breast.

At the lower hide the visibility – from an ornithologist's point of view – is much better: here the mud is full of Redshanks with hardly a Godwit to be seen. There are large numbers of Teal, Lapwing and hundreds of Wigeon marching inexorably forward step by step, feeding along the grassy bank separating the lagoon from the salt marsh beyond. Suddenly, with a great rustle of wings and flurry of water, they leave the bank for the lagoon. A sky scan reveals no wheeling shape of Peregrine, but there is now a Merlin, the smallest of our resident breeding falcons, on the far fence, a favoured perch where she is content to sit quietly enjoying the sun on her back. It breeds in upland, open heather moorland, becoming a regular visitor to the coast during winter when the high ground is largely forsaken by the Pipits which form its main spring and summer prey.

To the south there are several blue-grey muddy islands, each behind the other and with extended spits by one of which stands a Spotted Redshank, tall against the squat bobbing shapes of the multiduninous Wigeon. It's constantly on the move, bill probing deep, so that in the deeper water it appears almost up-ended like a duck, but in the shallower water it occasionally breaks into erratic lunging dashes, until finally it's lost behind another intersection of islands. Another tall wader stalks briskly along the margin of one of the larger grassy islets – a very pale, elegant bird, almost ghostly white in the shimmering light, the telescope just revealing the frosty forehead and slightly upturned bill of a Greenshank – it too gets lost behind the tussocks of an intervening set of islands.

Over by the railway line are two Buzzards, one perched on a wall, the other in a tall thorn bush. Their arrival causes a general unsettling, particularly among the Canadas which resettle when the Buzzards seem content to sit almost motionless in the sun. Another, much closer, sits on an old ivy-covered stump adjacent to the edge of the lagoon – a magnificent bird, with a full, deep creamy-white upper breast and a pronounced, darker 'necklace', or breast crescent, fading to streaks below. A rich brown above, the feathers look well groomed with that silken bloom which renders them almost purple-sheened as she turns in the light. She's a very large bird, content to sit and gaze until she just leans forward, gives herself a push and her size is revealed by the span and width of her wings – a large and strikingly beautiful female.

The afternoon unwinds towards evening and as we turn away there is an enormous shout from the far south of the lagoon as hundreds of geese rise clamouring into the air. Whatever caused this sudden panic, this 'dread' – a Peregrine, perhaps? The sky darkened by multitudes of wheeling geese brings a fitting end to our visit. The sky promises a superb sunset.

11 December

8.30am – Mild and still quite dark. The dense cloud shoved aside by the brisk wind reveals an illuminated sky with pale gold clouds in the east and great lumps of purple-grey cumulus accumulating behind Lingmoor as if there's an unseen barrier holding them back, ever darker and greyer, piling up like water behind a dam so that within the space of a couple of minutes there exists the most intense illumination and the most solid, impenetrable bastion of dark grey cloud. The Jackdaws have just arrived, flying restlessly about the village finding their regular perches on trees, chimney pots and slates, telegraph poles and television aerials, mostly by now in couples. They've come up in groups of half a dozen to fifteen, very low, like marauding black raiders, silent, intent, wrapped in a trance of destination.

The valley and trees surrounding the village are in shadow, so that the contrast between the brilliantly lit crags and fellside brackens is most dramatic, particularly when the very dark cloud from up the valley sweeps behind this theatrically illuminated ridge. A solitary Jackdaw flies up the valley chattering to himself a non-stop outpouring of 'spoken' rather than 'shouted' Jackdaw, highly entertaining but puzzling, for there are no other Jackdaws in the immediate area. Distant goosy noises from the south-west resolve into a silhouetted skein of about 80 grey geese flying high and north into the atmospheric gloom up the valley. Flight patterns change from chevrons to lines and back again – a rippling wave passes down the entire line as it becomes necessary for each bird to reposition itself in the slip-stream of the preceding bird whenever the formation changes.

9.30am – As the sun rises and the meadows are suddenly flooded with light, everything comes to life, and immediately

89

there's much more activity as small parties of tits and finches seem suddenly to appear, feeding in the mossy branches of the riverside trees with a renewed sense of vigour and purpose. A pair of Mute Swan takes off from the tarn; against the cloud-gloom they present a white so immaculate that they assume significance beyond themselves, no longer birds but some kind of mythic presence from an ancient story. The first Crows appear in the meadows. One perches on the extreme tip of the tallest larch's leading shoot, bending it under its weight. It looks around, moving its head continually, but seeing nothing to investigate for food, nothing to dismay or disturb, it settles to preening. When it brings its wing forward and down to preen behind its folded carpal joint there's a sudden flashed sheen of yellow as its hard, brilliantly reflective feathers catch the sun. It is as if everything has waited for that moment when the sun hoisted above the cloud, flooding all not only with light but the promise of even a touch of his fire.

By afternoon the wind is much fresher, but half way up the track to Little Langdale, by the big pine – an important tree of great age and size – it is so sheltered that nothing moves – not a twig twitches, not a sound divides the air; but only a few yards uphill and out of the lee of the wood there's a rush of big wind pushing great clumps of cumulus over the top of the watershed. The first signs of a Blackbird's anxiety – a quiet 'chook…chook' – issues from a track-side holly bush in which his shape is completely fragmented by leaves and branches. If he hadn't alarmed I would have remained ignorant of his presence. He resumes his soft clucking and moves slightly so that his yellow bill and eye ring become visible, and out he hops onto the top of the bush, not only revealing himself, very handsome, aristocratic, but ready for instant flight. There was a moment when, staring down into the interior of the bush, it was like focussing down a funnel at the narrow end of which was just a yellow-rimmed eye looking me straight in the eye – a rare moment of contact! Up at the summit of the watershed

Wetherlam looks very dark, a mass of heavy cloud caps it, pouring down into Greenburn like a waterfall. Despite cloud racing over the ridge, the top of the watershed is sheltered by the bulky shoulder of Lingmoor, but it's by no means silent up here – Jackdaws 'chak' and 'chek' down in Little Langdale and there's a tractor working (unseen) in Billy's fields along by Dale End. When it stops the silence is immense and resonant.

2.15pm – Two Crows fly over from the top of the wood. They fall out of the air with nonchalant aerobatic ease, the wings brought right behind and over the back at one time, spilling air, as well as the whiffling tilt from side to side reminiscent of geese. It looks quite light-hearted, frivolous even, the whole performance much more jackdaw-like than crow-like, lacking the sombre concentration on the bare essentials more characteristic of Crows. Down in the village at 3pm a group of about two dozen Jackdaws clamour into the air as if commanded by some unseen, unheard signal, and set off on their first leg down the valley to their roost.

12 December

A late frost last night, a beautiful blue, cold cloudless morning. Coming down to feed this morning was a most handsome first winter male Blackbird, the faint mottling on his breast almost as if a body-fitting veil of black transparent silk were drawn over him, so very soft and subtle were its colours and textures.

On the Common I was struck by the way a Robin, perched on a stalk in a jungle of dead brackens, actually stood out from that background. One might think a Robin should blend into such an environment, but the russets of the bracken are tinged slightly with a neutralising hint of blue, whereas the Robin's breast goes the opposite direction in the colour wheel, towards orange, producing an inevitable optical colour clash in which the yellows in the orange 'advance', whilst the neutralising colour in the bracken is, comparatively, recessive, so the Robin stands out instead of blending. This is how it should be; his flaming breast is vital to him – it is his standard, his battle flag, the banner of his way of life. Unseen within the brackens has been a continuous faint ticking, and suddenly a Wren appears on a bracken stalk – relative to the warm tones of the brackens he looks positively grey, yet seen on a grey-lichened wall-top he's quite a warm brown! Both these examples serve to remind us that we ought to think more about the nature of what we call 'local colour'. These Wrens have been zipping about, dropping down into the brackens and periodically surfacing, 'ticking' the whole time. There's a sudden outburst of Blackbird scatter-alarm – a Kestrel sweeps fast and low across the fell beneath us. Once at the top of the Common there's the obligatory halt to admire the view up-dale to the mountains. The sky is always different – changes in light renewing the landscape minute by minute. Today the north-facing slopes of Lingmoor and the entire northern face of Bowfell are all in deep shadow save for a small, intensely glowing patch of sunshine on the Band which magically brings the entire two-dimensional-looking, rather uniform mountain mass into three dimensions – this achieved by just a dab of light among the shadows!

On the lake half a dozen male Goosanders snorkel and chase with much splashing along the reedy margins of the Nab – behaviour often indicating the presence either of females somewhere nearby or of fish – whilst on the open water a pair of Goldeneye dive, surface and silver-ream their passage across the lake. The late afternoon swells imperceptibly into the vastness of a cloudless evening with a rim of pale gold all the way along the horizon towards the west where it fades up first into a blue washed with gold and then into a blue just touched with the faintest hint of indigo, transparent and beautiful. The moon is very bright behind us and we're probably walking as much by moonlight now as by the fading daylight. Venus looks particularly lovely, hanging poised a mere two inches above Fletcher's Wood, rising not from the blandness of a Botticelli shell but from the spiky, brush-like sky-line of a Cumbrian wood.

13 December

A dark, heavily overcast morning after a severe frost; I'm going down to the tarns. A low mist brushes the top of Fletcher. One or two Starlings sit in the big conifers behind Kitty Hall. When one brings its wing forward and down to preen behind its folded carpal joint there's a sudden flashed sheen of yellow as its hard, brilliantly reflective feathers catch the sun. It's quite an event to see Starlings in any numbers here now, especially when, on bright winter mornings not many years ago, every chimney held its glossy, wheezing rattlebag of a bird filling the air with sheer exuberance and vocal mischief. While one has been mimicking a Buzzard, the real thing betrays its presence – just a wing movement, in one of the big trees on the other side of the path, then a clear, sharp whistle, becoming the better known ringing call, prelude to its taking flight – a few flaps, gaining height, a few circles, then back to the same tree where it probably roosted overnight. It's quite a dark bird, brown bloomed with plum on its back, but with hardly any breast crescent, more barred than streaked on the upper breast blending down into a very darkly streaked belly and underparts.

On the lake two Mute Swans feed close inshore near Ashes Point, and three Cormorants, swimming just off the point, show only their necks and heads, like periscopes – the white face patch and yellow bill vivid against the dark water. Their three heads and necks emerge from the water, swaying close together – darkly rearing serpentine shapes, their evolution plain to see – still reptiles beneath the skin. Birds with such demanding appetites as these Cormorants and Goosanders would not come unless they could fill their bellies. The great post-moult winter parties of Goosanders come less regularly; Cormorants appear from time to time, evidence that despite having suffered from effluent pollution and nutrient enrichment over recent years the lake still holds stocks of both perch and pike. A quiet pair of Mallards swims away from the point; five drake Teal leap off suddenly from the little muddy inlet by Ashes Point, followed by one or two females whose grating calls sound distinctly querulous after the cheerful conversational tone of the males. They fly off to the top tarn. Two Goldeneyes leave the far side of the lake, wings whistling as they gain height. To my astonishment a hundred or so Starlings arrive with a rush of wings, circle overhead before resuming the arrow-straight destination flight on which they were set. Except for their wings, they fly silently, a rather ragged group, with no formation, and they're gone almost as soon as they arrived, like a visitation, as if commenting on my notes of only half an hour ago.

The lake recovers its peace and quiet, the water still and black, silky-looking. The barely moving swans cause just the slightest shake of the water surface, reflections near perfect. The day is definitely arriving and to the west the Pikes are clear. An hour later and the Buzzard is still perched in the same tree, calling – long, drawn-out ringing shouts. He moves into the top of a tall larch on a rocky knoll, revealing his boldly patterned underwing; lifts off, makes a couple of circles and back to his original tree – he emphatically does not want to move from this immediate area. The Starlings still wheeze and rattle in their trees behind Kitty Hall – they've obviously not attracted the passing flock – the same bird still chattering its Thrush, Buzzard and Curlew to the accompaniment of a distant 'pirrip...pirrip' from the Teals on the top tarn. It seems right now to go home, deeply content; a full circle has been made; both place and vocal background are much as found earlier – such symmetry is rare.

It's 10.30am – the village, too, is as quiet as I left it in the near-dark some time ago.

14 December

10.15am – It is a truly gorgeous morning here by Rydal Water. Immediately visible on the lake three darkly shining Cormorants with varnished-looking, yellow bills swim towards one of the little rocky islets to join the other five already there – it's a favourite place to 'hang out.' The sunshine glosses them to a burnished green-black iridescence. These particular colours, like those of the Starling, the Kingfisher's blue-greens, the purple-green on a Pigeon's neck, the various metallic speculum sheens in ducks' wings – these are all 'structural' colours, mainly without pigment, and made by changing the angle of view from which the observer sees different reflecting surfaces within the structure of the feather. The technical complexities of the optics involved may serve to explain how the colours are made and why they are seen by us as such, but, fortunately, we are still left with all the wondering and ad-miration due to a breath-catching phenomenon, a rather special magic trick and yet another facet of the attention due to the problems inherent in dogmatising in respect of local colour.

By 10.45am all this northern flank of Loughrigg remains in cool shadow. Robins flit about the fellside brackens and in the shade, without sunshine to illuminate the orange constituent of their breasts, they blend much more easily into their background. Loughrigg is a very craggy-looking lump from the Rydal/Grasmere side, quite unlike the gentle, rounded contours presented from Langdale. This split personality is a feature shared by many of its much grander near-neighbours in the area – Hellvellyn, Dollywaggon Pike, Fairfield – deceivers ever. The fellside is divided by several rocky streams falling from the higher crags, clad sparsely with juniper, ash, holly, rowan and straggly hawthorns, trees rich in ancient myth and meaning, all excellent cover, whilst the crags themselves are well vegetated with grasses, lichens, mosses providing food, shelter and breeding places come the spring. As we climb, the skyline to the north opens out to reveal the pimple of Sergeant Man – at 2,414 feet being the highest point at which I've found inch-long, newly metamorphosed little froglets!

We emerge from shadow into brilliant sunshine by a wall overhung by a magnificent old oak sporting great growths of polypody ferns along a branch which spreads outwards from the stem. The whole is back-lit by a very bright sun so that the ferns stand up and out as a fabulous (a carefully chosen word), semi-transparent, pale green fringe or comb – more like the imagined dorsal decoration of a dragon than a tree. The hazel catkins have turned a lichen-grey dusted with yellow ochre. A Magpie buries a beakful of acorn, probing, poking it into the soft ground, planting it, and then covering the site completely with carefully placed leaves. Will the Magpie remember or will this have become another fine oak in two hundred years' time?

16 December

Although our gardens may be visited by many different Robins over the course of a winter season, it is also obvious that among these may be identified those which are our resident birds. Much may be told by habit and body language. One Robin who invariably uses the same approach perches from which he frequently sings is certainly the owner of the territory, which holds our feeding station. He is, more often than not, puffed out flaunting that flaming breast; his entire body language in everything he does suggests a confident male within his territory. Although highly intolerant of most other Robins whose irregular habits suggest birds on the move, he is gradually becoming increasingly tolerant of one bird which displays a similar habit of behaviour and approach but whose breast-flaunting is less flagrant. A resident female, perhaps? 'He' still defends a personal space against over-encroachment by 'her', but that space is decreasing as his tolerance increases, as does his intolerance of any other Robin in the immediate area, the function of that flaming breast becoming glaringly obvious – it is a banner for all occasions, a battle flag expressing readiness for conflict, even to the death if necessary. We are approaching the time of year when Robins pair. Male Robins do not leave their territories and the females select their mates from within his territory. Who would dream that the lives of these little birds achieve such tensions and epic dramas!

Of the several established pairs of Blackbirds that visit us there is one splendid pair which dominates the feeding area. The 'boss' is a fine adult male, intolerant of the two first winter males but more tolerant of a first winter female when she comes down at the same time, although he will not permit her near the limits of what he establishes as his personal space, driving at her with an aggressive run, head and yellow bill extended with unmistakeable purpose. The male Blackbird uses the ridge of the facing cottage roof as a vantage point – a stage from which he may both observe and also be seen as assertive and dominant. Seen in silhouette, one of the physical attributes which makes him so impressive is the proportion of beak to head size. This impressive instrument is a tool evolved not only for probing, but together the blazing yellow bill – the colour of which will intensify with age – and jet black head enable a very powerful display combination. Like the Robin, this male Blackbird uses a combination of body posture, bill attitude and movement to assert his dominance, standing bolt upright, at the full extent of his legs on arrival, announcing his presence and superiority with total confidence.

21 December

Midwinter's day, the Winter Solstice – perhaps the most important turning point in the whole year and probably the real focus of intention at sites like Stonehenge. In our arbitrary divisions and subdivisions of time and the names we give them very few have much relation to anything real in nature like solstice, equinox, sunrise, noon, sunset and the monthly cycle of the moon. We have grown up within the endless cycles of these stupendous events and what they represent in terms of our relationship with light and dark. But we have grown away from the positive natural realities of what these words represent to all kinds of spurious metaphoric meanings by which the wholesome organic richness implicit in the words 'dark' and 'light' have been degraded into symbols and metaphors for the set of socially acceptable invented conventions we call morality – and a fear of death. The rich potency of darkness nourishes us and every other living thing in blood and earth; the powers of light are what make the seed grow and the Skylark sing. Consider a few of the realities of darkness. More often than not we are conceived in it and born in it; for almost one whole year out of our allotted span we develop in it, are cherished by its blood-warmth, even capable of first learning. The smallest seed, the bird in the egg, the greatest men – there's no difference. Wherein lies the gestating origin of Shakespeare's works, last quartets of Beethoven, or Michelangelo's *Pietà?* We see the glory of the constellations because only the darkness reveals them. Out of the dark everything is born; in the dark everything rests; and our death is not darkness any more than a tree's or a bird's death is darkness – it is merely the end of living, part of the huge life cycle. At the Winter Solstice the natural world turns from the depths of its necessary rest after its labours of the preceding year to preparations for the coming year and its climaxes of sex, seed time and harvest for all living things. This is why we should celebrate the Solstice – for all the wealth of life which has sprung, nourished, from the dark into the renewed bounty of its heritage.

Up by the quarry tip between two downfalls of rubble there's a wide horizontal grassy ledge, maintained in lawn-order by the local rabbits. Daylight is on the wane. Looking westward towards the Pikes, between Lingmoor looming dark along the southern boundary of the valley and the long high ridge to the north the river is a molten silver thread, linking woodland and meadow, marsh and moraine all the way to its many small sources high in the mountains – truly a thread. I relish these silent minutes in which the world settles slowly towards its hours of rest – the virtue of darkness. Out of this still silence there comes gradually the unmistakeable shape and flight-form of a Peregrine crossing the valley. He's pale-breasted against the darkness of cloud, with dark moustachial stripes, cold as a crag and bold against the white face, rowing the close, overhead air with his dipping falcon wing-flicker – one can almost sense a dimpling of ripples as he sculls across the evening – and which, even when not hunting, carries with it such an imminence of drama, of urgency and purpose, an ushering-in of climax. For him the present is infinite, living intensely in the now and now and now; he has no past and the future is the next second's space into which he hurls, streaming eternity across the sky. It seems almost as if he's been sent as a messenger this Solstice afternoon.

Within the wood among the stark, leafless trees there is a profound sense of utter repose to which one must listen with one's whole body. This sense of stillness and silence is almost hypnotic – one could be absorbed by it into a quietus of word-lessness, a poem of silence, unconsciousness. It is midwinter. Richard Jefferies wrote, "The secret with all living creatures is – quiet. Be quiet, and you can form a connection… with every-thing…." The capacity of these trees to withdraw into such stillness and silence, their animating force now fast asleep, is deeply moving. Gradually sounds, remote and just audible, begin to register – the rhythmic drip-drip from a saturated moss cushion into a small gutter, the distant tinkling of a Wren settling for the night. A Buzzard, barely visible, floats silently between the trees and is gone to the restorative darkness of its roost deep within this sleeping wood.

22 December

8.00am – A mild misty morning after a wet night, the light just beginning to edge into the dark. On top of a bush up the lane a male Blackbird sits bolt upright, trance-like almost, singing very quietly to himself, obsessed beyond safety by the compulsion of his utterances. It's rather squeaky in places, with both continuous and disjointed phrases interspersed with pauses and snatches of whispered silvery sound, his subsong unlike anything the Blackbird will ever utter aloud.

8.20 – The first Crows call – in this dense mist they sound very distant, and even the river sounds muffled as if between its articulation and my hearing there's some barrier I'm not allowed to penetrate. It is said that the first hour after dawn is the busiest of the day, but down here, this day, the birds seem either to be revising their definition of dawn – or they've simply not read the right books, which often happens! There are no Crows even in the meadows to either side of the river – and then there is a solitary, but single 'pink!' from a Chaffinch – a sound both huge and important within this dense silence.

8.30 – Overhead, following the line of the river, comes the first wave of two or three dozen Jackdaws in ragged formation, playing in the wind as they come but without pausing in their purpose of destination – simply linking their play into their common passage. A second wave of sixty or seventy sweeps up and over in a tightly compact group, performing similar aerobatics so that as a flock they swirl like dark smoke, tightly bunched, shape-shifting up the far side of the valley. No sooner have they arrived than yet another three or four dozen surge up this side of the valley, following the line made by the junction of the river with the meadows. No air-play, now, though. They come low, close to the ground, intent and silent as a dawn-raiding party. That's three different lots of 'daws bound for three different destinations within the valley area. They're hardly recognisable as the same birds which sit and clown on our chimneys, gossip on roof corners, erupting into great babels of alien excitement from the larger garden tree tops – what mysteries at the heart of these most common of our village birds! They are followed by a flock of about 60 Starlings flying fast and high above the trees. Whereas the Jackdaws give the impression of flying into a felt wind, the Starlings, like clustered missiles, shear through as though down a beam of inevitable purpose linking them to an already determined destination.

8.55am – Raindrops shine everywhere, and there's the persistent, fascinating mystery of how surface tension holds these drops in impossibly gravity-defying pendants which, were they attached to a tap at home, would surely plop off into the sink! Here they remain cherished under the curl of a grass tip, run down the vein of a leaf, poised, paused in their physics, at the tip end of every slender twig – all left by the quiet rain and mist of the night only now clearing the fell tops.

9.05am – It's still quite dark. Nevertheless, Robins sing through the village, Sparrows and Jackdaws chatter and gossip from any and every perch – chimneys, aerials, roof ridges, gutter ends, telegraph poles, wires and walls. The Blackbird who was trying out his subsong nearly an hour ago is still in the same bush and still working hard.

25 December

7.30am – Very cold and clear after a hard frost – in the next half-hour the first fragmentary indications of a new day starting: a shard of Robin song; a Blackbird moves from cover onto the roof ridge which is his main vantage point; a House Sparrow sits on a gutter end, utters a single chirrup; a Tawny Owl calls, wavering between dark and dawn, Janus-like, facing both ways.

This initial transition from dark to half-light, feeling surrounded by things coming awake, watching a long, slow dawn arrive and its rapid acceleration, ushered in by birds – mainly Robins accompanied by soft chunterings from Blackbirds – is a new adventure every day. Living in a mountain valley, our horizons are always close, so, although the official sunrise is 8.30, the sun will not rise above the eastern skyline until after 9am. All the way up the lane high-perched Robins sing loud, full and clear, turning their heads and singing alternately at each other with much wing and tail flicking. Down at the river there's the perfect contrapuntal matins, three voices in continuous complement to each other – the Robins' clear, shining treble over the never ending murmur and water songs of the river and silvery staccato phrases from the Dipper by the bridge, but the further one moves away from the village down the riverside footpath, son correspondingly, both bird voice and movement declines.

8.05am – A Buzzard calls from Fletcher's Wood, Sheep huddle in the shadow-zone of the meadow wall, strung out as if in the lee of stone they might find some thermal benefit – our hardy little Herdwicks usually know what they're doing! The grass is stiff, rimed bitter with frost, and sheep must pick this into their warm mouths, scalding to their tongues.

8.15am – The tarn is really steaming now, visibility reduced to almost nil. It's impossible to move quietly through the Tanglewood to where the river flows into the lake – everything crackles with frost, the rushes tall and stiff, rattling like spears. Emerging from the little reedy island in the mouth of the river swim three male Goldeneyes in line ahead. On the dark reflecting surface of this steaming water they look superb, majestic even. The development of this little island has been fascinating. It started many years ago as a bank of river-shillets deposited after a huge flood and has since expanded as subsequent floods have found it a suitable barrier on which to deposit the silt to nurture the first algae and seeded grasses. Where I stand now was once a good viewpoint from which to watch Sandpipers in the summer, and the local Goosanders brought their small young to sit, doze, preen and generally relax on the smooth, sun-warmed shillets. It is now rank with phragmytes and other grasses, and there is even a six or seven-foot alder sapling – a fully vegetated and secure little island sanctuary about 20 yards from the rim of the bay.

8.30am – Officially sunrise, but all remains in cold shadow here. Two Crows forage in the meadow, but instead of probing into the cold, hard ground they walk among the sheep looking for anything edible which might be overturned, disturbed by their passage. They stop foraging and together indulge in a strutting display, looking more interested in each other than in foraging at the moment.

8.45am – There's no sun yet, but if I stare hard at the north ridge of the valley – always the first-lit – allowing what colour there is to flood onto the retina, the beginnings of that first glow on the bracken breasts, prelude to dawn, is just discernible; but renewed sunlight and an illusion of warmth will not happen until 9am. This makes for a very short day for such small birds as Coal Tits and Goldcrests. Many birds go to roost at about 3pm which gives them a short six hours or so in which to eat and metabolise enough fat/energy to last for 18 hours. Many of our local birds find much more food, shelter and security in the village gardens than in the surrounding winter countryside.

27 December

1.15pm – Bright, but with a bitter east wind following a very hard frost. From the Colwith road under Fletcher's Wood one can look down across the rough pasture to where the old boathouse still stands, albeit shakily, by the top tarn. It is a favourite personal landmark, not only as a subject for paintings, but also as the basis of a hide for photographing Water Rails. The local Barn Owls nested here for many years, leaving behind a huge compacted slab of castings 'cake' which provided many hours of dissecting pleasure.

Fletcher's Wood, or simply Fletcher, as its name testifies, is an ancient wood, at one time yielding wands for arrows, crops of coppice hazel for fencing and hurdles, as well as charcoal for the local gunpowder industry. The charcoal-burning pit steads may still be found, some of them now platforms from which large Douglas firs rear high above the skyline, providing the local Buzzards with territorial high-perching sites. It was part-felled many years ago, the lower part planted up with fast growing, now well-grown Japanese Larch, interspersed here and there with large, dark conifers – Douglas firs, spruces – whilst higher up there's much good oak among the other native hardwoods. These sit astride the summit of the watershed between Great and Little Langdale. In 1977 I spent many hours here 30 feet up an oak photographing Buzzards from a high hide, hours which also gave me wonderful moments with Red Squirrels and deer. Half a dozen hours at a time, day after day, sitting perfectly still, watching and waiting – much, much more waiting than watching! – became a regular routine over the five or six weeks from eggs hatching to young leaving the nest. One enters a kind of timeless zone in which every sense is permanently pricked and alert, the ears particularly, so that not a sound goes unregistered, from the crepitation as small things moved about the woodland floor litter to the zoom, hum and whine of insects all around. A few years earlier I found the remains of a shot Buzzard near this site.

The top of the wood suddenly opens out to a number of beautiful little upland sheep-grazed meadows. Undulating, with scattered rocky outcrops and occasional wind-blasted trees, these miniature alpine grasslands constitute my 'Delectable Pastures' where it's bliss to bask on a summer's afternoon, surrounded by the most magnificent scenery possible. Across the shadowy depths of Little Langdale the Tilburthwaite hills rise to the dominating hump of Wetherlam and the scything curve of Wetside Edge sweeps down to Fell Foot, enclosing between them the combe of Greenburn and its delightful beck jewelled with little craggy waterfalls and autumn-fired rowans.

This combe is often a seething bowl of concentrated atmosphere, cloud boilings, where the Raven kronks on the wet crag-ends in the churning mists – like Goatswater under Dow – a wonderful, often mythic place. Five superbly camouflaged hen Pheasants rocket up from the bottom of a bracken-skirted outcrop. The status of the Pheasant as a true member of our Cumbrian avifauna is a matter of continuing debate. The bird originally introduced by the Normans in the eleventh century – what we consider now to be our 'native' species – is a handsome bird lacking a white neck ring and of which there is a melanistic variant. An Asiatic subspecies – with a white neck ring – was subsequently so successfully introduced, bred and released that wherever there are shooting interests this bird can now be said to be very common – that is, all around the periphery of the central Lake District and up into those valleys where estates maintain shooting interests – but very sparse in more upland areas.

Back in the wood an old drovers' road leads diagonally down past former charcoal-burning pit steads where now the most magnificent Douglas Firs rear, tall, perfectly tapering columns, elegant and aromatic with high crowns of dark green foliage, where flocks of small birds gather and flutter, their tiny voices lively as sparks in the dark green gloom. This is Sparrowhawk country, and there is safety for the birds in such numbers – they could have been met with almost anywhere during their group wanderings about the wood and in a few minutes they'll all be gone. Further up the wood a Buzzard calls; a minute later it circles directly above and the small birds have disappeared, vanished in the space of making that observation, displaying their inevitable, inherited raptor response. Two Crows cross the sky in pursuit, their mobbing call unlike any other Crow utterance, a deep, gutteral, almost gargled sound, raucous and persistent until either the Buzzard leaves their territory or they leave its. Sometimes they just get tired of what is usually a quite ineffectual protest, breaking it off but satisfied to have made their point. The Buzzard has flown out of sight. Sky and wood are silent, darkening.

29 December

12.30pm – A very cold night and freezing morning. The lake is shiny with ice save for occasional patches of very dark water at the Nab and where the river runs out of the lake. The unmistakeable whistle of Goldeneye wings reinforces the silence, enriching the sense of solitude which has its own vibrations, welling outwards from self, welling inwards from surroundings so that one is wired, earthed, linked up, connected in a way that only solitude can generate. Just below the river pool the river itself is frozen across with about an inch thickness of ice, then free; frozen yet again just above the weir. On the 'Tuonela' pool – looking very dark in the cloud gathering rapidly from the north – a male Goldeneye displays to one of the two females. It's a strange display in two parts, not necessarily linked together. In one the male simply extends his head and neck outwards and up to an angle of about 45 degrees. In the other the neck is thrown vigorously back along the dorsal surface so that the large bulbous head is thrown into a vertical position with the beak slightly open, whilst simultaneously kicking back and splashing with his feet. With the water so very dark, reflecting the tall conifers at its edge, the Goldeneye's black and white reflections wobble and inter-sect, creating a constantly changing, fluid series of abstract shapes on the water.

Two Little Grebes and a solitary female Goldeneye paddle about the edges of the iced river pool, whilst at the river's exit from the lake a group of four sombrely dressed female Tufteds drift about with a rather morose-looking lack of purpose. Surprisingly, a Grey Wagtail – that most charming of our up-land stream birds – flies down to the gravelly lake shore, a glad accent of warm lemon in an otherwise grey scene, graces us with a few elegant wags of her non-stop tail and flies on down river. During the winter many of our Grey Wagtails choose to leave the upland waters they share with the Dipper; this is the only one I've seen all winter hereabouts. It fares very badly in hard weather and has never really recovered from the decimation it suffered during the winter of 1962/63 and succeeding hard winters in the 70s and 80s. In Cumbria, however, it seems to be doing quite well, with even a suggested increase (new *Atlas*) to about 5,000 pairs. I wonder how far she will go, this little wagtail, for the weather is on the change and if I'm not mistaken, snow is in the offing!

January

2 January

There was snow indeed – about five inches in the village – but it didn't stay long and 2006 came in very mild, ending the current wintry spell.

1.30pm – The lake-side meadows are bone hard and the top tarn is still frozen, ridged here and there by the stiff leavings of snow, thaw and frost, and exhaling a quiet, slow mist. The setting is bleak and inhospitable. Beyond the tarn, Lingmoor gathers mist as if drawing a cold grey mantle about its shadowy flanks. Under the grey overcast all colour seems to have leached out of the landscape, which today seems sunk in an almost ultimate dormancy. Nothing expresses its own identity with any clarity, colours merge without individual song. A bundle of sheep feeds from the fodder troughs up by Kitty Hall and steam rises from this concentration of densely wool-warmed blood.

It's so still that the surface tension of drops pendant from the tarn-side willows seems to hold them in defiance of gravity, so that what would normally drop merely wait to be frozen. The only signs of life are clues in lieu of presence, filaments of swan's down hanging from rush ends – evidence that the second winter youngster is moulting into full plumage. Ashes Point is covered with great ice slabs, things of strange, spectacular beauty, filigreed with stellar frost patterns caused by the touch of grasses beneath, etching the ice. In places the ice is as clear as glass, the grasses beneath seen as within a specimen cabinet. Only a few days ago these ice plates, only window-thin, vulnerable to the slightest exhalation of the earth or movement in the air, formed a continuous sheet, but now the thaw is coming, they lose their tension, the plates crack and break open. If one stands quite still, focussing the senses, it is possible to hear this ice – tiny, almost imperceptible creaks and groans as a hitherto trapped blade of grass spring back into position, the movement causing a reciprocal in the ice and the ice speaks of change in lie and balance.

A Heron has just come up from Dead Sheep Bay, shouting a continuous harsh, gutteral alarm; its flight expresses an air of panic disturbing the usual sedate rhythm of even its great ballooning wings. Suddenly a 12-bore shot cracks the air somewhere in amongst the carr and reeds of Dead Sheep Bay – I am outraged at the presence of a gun here! Goldeneye wings whistle and Woodpigeons erupt from the trees, clattering an escalation of shock all along the shore and a Green Woodpecker now, like some unexpected tropical flash explodes out of the wood and up-river, a sharp-pointed missile targeted upstream in long swooping undulations. A sudden Woodcock rockets out of the marginal tangle. With a slight whirr and rustle he accelerates, jinking, over the trees. Fortunately there's been no further shooting and many of the birds have re-settled.

By 3pm the afternoon is darkening by the minute and at Ashes Point the tarns are heavily misted as the ice exhales in the milder temperature. Four Crows perch close together in a dead pine by the top tarn and there's much noise until one pair, objecting to the presence of the other, finally succeeds in driving them off. It's got to that time of day when many perched Crows seem unwilling to move, an unwillingness not overcome even when passed close by a Buzzard as it approaches roosting time, and for a Crow that's real unwillingness! Back up by Kitty Hall many of the sheep are now fed and lying down, but there are still two rows, heads into the feeders, of broad, bunched woolly bottoms – Herdwicks mainly, with lovely soft blends of grey and very strong legs – wonderful animals. The village Jackdaws demonstrate their daily communication mystery as out from their incessant social chatter there suddenly erupts a great unanimous clamour like a huge shout following which the whole flock erupts into the air at the start of their erratic evening flight down the valley, an event which marks the end of every winter day.

4 January

1.30pm – After a very hard frost we've come down to the shore at Rampside, the most southerly point of the Furness mainland, terminating in the low, banked causeway leading out to Foulney Island and its continuation of mussel beds with wonderful names like Blackamoor Ridge, Conger Stones, Foulney Twist and Ragman guarding the entrance to Piel Channel and Walney Island. The romance here, however, is all in the sea and the interplay of sky and light reflected off Morecambe Bays' immense mud flats and, of course, the birds. Now, the soft perfection of this blue-gold afternoon with its only just haze-filled sunshine is ignorant of limits and boundaries; sea and sky become each other, breathe gently each into and within the other, so that there is no horizon to be endured – only the endless, elemental communion of air and water. It's three quarters of an hour to high tide and all along the salt marsh birds are gathering – Oystercatcher, Knot, Redshank and Dunlin. The sea edge of this bit of salt marsh is fretted with promontories, inlets and lagoons enclosing little islands full of huddled birds, from as many as fifty to as few as a dozen, all of which will go when forced by the tide.

Some are very unwilling to move, as if deep within a doze induced by some potency inhaled from the shimmering air, and remain standing until the water flutters about their bellies.

110

A large flock of tide-displaced Redshanks swirls by, low and fast, alternating light and dark as they twist and turn in unison, shape-shifting as smoke swirls in the slightest breeze. They move restlessly back and forth along the water's edge, dropping to the shore momentarily before taking off again, but each time leaving one or two behind so that the flock gradually decreases in a continuing process of settling, flying and re-settling. The soft powder-blue water produces the most subtle and beautiful reflections. The white bellies of the Dunlin in their midwinter plumage are only just flushed with the faintest haze of reflected light, and their slightly down-curved bills, constantly wet with being dipped into the water, shine as if freshly black-glossed. The birds maintain a constant chatter, the variegated sound dominated by the Dunlins' soft calls – an incessant, soft background to the long, rather melancholy, drooped, pure wilderness calls of the Redshank, the grating of gulls, a distant Curlew. It's nearly full tide. It's quite instructive to look along the length of some of the more elongated islands – there's a group of three Oystercatchers at the right-hand edge of this seven-by-one-foot length of grass: one stares into the water, the others roost with their beaks tucked back. Then there is a line of Redshanks; some roost, some preen. Then come one or two Dunlins – the size difference is very striking, as is their immaculate whiteness beneath. There's a definite pecking order even on these little temporary islands – if a Redshank comes down, Dunlins move off – as well as a defined order of precedence among the Oystercatchers.

Between Newbiggin and Rampside hundreds of Eiders float gently on the full tide covering Roosebeck Sands – mainly drakes, the solidity of their rafted bodies seems to press down on the water, their silent serenity enforcing an even greater calm. Here at Newbiggin are two fields full of high-tide Oystercatchers and Redshanks, the latter again very restless, and suddenly all the birds are up, hundreds of them, swirling around in the most complex of smoke-blown configurations,

111

brilliant flashing-white beneath, whirling and twisting low across the fields, a 'dread' caused by the arrival of a Peregrine, high enough to catch the light beneath him, his body thick-set and dark, broad-based wings flickering like oars dipped in the flowing current of air. He appears and disappears just as rapidly, lost to sight following the coast-line, his passage marked by a succession of such 'dreads' until they pale into misty smokiness in the distance. Far out to sea in the changing afternoon light there's what looks like a dusting of white powder widespread over the water. The furthest 'powderings' resolve into uncounted multitudes of gulls floating out the calm height of the tide, stretching as far as even the binocular-aided eye can see. The nearest, when viewed through the telescope, resolve into yet another large flock, mainly drake Eiders shining with a soft, hazy brilliance in the sunshine. Beyond them, far and wide, scattered rafts and lines of white birds are discernible only as white dustings in the mysterious haze where air and sea meet.

But the afternoon is changing fast – a large overcast spreading from the south-west, with still no horizon save for a long drawn out gleam of cold silver scratched, as if by a needle, where the horizon might or might not be. Whereas earlier the water was a soft smoky blue, it is now grey, with a pulse of restless little ripples just catching fleeting silvery sparks along their crests.

At 3.15pm we leave for home. I note that on December 21st the solstice sunrise was at 8.30am, sunset at 3.48pm. Today sunrise was at 8.31am, but sunset at 4.01pm. The mornings have gained one, but the afternoons have increased by thirteen minutes!

8 January

7.45am – Light just breaking in a heavy grey overcast. The first Robins sing, probing the dawn space with thin exploratory wires of sound; Blackbirds flit darkly across the lane on seemingly urgent, mysterious errands; a Tawny Owl hoots from over by Fletcher and is answered by another in the village; a disturbed Wren scolds.

8.20am – The Hall corner Nuthatches add their shrill contribution to the morning sounds – a Great Spotted Woodpecker drums nearby; the thin note of a Goldcrest calls from within the dark conifers by the gate. Both Jays from the Hall woods have flown into the large gateway oak; moving about the branches in a series of springy, flapped leaps which create an air of restless unease. The light is still poor and birds remain only moving silhouettes among silhouettes of tangled branches. There is considerable vocal interplay between Crows, demonstrating the often overlooked, but considerable range of tone and tempi in their vocabulary, in addition to which there's the accompanying body language – particularly impressive is the bowing call in which the sheer force of intent produces a bowing motion with tail fanned, nictitating membrane drawn over the eye with the effort of projecting the voice as far and wide as possible, so that the whole bird and what he represents at that moment is focussed right down to this extraordinary assertive bellow – a sort of vocal missile!

Noteworthy about this morning is that there's been little seen of the birds themselves – merely silhouettes among black tangled branches. This demonstrates the great importance of accurate hearing, and if all you want is to 'bag' birds, see them and tick them off a list – bird spotting – then this morning would count as a very poor result for the effort involved, particularly if they're what some discard as the 'only' types of birds – only a Blue Tit, only a Chaffinch, etc. – you see every time you step out of doors. These, however, are the endlessly fascinating bread and butter of local birdwatching, and if you're trying to build up a more realistic picture of the life around you, the small, often overlooked routine and 'only' bits of call and behaviour such as recorded this morning become part of the pattern of life.

12 January

9.00am – Very mild, but heavily overcast and threatening rain. Watching our local Dunnocks, I feel very disinclined to use the British Ornithological Union's (BOU) recent vernacular updating – *Hedge Accentor* – there's an implicit diminutive in the word 'Dunnock' that characterises not so much its size, but the appealing nature of its behaviour. To the tidy taxonomic mind, however, to have five European members of the Prunellidae of which four are 'Accentors' and one is a 'Dunnock' must be agonisingly improper! Whereas a fortnight ago there was a period of much wing-flicking and waving with pursuit flights – an activity from which it derived its Old English name 'Hegesugge', the name used by Chaucer, meaning hedge-flutterer – they appear to have resolved something, for two of them now feed close together without overt tension. Dunnocks, however, have their own very peculiar pairing system which must necessarily be anticipated here. Territory quality is everything among Dunnocks and on it depends the number of mates a male or female may acquire. It may well be that one territory will support one monogamous pair, as is the case with most of our garden birds. However, a male Dunnock with a really good territory may attract two or three females, each of which has a cunning plan. A female will try to mate with more than one male, because any male she mates with will help her with the domestics of brood-rearing. If two males mate with the same female the territories tend to merge and a dominant male will emerge from this ménage à trois. Extra-marital copulation is the order of the day in the rather matriarchal Dunnock society. Even so, a male who mates with more than one female might well be run off his feet assisting at two broods simultaneously, even at broods he has not fathered. To avoid such undesirable labour-intensive situations therefore, the males, too, have a cunning plan. Before mating, a male will peck at the female's cloaca forcing her to eject the sperm bag of any other recent male in order to ensure it is his own which will fertilize her eggs! Dunnocks are the avian still waters which run very deep!

The spread of Goldfinches in gardens throughout the land has generated much comment. Three or four pairs nested locally last year, bringing their broods to feed. They come in pairs or in families and will not tolerate the presence at the feeders of any other pair or family. The slightly brighter males are very pugnacious and for birds of their size and delicacy are well able to look after themselves, successfully out-facing Chaffinches, Blue Tits and female Great Tits which may threaten them, but are themselves outfaced, with varying degrees of success, by House Sparrows.

13 January
Heavily overcast but dry. In the gardens there is increasing vocal activity, with both Blackbird and Song Thrush working at their forthcoming songs. There's a Blackbird now within a favourite bush – as hidden and private as he can be, rehearsing with such an air of intimacy and inwardness it is almost not heard. The Song Thrush is more audible. He, too, is out of sight in a holly bush, quietly assembling and re-assembling short phrases as if sorting the basic elements of his song. His tone is not yet as clear as it will develop in his matured song utterances. This is what coming into song really signifies. The gradually increasing light stimulates the sex hormones in preparation for spring, preparations which must begin early because once the breeding season starts it is short and intense with a great deal to do within a limited time. With birds like Blackbirds and Song Thrushes which seem to take such pains to get their songs 'right', we must ask, therefore, how do they assess the current status of their song day by day until it is biologically ready for proclamation? The reason for their song in the first place is purely biological – impress a female, take, defend and hold a territory in which to breed. Therefore, as long as a song can be recognized within the species as fulfilling

that function, why do these birds go to such pains to 'improve' and 'develop' their songs beyond what might be interpreted as biological necessity? Female Great Tits respond positively to the males with the widest vocabulary; female Willow Warblers actively seek out those males with the most persistent song, and we must suppose that female Blackbirds and Thrushes respond positively to the finest songs, or what point is there in all this rehearsal? The point of the widest vocabulary, the most persistent song and the most musical performance is that not only do they proclaim ownership of a territory, but that both territory and owner are optimal – the best bird advertising ownership of the very best territory available. How does a male Blackbird know when he's developed the ultimate in song of which he is capable? Can he judge his progress? If so, does this imply some degree of musical awareness? Or even pleasure? Such matters are deep and difficult. And what of the Starling – how are we to construe his exuberant blue-morning midwinter prattling as anything other than sheer high spirits, joie-de-vivre beyond the necessities of the day? Who knows the answers to these things – mysteries they are. What is beyond doubt is the immense pleasure they give us.

14 January

12 noon – Leighton Moss. After the dull morning it has developed into one of those glorious gold and blue afternoons which provides the most exquisite light, but makes detailed observation very difficult. Down at the estuary the main island holds half a dozen Shelducks; the other has a row of Black-tailed Godwits backing a mass of Redshanks and a single Dunlin – a small bundle bunched up beside the huddle of bigger birds dozing the tide through. The many Lapwings are very restless, erupting into unpredictable aerobatics which disturb the dozing poise of the Redshanks, so that their exhilarated 'comb-and-paper' 'pee-ee-whit!' are counterpointed by the more drawn-out, slightly drooping calls of the Redshank

as some of them too seem urged to a restlessness by the activity of the Lapwings.

There are many Wigeon on the water, several on the banks projecting that sense of slow, but inevitable momentum as they feed their way forward inch by relentless inch. Suddenly, with a loud sigh of rushed wings, all the birds take off into a wheeling, whirling mass. The 'culprit' cuts through, dividing them as a boat bow cleaves water, and lands on the far bank – a young Peregrine, a 'brown boy'. His first action, suggesting he has taken prey, is to mantle over it for a moment or two before skimming off low over the marsh, twinkling in and out of visibility among the tussocks. The birds are very reluctant to re-settle and there's much whirling, circling and calling.

Beyond the boundary fence a Kestrel hovers, brilliant against the dull aubergines and browns of the leafless trees behind, his grey tail fanned, his wings working hard in the not very big wind, gradually making his way towards the few spiny twigs protruding from an old ivy-covered bush. Sitting in the sun, he looks as imperious as any Peregrine, one lifted foot fisted and clenched, sun-varnished yellow, the burn behind his eyes pulling his territory around him, a glorious sight! Below, on the lagoon edge, a Snipe relaxes in the afternoon sunshine, long beak snugged down into its dorsal plumage, the pale golden-ochre feather-edgings of mantle and scapulars breaking up its shape amongst the dead vegetation. Despite the relaxed posture – its eye is wide and very alert. Down the telescope this eye looks locked onto mine, disproportionately large, moist, shining with a reflected patch of sky.

Suddenly there's another great 'dread' – another Peregrine alert and, sure enough, at the edge of the twinkling, circling Lapwings the large, dark, looming shape of a Peregrine, bullet-bodied, streamlined, those long wings flickering in urgent counterpoint to the more measured beat of the Lapwings. He harries overhead and his onward passage is measured by the equally panic-stricken air-massing of thousands of birds,

117

receding in intersecting planes, gyring hypnotically into far, smudged spaces. It took some time for this clamour to settle, and the settling was continuously disturbed so that for nearly half an hour the entire spectacle was repeated several times. It's very hard to appreciate the realities attending this 'spectacle' of movement and sound, the magical beauty of it all. With what easy lack of consciousness we betray our alienation for, of course, this is not a wildlife spectacular – it is the reality of life and death.

Slowly the afternoon swells to a magnificent *Götterdämmerung* sunset. Walking back in the twilight, the very last sound is that of a Water Rail sharming as a huge full moon rises over the reeds beds, reflected wobbling in pools and ditches as we pass, and I thought, inevitably, of Birkin's nocturnal visit to Willey Water where "the water… was perfect in its stillness floating the moon upon it." Unlike Birkin, however, I had no desire to fragment this image as he stoned the moon…

"…the moon had exploded on the water and was flying asunder in flakes of white and dangerous fire….like white birds, the fires all broken rose across the pond fleeing in clamorous confusion."
(From *Women in Love*, D.H. Lawrence)

…and I thought of all those thousands of waders which earlier had fled in "clamorous confusion", now feeding quietly on estuary and salting, mysterious under the dark silver glow of the full moon.

17 January

8.15am – Just past dark, and the sky is beginning to clear after rain. Down in the south-east the unfolding pre-sunrise sky mutates from salmon-rose into gold, each change reflected a million times in shining drops pendant from hazel catkins, still bunched like mute fingers, but now with tender fresh greens replacing their winter lichen-greys. There's a sprinkling of fresh snow on Wetherlam, but the Crinkles and Bowfell along to Esk Pike and Great End look remote and positively alpine on their north and north-east faces.

Our Song Thrush is still in rehearsal for the main event, practicing and reassembling his repeated phrases, but, although he's singing aloud, it remains more a private than a public utterance. The gardens now are full of bird sound – bits of the avian orchestra tuning up. Gradually, over the ensuing weeks – months even – each instrument will find its true voice, the song chorus building to its peak about the middle of May. In the village centre House Sparrows and Jackdaws appear to dominate vocally, but stand and listen hard enough and the multi-tonal babble becomes merely an accompaniment to the song of the Great Tit whose particular frequency, volume, clarity and persistence enables it to over-ride this background, not only in the village but also penetrating the distance across the meadows to the river bank.

The middle tarn is well up over Ashes Point, and the tarn meadows hold extensive lagoons of flood-water. A few years ago they would have been rimmed round with Lapwings and gulls; ducks would be dabbling and Crows picking about the margins. It's sad to see nothing there now. Other than distant Crows, the almost unobserved step-by-step forward move-ment of grazing sheep and the constant soft, multi-toned swish and rustle of moving water, all is still and quiet. A Heron glides high all the way from the ridge overlooking Grasmere and out over the middle tarn in a dead-straight line without a single movement of his great wings – that's at least three quarters of a mile – so accomplished, so professional! Henry Williamson (*Tarka the Otter*, 1927), no mean observer of wildlife, defines straightness in terms of a Heron's rather than the clichéd Crow's flight – "straight as the fed Heron flies." Nothing could have been more ruler-edged than this bird's flight this morning – a serene, slow, perfectly controlled glide by a master.

Up valley the Pikes' brackeny breasts glow in response to the soft fingerings of the first real light, and the bronze-green alder catkins hang with drops shining against the dark water of the river. The rising sun lights first the gateway wall and trees and then in an astonishing accelerando light and warmth flood the meadows, and the day can truly begin. Strangely, it seems not so much that light is washed on to the landscape, superimposed, as that a 'skin' is peeled back and some virginal quality of original luminescence, newness, pristine light and order inherent in the land for daily renewal is revealed. This diurnal revelation is one of intense wonder, and the emotional response thus illuminated comes each day with equal wonder as something quite new, as if yesterday had never happened and tomorrow is utterly unimaginable; it is of the moment only, ephemeral.

Above the meadows a pair of Ravens slowly swings about the huge sky in synchro-flight mode, gliding their gentle curves and arabesques without wing flap, each maintaining exact station a wing span distant from its mate in one of the most beautiful and moving of all display flights. The more one watches these mighty birds, Odin's birds, the more they command respect and wonder. They pair for life, renewing that bond each successive spring with these majestic, intimate flights, anywhere writing their runes upon the sky. A bird rich in myth and folklore, to the Anglo-Saxons he was the Hrafon and Odin was the Hrafongud – the Raven God. He had two Ravens which flew all over the world and on their return perched on his shoulders, whispered to him all that was happening. Below them a Heron sits high on a dead tree overlooking the narrow neck of water between the top and middle tarns – a special sunrise tree favoured by this one bird. He sits high enough to catch the very first rays – adult, fully plumed, hieratic; the morning, in Dylan Thomas's birthday words, truly "heron priested".

20 January

7.30am – Just beginning to break a little light into a dark sky, although the moon is still bright. Down in the south-east the sky soars to an unbelievably pure ashen indigo, not yet a true blue. The strong south-westerly does not encourage loitering too long or scanning too intently – it's a hard wind, bruising the eyeballs, snatching song from the village gardens to be shredded by the roaring trees. The river is swollen after last night's rain, and it and the wind together make a roaring, both above and below.

8.00am – All the way down river there's been no sound of birds, but at the sheltered corner of the Tanglewood a Robin shatters the dawn with his astonishing song, so rich and loud it fills the air because of the manner by which he spreads it round, turning his head from side to side, distributing his riches left, right and centre – a superb, dominating per-formance and worth coming out for this alone! The sheep huddle under the meadow wall, sheltering from the wind, Herdwicks most of them, with a sprinkling of last year's lambs. They're not feeding. The grass looks very unappetising, uninviting in this pre-dawn yellow windy light. There is also a whisper of Blackbird subsong from a thicket of lop and top, the thin sound of a bird hesitantly exploring his voice, possibly a first winter bird with a virgin syrinx – experimental, un-certain-sounding, discontinuous; not even shaped into phrases but a few notes put together very *sotto voce* and high pitched – and there he goes, a dark shadow moving from his thicket into the furthest recesses of the wood – for Blackbirds the business of learning one's voice is an intensely private thing.

8.15am – Up in the wind-stream the morning's Jackdaws surge up-valley with an almost blind-seeming, destination-linked darkness of purpose, the birds clenched close together for aerodynamic efficiency, their flock benefit in stark contrast to two Crows struggling to make headway against the roaring gusts which barge them first to one and then the other side of their desired flight-line. They change tactics, enter a close-hauled glide mode and slant down rapidly to the fields behind the wood, shearing the wind, but even these sturdy birds land only briefly, finding little hospitability in the cold wet meadows. Looking back down the length of these meadows, all the way across to the woods below Loughrigg, the entire landscape, wild, stark and bone naked, looks dead and scoured and lifeless, flattened by this wind as if it devours for itself any vitality which might yet linger in the grass. These are still real midwinter meadows.

21 January

10.00am – A bright, mild morning, the most pre-spring-like so far.

On the Common it is necessary to stand still for some time before the ears detect the tiny sounds and mousy movements as Wrens 'tick', emerging from the tangles of dead bracken stems just long enough to catch the sunlight before bobbing down again. The recent winds and rain have so beaten down much of the standing, though dead, vegetation that it is now possible to see the extent to which last summer had been exceptional for Bog Asphodel, their stalks stiff and vertical, shining like forests of little gold pillars in their hundreds down all the soft acidic flushes. The illusion of pre-spring is shattered up here, however, by the lack of bird call, never mind song. Apart from Crows and Jackdaws, the woods and gardens of High Close are silent until we really enter the wood where all the Robins prove me wrong, and walking down the path is like entering an overgrown corridor of glorious three-dimensional song!

Loughrigg Tarn is very still with perfect reflections. But I am almost blind to them for in the distance – a Mistle Thrush!

He sounds better now than at any time later in the year, even though his song may improve with more singing, simply because after the long song-silent months it rings so, commands the attention, gladdens the heart, throwing whatever 'weather' there may be in his song back to the windy skies with sheer zest for life.

22 January

7.15am – Set off for the top of Hullet's Nest to explore the unfolding of the dawn hour. It's dark but very mild and misty.

7.20 – The first Robin sings, stimulating the next Robin up the lane. From the cottage to the bottom of the Hullet's Nest track is 13 Robin song-lengths.

7.30 – The first Blackbird 'scatter' alarm.

7.34 – The first Crow calls from down by the lake.

7.35 – Tawny Owl calls from Fletcher.

7.41 – Other than Blackbirds alarms, Robins remain the only birds singing despite the fact that there's woodland to either side.

7.46 – The first Crows fly silently over the wood. In this misty half light visibility is restricted to a wash of receding blurred conifer spires; flanking the path, the woodland oaks become tall dark pillars of ancient silence about which bird calls flash through the mist-like sparks.

7.50 – Crows materialise out of the mist, fade back in. A Blackbird flies from the hedge into the holly bush with the most gentle of protests which gradually become a little more anxious as I walk beneath the overhanging spread of his bush. Now there's sub-song – he intermingles his 'chuck…chucks' with fragments of sub-song, caught between the need to register his unease and his impulse towards song. The two blend strangely, the sub-song being a combination of hushed high-pitched squeaks and small, liquid golden phrases, a thin thread of sparks sizzling up into the air from the deep igniting caverns of his mystery, tender and intimate as the distant stars.

7.55am – Great and Blue Tits call and sing in Sawrey's Wood. From 7.15am the growth curve of light increase was quite shallow; now the rise is sharper. At the top by the gate it's very still except for the incessant drip of mist-dew beads on to the dead brackens and leaves below. A Crow comes in low following the line of the track, sees me rounding the bend, performs a very abrupt, powerful and audible wing adjustment to swing him rapidly from his flight-line, the 'thrum' of a wing used in extremis.

8.15am – It's misty, silent otherworld up at the top of the watershed (about 600 feet a.s.l.). The grasses and rushes retain some vestige of colour to a distance of about 20 yards, after which everything fades into a misty infinity in which nothing claims or reveals identity save an occasional stunted tree and that only as a blurred mound. All's a mystery, shapes which materialise and float away into the shadowy silence of infinite, enveloping mists.

8.35am – Past official sunrise time, but no sunrise this morning – it's very cold and time to move on. Walking back down the track, one re-enters the main zone of call and song. A Great Spotted Woodpecker drums in Fletcher, a sound signal in lieu of song. A solitary female perched on the Blackbird holly bush 'chucks' softly as I approach. Her tail betrays her increasing alarm as her call sharpens to 'chück', the syllables escalating to increased urgency as I approach her very slowly; her tail flicks increasingly rapidly – she does, after all, have the option to fly! I stop, stand still and the alarm begins to downgrade. She remains perched as I come very slowly to stand right beneath her, a most beautiful adult female. Standing still once more encourages her to downgrade her alarm to a soft sequence of 'chucks' with an admixture of 'chücks' just to let me know that she's still rather wary. The bird to person relationship which develops, however briefly, during the course of such meetings has a degree of intimacy which I have found impossible with other birds; you know that your presence and her changing vocal responses are inextricably locked together in tense moments of intimate mutual awareness.

8.50am – A very deep-toned hammering reveals where the Great Spotted Woodpecker has found a particularly resonant sounding board, but it elicits no response. Hidden in the bottom of the hedge a Dunnock is busy with his sub-song. He's never still, putting his bits of private whispered warble and whistle together in combination with a considerable physical restlessness which might be thought unproductive when compared to the Blackbird's concentrated, still, self-absorption – some of us, however, think sitting still, others must pace about! A noisy chorus of House Sparrows and Jackdaws accompanies me into the village centre and suddenly there's a resurgence of bird sound from all around.

24 January

Taking advantage of visiting a friend in Lancaster hospital this afternoon, we visit the northernmost end of Morecambe in order to look out over the vast expanse of the Bay, but the visibility is poor and beyond the great channel everything recedes into a blue haze.

Five or six hundred Curlews, and smaller numbers of Redshank and Knot, are slowly being forced back from the edge of the great channel by the flooding tide – an exquisite picture in this hazy light. On the far side of the channel thousands of birds dot the mud, regularly spaced so that each moves within its own constantly moving feeding space, rarely impinging on that of any other bird. Morecambe Bay is a huge area of nearly 200 square miles, of which about 130 square miles of sand and mud are exposed at the very lowest tides – one of the largest continuous intertidal areas in Britain. Like all true estuaries, it is an area in continual flux in its changing proportions of water to mud as the tide flows and ebbs. Each full tide cycle, moreover, brings changes in surface, texture,

125

content, of which the thousands of dependent birds must be aware and quick to exploit. It is a habitat of endless fascination and excitement – quite apart from the birds – with its vast mud flats varying everywhere in tone, colour and texture – dark and pale purple greys, light-reflecting wet mud, the intrusions of harder, drier sand-bars and rocky scars, and always giving back to the eye what it receives from the sky, all blending into a presence and an atmosphere which is utterly spell-binding. This vast desolate, dangerous area is a huge powerhouse of energy containing food resources so prolifically abundant that some of the largest concentrations of birds in Europe, mainly waders, assemble here year after year. Each cubic metre of mud may contain over 20,000 various food items – small bivalve molluscs and marine snails, lug- and rag worms and various shrimp-like creatures, whilst in some parts of the Bay are large mussel beds and immense numbers of small mussel 'spat' which settle in late winter and early spring to be taken in vast numbers mainly by the huge wintering flocks of Knot. Add other small molluscs, a wealth of cockles, shore crabs and small creatures like the shore-living sandhoppers, and we begin to get some idea of the truly astronomical food resources available during the intertidal hours, and taken by vast numbers of birds according to their food preferences, their leg length, bill length and structure, and their feeding habits which finally resolve into those which pick and peck on the surface – short-billed birds like the plovers, continually on the move from one surface area to the next – and those which probe deeper. Some birds combine both methods – the Curlew, for example, takes many small crabs from the surface while able also to probe down into the mud for deeply hidden delicacies.

As the bay fills, there is everywhere a continual movement of birds off the mud. Restless flocks of Lapwings climb in tightly packed pied flickering circles until lost to sight. The Knot look even more hunched than usual, very pale against the darker Curlews and Godwits; pale-breasted, too, the relatively few Dunlins. From time to time little groups of up to a dozen Curlews leave the flock, heading for inland pasture land where they will sit out the tide. Despite their dark appearance against the water as they fly past, one after the other displays pale belly and underwing, nearly lost in the afternoon sunlight with only the dark wing tips indicating their motion through the air. Oystercatchers pipe, adding an escalating sense of urgency to the now rapidly changing tidal situation. Out where the mud bank curves over and down to the flooding channel a solitary Greenshank appears almost white headed. The whole bird provides a wonderful example of counter shading – dark bill, slightly recurved, against pale water, pale body against dark mud and the more distant background of darker Godwits and Curlews against which it seems almost insubstantial, wraith-like.

5.00pm – The tide is full and every little scar and island holds its tight huddle of Oystercatchers with huge numbers assembled at Hest Bank where the entire shoreline is black with birds. Not far off the breakwater swim a Mute Swan and a couple of Shelducks. It's a very soft tide, glazed with hazy light. Just as earlier, the mud was densely populated with evenly spaced waders, so now the glassy water is flecked with quite evenly spaced gulls riding the quiet tide. The Swan and the gulls, being white, look glazed over with light reflected from the glassy water, so each bird rides in its own faint haze as though seen through a soft-focus lens. But it's the end of the day – this light does not last long. The sky is pale above, the very palest blue imaginable, blending to gold in the west. Behind me an evening Mistle Thrush sings. It's time to go.

25 January

A clear, perfect pre-spring morning, with that rather special 'something' in the air stimulating the start of another Buzzard year, with birds becoming active about fellside, field and winter woods.

Many Buzzards are already indicating that it's time to begin the long process of territory declaration and pair formation (or consolidation) by 'high-perching', often on top of some conifer – "I'm here, I'm visible, I'm available (if not already one of a pair) and all around me is my territory – keep out!" When conditions are right, particularly during a rising pressure system, he will also begin to soar, advertising not only the area of his territory, but also its vertical height above which is common air space. This is also the time when the birds initiate their first bonding procedures, and a day such as today might even see them in the air together. When one considers that by April the larger, more powerful female must actively solicit an apparently aggressive series of copulations by a smaller male one realises that this must be worked towards very gradually and with great care. One of the first steps is counter soaring in which the birds soar together in opposite spirals which expand and contract as the birds wheel, allowing them to participate in a joint effort without touching, maintaining critical tolerance distances, both birds knowing that there's space to lessen the tension if necessary, either by diving out of the situation or going off to soar independently, before resuming counter soaring. The onset of counter-soaring marks an important stage in the developing annual cycle, not only for the birds but for me, for it symbolises reassurance that everything is still going – however roughly – to plan!

That 'something special' in the air today affected not only the Buzzards, for as we watched the skyline of one hilly pasture, a long, seemingly never-ending line of Herring Gulls streamed over its crest, thronging the sky overhead with hundreds of shining birds, for no reason we could see – there was no muck-spreading, no ploughing. They whirled in counter-soaring layers arranged in a series of vertical planes, wheeling, weaving, catching the light with brilliant flecks as they turned, their wings almost transparent, the pure white trailing edges brilliantly lit against the blue. This whirling white-lit soaring gyre continued for some minutes and then, strangely, dispersed as quickly and mysteriously as it had formed and the gulls were gone, leaving behind a sense of meaningful visitation, but cryptic as an oracle.

26 January

Another beautiful morning after a hard night's frost, the cold stretching skin tight over bones. On the knoll the shadows are very cold, an arctic blue-grey glazing the chrome-green rush stems. The shining, sunlit meadows beyond, however, although heavily frosted, were flushed with a hint of green as though it were trying to wash its way through the blue-white glaze.

Down by the bridge a Chaffinch starts his song – in the well-known bowling analogy, just starting his run-up, and probably a first year male as yet without song. He gets as far as the first 'paces' and then stops. He repeats it, trying it out and gets a little further. All the Chaffinches in the area listen to each other, because, although a Chaffinch is born with the basic pattern of his song, he must learn its sound details from other Chaffinches. This explains why we hear so many incomplete struggles from males at this time of the year, especially in the middle and most problematical phase of the song, also the phase in which individual variation is most likely. It is astonishing, after long weeks of hearing nothing from Chaffinches but various 'pinking' calls, that suddenly, one morning – this morning of mornings – they are all apparently overcome by the urge to sing! It's good now to be able to add just a little bit more to the developing chorus of bird voice as gonads respond to the light increase by two or three minutes every day. On the other side of the track the Buzzard is in his usual tree apparently drowsing in the morning sun – he looks so casual, content, so deserving of the French falconers' epithet 'lazybones' – but I know him. I know that those eyes are his consciousness focussed down long bright tunnels over the arched bridge of his beak, focussed to every present moment. He may appear as if in a daydream of new warmth and light, but he is present, in this moment now, absorbing his surroundings, intensely aware of every changing detail moment by moment and of what might benefit him, what might be to his advantage…

"It took the whole of Creation
To produce my foot, my each feather:
Now I hold Creation in my foot
Or fly up, and revolve it all slowly –"
(*Hawk Roosting*, Ted Hughes)

He hears something beyond my range, leans forward, pushes with his bright yellow feet and with a flash of pale sunlit underwing jumps into the still air, beats slowly over to the tangle of carr round the old boathouse where, with hoarse, throaty shouts filtered through the whisper of reeds, a couple of Crows mob the Buzzard on his new perch.

The top tarn is still deeply shadowed by the surrounding trees. Pausing to look back – always essential! – Lingmoor and the high fells behind stretch clear and hard lined against the sky, details of every crack, crag and gully etched with an almost Dali-like precision, so that it seems for a moment like walking through a dream, somehow apart from what people like to call 'real life' but, of course, this is real life where every second life is lived on the edge of death; this is the arena for survival at its most basic and raw.

Among the pines of the top-tarn wood, snug and dry where the rock gives cover, a flat, two-dimensional jumble of last autumn's leaves re-assembles – as if in obedience to a muttered spell – magicked into a Woodcock almost under my feet. As it weaves through the trees, light shines along the length of his down-tilted bill. In the quiet corner of the top bay the local Mute Swans and their second-winter youngster swim together. The pair did not breed last year and this youngster from the previous spring has stayed around the tarns all autumn and winter so far, tolerated against all the odds by this particularly aggressive cob. A Cormorant swims, low in the water, only his head and neck showing. It has a cold, calculating eye, green as the water it rides, bearing and bill clinical as forceps. Coal Tits call as they feed in the tops of the tall alders and pines, their calls pert and defined as the birds themselves.

After the shadowed wood the meadows are radiant. Grasses twinkle with frost pendants bent over, hung with crystal drops which, as the sun works on them, exchange their icy translucence for shining water droplets, hung globes reflecting the sparkling world about them a myriad times – the near immortality of memory and experience sown among stars. A Crow sits on top of the tallest tree by the riverbank, looking around, watching for whatever may be to *his* advantage. He's burnished almost yellow in this brilliant light. Down towards Ashes Point there's the companionable chime of Teal-talk – about 20 males in a sunny, secluded bay overhung by stunted willow carr, a favoured spot for these little ducks, and more than I've seen here for a long time. A drowsy male Goldeneye on the far side of the tarn slowly revolves his world of unexpected, but apparently pleasing eddies spun by some mystery of increasing warmth into his bit of water. A pair of Goosanders swims down the sun-glare, path-fading from sight into light like the magic end of some myth.

A slight mist rises from the water and visibility becomes difficult. The lake surface is covered with little feathers which also hang like small bits of washing from the reeds and grasses – probably from this second winter bird in its gradual moult towards adult plumage. It is truly glorious here this morning, listening to the companionable Teal, surveying the ancient, surreal sculpture of the mountains, the silence of the dense shadows on the far side, the calls of small birds going about their morning business. A Blue Tit has arrived in the alder

131

behind me, perched up against the pure blue of the sky. The caeruleum of his cap, tail and wings – the latter partly opened and drooped – react against the almost pure cobalt of the sky, somehow brightening and intensifying all his colour and presence, re-defining the concept 'Blue Tit', stunning the senses with revelation, a catalyst energising the consciousness to wonder at the recreation of the known commonplace into something emblematic, as Blake saw the grain of sand or as Boethius established his terms of reference for eternity –

"…to hold and to possess the whole fullness of life in one moment,
here and now, past and present and to come."

There's no wind down here and for a few moments there is silence – nothing moves, no sound of distant traffic, no talk of Teal. This is how this place has been for hundreds of years, unchanging save for adjustments in water levels, vegetation and the calls and movement of birds in due season, and it gives one a momentary, potent perspective through time. Such a depth of silence is very rare and an adventure into which each one of us enters, responds to in his or her own way, depending on what the imagination or one's sense of connection whispers in each different situation. I've seen responses range from tear-filled wonder to panic-stricken terror even. One of the most astonishing places in midwinter conditions is Tarn Howes on midweek midmornings when one usually has it to oneself. There is a sense of being up in a rarer space, high above the unseen valleys and ringed round by the alpine iron of the high fells. The tarn is as iron-bound with ice as the fells, the frozen water a membrane against which the intensity of silence generated by nights under remote stars resonates in sympathy with the ear drum. Windless, the still, dark column of a tall pine seems to act as a receiver for all those wavelengths of silence sighed at the hub of space, and the air about it, unrelieved by Raven or Robin, pulsates. One such morning I was up there when a young man and his girl embarked on a walk. Away from the car, suddenly alone within this vast pulsating, silent space she very soon felt vulnerable, distressed to a panic attack beyond the ministrations of her companion even. Putting her hands to her ears to block out the screaming silence she stumbled back to the car and immediately switched on the radio to regain some sense of her own normality and self control. I had never before seen such an extreme reaction to the realities of intense space – I hope never to again. Truly, silence has its own way of speaking individually to each and every one.

A small party of five Teals springs from the reeds by South Bay, flies off low towards the bottom tarn; their launch-ripples lap ever-outward, their wavelengths widening and subsiding until once again they become the glassy stillness at the tarn's centre. The trees are perfectly reflected, and if ever there was a platonic ideal of perfection in time and space this would have to be it absolutely, but this is not ideal, it is real, vibrant and alive and I'm here with it!

Back up by Kitty Hall copse the Buzzard comes up off the ground and into the sunlit branches of an old oak, only some 30 yards away. He is a dark bird, possibly the same bird seen on December 13th. His breast is much barred, lacking the usual definitive 'necklace' – that dark and creamy crescent seen so often about the upper breast. He goes off into his morning calling tree from which I dislodged him earlier and now glides slowly, with an occasional flap, the light shining under his wing as his primaries feel for the support of air over the morning meadows.

27 January

A cool, slightly damp morning after a night's frost. Three song-related items this morning. Up the lane into the village a Mistle Thrush sat singing on top of a Lawson's Cypress, his phrases flaunted, rolling out one after another. He's rather late this year, and I've heard no sub-song, his full song apparently springing – like Athene from the split skull of Zeus – fully formed, matured and proclaimed as if it were not there yesterday but here today! – quite unlike Blackbirds with their intense sub-song rehearsals, or Chaffinches who work at their song one phrase at a time. Another song I've been waiting for also matured this morning – that of the Dunnock. I've heard his sub-songs, his rehearsals in the dark, secret depths of over-grown shrubberies, but today it too arrived. It's been described as a 'bright but rather monotonous warble', but it pleases my ear with its clarity, definition and not a little swagger, what Grey described as 'spirit and uplift', surprising, perhaps, considering the unobtrusive nature of this most remarkable little bird. The third song item this morning relates to a Song Thrush – sitting openly in a larch quietly rehearsing a limited number of repeated phrases, rather louder than that sense of total privacy generated by the Blackbird, but enough to be heard only a few yards away, yet by no means a song.

29 January

7.15am – Off to compare last Tuesday's damp, misty walk up to the watershed with this morning – clear and cold after frost, stars still firing the pre-dawn glow and brilliant Venus for company high over Fletcher. The first Robin sings, a voice sharp-fired, caught from the stars, initiating a constellation of Robin song all up the lane. A distant Tawny Owl hoots, rounding out the air; another calls from the opposite direction, its outward-lapping, rounded bubbles rebounding against those of the first call. The volume of song decreases outwards from the edge of the village to the bottom of the track.

7.40 – At Andrew's Field now, and today, instead of dim receding spires of pale misted conifers beyond the top of the field and the watershed, Wetherlam bulks up against a pale, gold-flushed indigo tinted sky. There's much less song/call up here this morning than a week ago when, although there was a lot less light, it was also several degrees warmer.

7.41am – Great Tits and Robins sing up by Sawrey's Wood and across the field Fletcher sleeps. I had expected much more vocal activity – not necessarily song – this morning, because this aspect of the wood faces straight into the sunrise. The other thing to consider is that it's no good waking up to a world in which the temperature is so low that food is not yet available!

7.45 – Up here it is a brilliant morning; looking down across Elterwater and towards Windermere a thin mist rises in vaporous layers. Above the head of Windermere the dark, sharp blade of Wansfell Pike cleaves up towards the light, yet it still manages not to look like a piece of cut-out, super-imposed stage scenery. Whereas in nature the hard edge of a mountain horizon exists as a visual fact, such hard edges are shunned by 'painterly' landscape painters because they destroy the illusion of a dimension over the top and down the other side. Art must preserve our illusions because we take images from the context of the surrounding world of sensory experience, each fragment of which – the feel of wind on our cheeks, the scent of a flower, the calls of birds, the perspective and over-roll of every visual object from foreground backwards – contributes to our knowledge that that distant cardboard cut out of Wansfell stuck to the dawn sky does in fact descend to unseen Troutbeck on the far side, and you won't fall off that apparent edge of the known world! Many hazel catkins now are loosening and unfurling, but there's a great deal of individual difference here – it's possible to find one tree with the catkins still bunched tight, whilst its neighbour, benefitting from identical conditions, displays fully open catkins.

7.47 – The first Crow calls from further down the track and one flies overhead.

8.00 – Across the top of the watershed it is, for a few moments, totally silent – the impact after leaving the wood, the sense of suddenly achieved, unenclosed loftiness, cracking open the consciousness and flooding it with new space is so great it drowns out for those few moments the hitherto unheard bleat of a sheep on the distant fell, even the bellow of a Crow, the drumming of a Woodpecker down in distant Little Langdale.

8.03am – At the summit of the watershed it's a white, frozen world. Even the sheep seem more like metamorphosing rocks, slowly coming bitterly awake from the secrets of an ancient sleep. The sun has yet to rise (official sunrise is 8.05). A Snipe rockets harshly from the track-side rushes, jinks across the stiff marshes towards the top of Fletcher. Nine Pheasants glide in a long slant down from Howe Banks like a fusillade of missiles, so direct and swift are they in their elongated, concentrated aim, as a single body, for one particular, seemingly pre-chosen target in the rushy meadows below Black Wood.

8.10 – The very first sunlight strikes Wetherlam and Great Carrs, flaring roseate and rosy-grey all the way up Wetherlam Edge, whilst Lingmoor's upper crags and brackens glow as if hardening off a molten dawn-flow of volcanic renewal.

8.15 – In an old yew high on Lingmoor a Chaffinch struggles with his song, and one might think that if a Chaffinch can almost perfect his song up here, half-way up Lingmoor on a frozen morning they ought to be managing better down in the village! Distantly, down in Little Langdale, a Green Wood-pecker yaffles.

8.20 – High above, their voices muffled in the cold air, 20 grey geese, the skein shape-changing with a ripple that trembles down the chevron's arm as bird after bird adjusts to the slip-stream of the preceding bird, disappear over Ling-moor's fiery shoulder. The light on Great Carrs is now an intense, buttery yellow, defining each groove and gully, folding round each buttress and spur, whilst the shadow line on Ling-moor creeps ever lower, the fellside above flooded with light.

8.30am – The tip of the new sun rises above the distant hills, climbing fast, pumping out light, the ice-tipped grasses and rushes suddenly twinkling and chiming with tiny ice crystals. It's exhilarating to be standing in a golden pool of the day's first sunlight, but it's very cold after half an hour's standing and waiting!

8.40 – Back at the top gate, and the wood is now flooded with a soft buttery light and small birds shoot like stars among the branches, materialising and disappearing as they flash across the retina, lingering neither in the eye nor in space.

8.45 – The valleys below are swathed in a cold mist. A Green Woodpecker's manic shrill shatters the still air among the trees in the Hall wood, is answered by another in Fletcher, and yet another from deep in Bayesbrown Wood – it's good to know that there's no shortage of these locally.

9.15 – Back in the village there's no sign of human life – nobody in the lanes, no vehicles. Smoke rises in vertical blue plumes and Jackdaws are busy about the chimneys. Sparrows chatter on spouts; a Greenfinch wheezes; a Chaffinch works indefatigably at his song.

(Note: A comparison of the times at which different birds started to sing/call on 22nd and today, covering the same ground at the same time, shows that although 22nd was damp, dark and misty, today's clear, bright and very frosty conditions with a temperature drop of about 1.5° over a climb of about 450 feet had not been the inhibiting factor I had thought it might be.)

30 January

2.30pm – A beautiful afternoon after a very hard, frosty night and morning. The tarns are frozen and the river is iced over below the pool. Standing at the bridge now, between village and meadows, those few yards from sunlit to shadow make all the difference, the difference between a volume of varied bird sound and total silence. Robins sing and Chaffinches 'pink' on

137

the sunlit far side, but along the shadowed bank of the river all is quiet. The beck is quite low, the water clear and transparent, the sunlit pebbles on its bed presenting a green-ochre illusion of warmth. The alder catkins are a rich plum colour in the sunshine, but unlike the hazels which daily show signs of unfurling, these are still stiff, tightly bunched.

In the bridge pool a series of expanding ripples and concentric circles materialise into a Dipper swimming under water in a pool at least three feet deep. When submerged, a trail of bubbles betrays his position. Sometimes these dribble up vertically, showing that he's dived straight down. Underwater he has a silvery sheen due the air bubbles trapped between his feathers, like a water shrew. Although this helps to preserve his temperature in very cold water, it also gives him buoyancy problems in that he must work hard, using his wings, to remain underwater, so that when he re-surfaces he bobs up like a ball that's been held underwater and let go! Over the bridge and across the road the Gala field has just been mucked and six glossy Crows strut their stuff, shining in the low, late afternoon sun.

3.30pm – Up at Walthwaite on the old road above Chapel Stile the south-facing fellside is still radiant in glorious sunshine, the brackens a richly saturated russet, the rocks of Raven Crag soft, warm ochre-greys. From where I'm standing the sun sits plumb on the ridge of Lingmoor. At any moment it's going to roll down the other side. A last ray slants, almost horizontal, across the summit, drawing a defining line across the dark, frosted shadow of Lingmoor's north-facing slopes which will see no sun again until spring. How very quickly the sun sinks once it starts – the lower it gets the more intense this beam-shine across the top of the fell, until it's gone – it takes only one and a half minutes for the sun to fall off the edge of the visible world! Straight up the valley Bowfell looks magnificent, saturated with both sunlight and shadow tone. It changes colour from one minute to the next, from buttery to a kind of hazed milky-blue. The reason for this lies in what one looks at first. If I stare unblinking at the blue, shadowy depths of the north face of Lingmoor, and then at Bowfell, it looks yellow. If I flood the retina with the warm glowing russets of the bracken and then look at Bowfell, it appears milky-blue. There is surely no such thing as fact, perhaps not even truth, and reality is a truly individual perception.

An old thorn grows out from a small fellside crag. Perched on top is a Kestrel, making the most of the last sunshine. In the low evening sun among the glowing brackens he almost assumes their tone, the rich buffs of his breast washed with some of the reflected light from the brackens below him. He looks around and he's off, swinging about the sky, alternately gliding and flapping and the play of light and shadow as he swings about in this low evening sun flickers underwing like a code. Sliding fast down the ridge eastwards towards Hunting Stile and Hammerscar, he's suddenly no Kestrel, he's just falcon, Horus riding towards sunrise as the sun falls out of the western sky, gone to meet the sun, focussed like a dream between his eyes, brown and gentle as death itself, and drag it up the eastern sky of morning.

February

1 February

Those of us brought up within the old folklore memories of what characterised the sequence of months will remember 'February fill-dyke', having its roots in the Old English 'Solmonath', from the prevailing conditions of the soil in this month, 'mud-month'. After a night's hard frost, a raw sunless morning.

7.15am – Up to High Close Wood. A Mistle Thrush sings with a rich flutey tone, occasional repetitions and already beginning to achieve that ritualistic proclamatory style so enjoyably characteristic of both Mistle Thrush and Blackbird, as yet imperfect, but promising. A Tawny Owl calls from the bottom of Fletcher, is answered by Owls from both the Hall and over Baysbrown way – three birds in the process of defining territory that from the Hall woods being exactly between the other two.

7.39 – Occasionally, in this crepuscular world a darker shape detaches itself from the layers of banked-up dead leaves and a small bird bolts up into the trees. I've been sitting on a log for several minutes surrounded by an almost tangible silence. What by now is a noisy pre-spring morning down in the village is still a quiet midwinter wood up here. From higher up the wood there's a sudden uproar from Carrion Crows – a Buzzard moving about, perhaps…

7.44am – …followed by the first ringing shout and sight of a Buzzard moving darkly down the wood's edge, calling a chain of bright ringing links from cover to trembling air. It had been perched at the wood's edge overlooking the collection of fresh, crumbly mounds left dark on the frosted meadow by the local moles on the other side of the fence.

7.57 – It's very difficult seeing birds in here, even when they do move – they are all up in the tree tops, a place of black, up-ended besoms and little to see except in the blank spaces of sky between the trees, where, at times, a small black flake detaches itself, moves, re-attaches to a larger bit of black! A family group of seven Long-tailed Tits darting about with their usual mercurial air of erratic unpredictability is, at first glance, merely a number of dark motes in the eye before they become birds. A Coal Tit chimes – his high-pitched, clear voice totally appropriate to the jaunty charm of this little bird. Ears are so important. Sound, its recognition and, if possible, its understanding, determines the extent of one's immediate environmental knowledge. More often than not the ears provide a first focus for the eyes. The inability to recognise song and, to some extent at least, identify and interpret call imposes severe limitations on the observer, and even after many years' field experience I feel I'm only scratching the surface.

8.05 – The top of the wood is also the centre of a Roe Deer's territory, and I find two in their usual place among the thickets below the top wall. One disappears immediately, but the other, typically inquisitive, stands still, ears erect, alert, looking directly at me with an intense concentration which I return, so that there is, for the eternity of almost a full minute, a strong sense of link from eye to eye. She eventually turns her back, her caudal disc shining out like a signal, but keeps her head turned, maintaining her stare. She's the first to move, casually almost, breaking off the exchanged intimacy, following the other into the thicket but unable to resist a last inquisitive

141

look! Their white caudal discs shine through spaces in the dark thicket, until the last all I see is an intermittent flashing white rump as one of them bounds down the wood and out of sight, followed by the carrying voice of the buck – an explosive 'böh!', a gruff half-cough, half bark.

8.25am – Here, out on the open fell at 600 feet, the creeping edge of a chill mist which has settled into and over the valley, blanking out the surrounding hills. The air is empty; there's not even the usual ticking of Wrens from the brackens. A Robin bursts from a bracken clump only a few yards away and flies straight into a dark hole in the wall, a thing done at speed and with unerring accuracy as if this were something he's well used to doing. Some quality of air seems to inhibit flight this morning, even the local Crows and Jackdaws are unwilling to take flight. Re-entering the village from the Common, however, the contrast could not be greater – Sparrows gossip, Greenfinches wheeze, Chaffinches work their songs to triumphant conclusions, Robins and Great Tits sing whilst somewhere unseen a Starling rattles and bubbles his usual boisterous joie de vivre no matter what the quality of the morning affecting dour corvids!

9.15 – At home a cock Blackbird sits on the roof edge of the gutter. He chuck-chucks and then goes straight into a type of near scatter-alarm, but higher pitched than usual, and tending to diminuendo instead of the usual crescendo. He repeats this before beginning a sub-song bearing no resemblance to the kind of phrasing or note sequence one might expect to hear in an ultimately developed song. It's very high pitched, full of little piping sounds, some quite squeaky and unmusical, only just audible, uttered as it is with bill closed. From this again back into the strange alarm preceded by quiet 'chuck-chucks', thus completing a full cycle of sounds. He may be bothered by my presence, but not bothered enough to affect the very private intensity of his almost introspective-seeming practice – a bird caught in a conflict between the urge to alarm, possibly even to flee, and the demands of his gonads!

3 February

1.30pm – After a complete white-out this morning. The fog has thinned to a softly beautiful, mild afternoon, an almost milky haze softening the light on the fellside, truly exquisite!

Chaffinches are still in various stages of song development. Many finding their song now would have fledged last spring and at some critical period during their infancy – usually between fledging and independence – attempt to match an inherited, roughly formed template for the species song to repeatedly heard adult songs, until, during a memorisation process, that rough template is transformed into an exact template. Those birds now feel the urge to sing, gradually improving the efficiency of their first performances until they begin to match the memorised, exact template. Whereas most Chaffinches are quite open about their 'struggle', others prefer privacy. Somewhere within the dark interior of a tall *Cupressus* another Chaffinch tries his song, the sound dwindling away into a quiet little sub-song of small pipings and squeakings which bear no resemblance to any kind of ultimate song. Everywhere Crows and Jackdaws sit upright, close together in quietly intimate mutual preening. A pair of Crows sits together on a sunny branch, he slightly above her, nuzzling and preening her head and neck to which she responds by leaning into the pressure as does a cat when rubbed behind its ears. I thought he was a bit rough with his great bill for splitting small skulls and digging out eyeballs, but this was rough tenderness and she seemed to enjoy it!

In the shallow rapids at the tail of the bridge pool the resident Dipper bobs about on the boulders, picking at bits of moss, gradually making his way downstream. He sings, he bobs and preens, nictitating membrane flashing like an Aldis-lamp. In the low, almost grazed light his mantle and tertials

143

appear almost scaly. It's only this kind of light that reveals the complex blending of very deep chestnuts and matt sooty blacks within his plumage. The pool is his treasure, however, and he soon returns to its mossy jewelled depths – I could watch him all day, but it's time to move on.

Further upstream the river makes a sweeping turn westwards, its surface glazed with mother-of-pearl in this hazy afternoon sun. Overhung by mature alders and oaks, this is one of my favourite bits of 'orchestral' river as it ripples over shallow shillets and small cascades – a whole score of sounds. Half a dozen well-whitewashed mossy boulders testify to their habitual use by Dippers, evidently anything but casual in their use of the river, creating, as they must do, their own 'mental maps' of the way they use the river. A pair of Mallards drowses in the sunshine, their heads tucked in, the sunlight brilliant on the structural greens and blues of the drake's head and speculum. They're not asleep, however, and the duck has me fixed with a very beady eye. I leave the footpath and the ducks to their dreams and follow my own way through the wood to Baysbrown Tarn.

During the summer this unsuspected entrance to the lower wood is well disguised by a curtain of greenery which must be lifted like a ceremony of admission, an 'Open Sesame' to a trail of hidden secrets and adventures totally different each time it's travelled – a portal to an interface of habitats. Within the entrance lie many massive old boulders, humped and huge with mantles of moss, the low sun catching their rounding-over, as if they're blanketed sleeping forms such as Henry Moore might have enjoyed. The shadows are soft, and the moss has claimed them gently and completely, with an intimate reverence for their forms and slumbers. Here's one like some ancient figure sinking slowly down to the centre of the earth, embryonic in its pre-birth dreams of life – some ancient mythic thing waiting for the right signal to rouse and rise. The mythic atmosphere generated by the stones is confirmed by the overhead calls of a Raven writing his runes upon the sky, his harsh call somehow smoother than his usual call as if the soft sunshine had blunted the rough corners of his rocky shout, and there, very high in a bit of blue between the trees, a pair of Ravens in their wonderful intimate bonding flight, wing tip to wing tip, swinging, sweeping as one organism in stately arabesques over the high ridge of Lingmoor pale and milky-hazed in the soft sun. There is an excellent sitting stone here from which to stare into and beyond the surrounding trees towards the rough ground where quarry tip and wood edge meet in a rushy marginal area. This interface of two contrasting habitats is sometimes revealing for there's a change in tempera-ture zones, as from the coolness of the wood one can feel the radiation of warmth from the sun-warmed rocks of the quarry-tip downfall.

As the sun goes down behind the ridge, this northern aspect of Lingmoor loses that soft downfall of misty light and hazy outline and is now a hard-edged milky indigo against the high drifting blue and white. The boundary wall between the wood and the fields outside is a wall with posts and wire – the 'Cuckoo wall' I've called it from the many years I've watched Cuckoos perched looking out across the upper Baysbrown meadows, the little conifer copse by the tarn, Lingmoor's deepening indigo shadow and away westwards to the Pikes so softly milky in this lovely afternoon light. No Cuckoos this afternoon, of course, but a single Robin, bowing and bobbing, watching my entrance into the rough ground above Baysbrown Tarn like some approving janitor. The small tarn is grey and frozen. From the outliers of the wood on its far side floats a Buzzard – more a floating drift of soft tone than a bird, weightless almost, a brown shadow over the mixed conifer copse, floating and gone, low across the ground, hugging the shadows.

3.00pm – The only movement is that of a group of Herd-wicks crossing the dam from one pasture, via the wood's edge, to another, their neat little hooves rattling on the stony track. There's the beginning of a mist in the atmosphere now, a milky transparent haze-filtering tone and colour from the more distant fellsides. The Sweet Gale around the tarn is a glorious tone of purple rich against the dead *Molinia* tussocks out of which it grows. Its buds are full, some green, some brown-scaled but all ripe and juicy within. I've taken the liberty of picking one, opening it out and rubbing it on my palm – fragrant and aromatic, waiting for the right day.

3.25pm – Baysbrown Farm is shadowed now, but to the north the valley's main boundary ridge is gradually acquiring a most delicate light, soft and made slightly opaque by the milky-hazed atmosphere creeping up the hillside from the valley bottom. Huge areas of this broad, fertile stretch of the valley are now under soft rush, beyond grazing – but useful for Snipe, and the delicate grass of Parnassus grows here in due season.

Back at the river a Dipper stands on a small mossy stone and, after depositing a fine, white juicy squirt, begins to work his complex way down river alternately allowing himself to be floated downstream by the fast current and executing the most complex convolutions – fantastic as a weasel before a young rabbit – with wing-flickerings, flutterings, whirling round like a dog chasing its tail – a remarkable sequence of fantastically energetic writhing flurries both in and under the water. By contrast, two unobtrusive pairs of Mallards slowly forage their way upstream, working between the mossy boulders, swimming where possible, walking where too shallow; dabbling down among the underwater mossy boulders. They're quiet, busy and very self-possessed, looking for what's just in front of them, quapping with their bills, taking a bit of water, a bit of moss – unconcerned, unhurried, self-contained, beauty-ful.

4.15pm – At the footbridge there's Robin song. I stand still, listening. Here come the first people I've seen all afternoon. A woman asks, "What've you spotted?" "Just listening," I say. "There he is!" and point out the Robin singing from a branch above the bridge. She stops to listen. "Lovely," she says. "I've never heard that before; lovely!" She nods appreciatively, moves on and I wonder if there's been a revolution or just a momentary pleasure – which pleases me too.

6 February

1.00pm – Overcast, much milder. This morning the lane rang with Mistle Thrush song, a commanding, perfectly phrased performance as dominant solo to a mixed band of the usual local songsters, the Dunnock's song – hitherto only fragmented bits – now much more continuous and defined. Up on the fell it is totally still and silent under a bland, motionless sky. The silence is not a dead silence, rather that of withheld life with the added ingredient of tension. Even in High Close wood there's neither sound nor movement until under the wall two Roe does materialise, one possibly last year's kid, very grey, with little colour variation within the grey and lacking the white muzzle patch very obvious in the other, whose coat is more subtle in its blended greys with even a hint of ochre on its flanks. They seem content to continue grazing on the straggles of still-green bramble, but there's a sudden tool-clatter from beyond the garden wall and they canter off down the wood. They remain the sum total of wildlife met so far and only on the approach to Loughrigg Tarn does the bellow of a Crow relieve the, for the most part, unbroken silence. Birds are very aware of changes in atmospheric pressure, and within this sort of high tension silence – like a suspended charge in the air – come occasional distant small high-frequency bird calls flying through the charged, conductive atmosphere like sparks and with the same sharp bright impact. The surface of Loughrigg Tarn changes its texture and tone continually according to conditions stimulated by the gusting winds. Birds are difficult

147

to detect – two pairs of Goosanders, almost miraculously materialising out of a sudden dark on the water which only a second ago had been glittery bright. The males dive and splash enthusiastically. There's so much bright shine that when they dive they disappear from the dark tones that reveal them into the almost blindingly glittery light which hides them, and the lake looks totally empty!

Down near Skelwith we are treated to an exceptionally fine view of a Great Spotted Woodpecker foraging along the branches of an old oak, punching it very hard, putting his skeletal shock-absorbers to very good use. Woodpeckers are noted for their ascent of branches but this one suddenly goes into reverse, unusual behaviour and not easy because his tail is structured to be pressed against the bark for support during ascent. The caudal discomfort of those couple of steps, however, makes him pause to re-adjust his tail feathers before he resumes the upward climb for which he has been designed. Nearby a Treecreeper provides contrast, moving up the trunk in little runs and dashes, sharp, erratic, and flying off to the base of the next tree when whatever it is that determines his upward limit has been reached. The atmospheric tension increases, with an almost tangible sense of 'something' held in abeyance.

8 February

7.10am – After a day and night of very heavy rain – the first for nearly three weeks – the day dawns dry, but very cold. In the lane a Mistle Thrush sings, stimulating a response down in the meadow. The difference between the two birds is very great – one obviously already an experienced songster now re-covering his full range, scale and tone of performance. The confident style of his singing is enhanced by the fact that he chooses the topmost branch on the tallest tree in the area from which to sing, exhibiting to the full those two essential qualities of all Mistle Thrush song – a vigour and musicality of phrasing, and that suggestion of flung-forth challenge, particularly on a wild morning, which has given him the well-earned title, 'storm-cock'. The bird in the meadow, on the other hand, is a comparative novice and he does well to position himself close enough to be able to learn from a master. His phrases tend not only to tail off into unintelligible squeaks, but they lack that full-throated, rounded sense of inevitable completion we get from both a master Mistle Thrush and a master Blackbird. Even down in the very wet meadows over and through the great wealth of village Robin song peals the pure, powerful music of the Mistle Thrush. His song is often enhanced by slight distance. From the darkly silhouetted trees a large broad-winged bird drops almost to ground level before flapping hard and heavy over the rushes to gain height above the riverside trees. Unusually early, this pre-dawn Buzzard, the same bird I've seen several mornings perched in a near-by oak, climbs above the village, circles slowly, claiming this area for his winter territory.

7.25am – Six Greylags fly fast up the meadow, low, direct, clanging as they come. Initially, against the pale gold of the eastern sky, they are merely silhouettes but as they curve round against the dark background of the wood the dawn light so strikes the flashing pale wing coverts that they shine almost white as first one surface and then another is illuminated, almost as if this circling were a kind of ritual ecdysis stimulating a necessary dawn metamorphosis from the nocturnal to the diurnal condition.

The meadows have softened now and the Snipe are back. They explode from the rushes, dragging their harsh call over the stunted lake-edge willows, dim shapes at best this morning; they whisp away as quickly as they had materialised from the dim grasses. A pair of Goldeneyes whistles off the water, they too having lost the peace of their dawn, but a pair of more phlegmatic Mallards swims out into the restless water this windy morning, jaunting on the short uneven chop.

Periodically I cannot but help reflecting on the sad decline in Elterwater's winter waterfowl over the last ten to fifteen years, and this difference is documented in my counts for the same date in 1997, with those for 1990 bracketed:

Mute Swan – 2 (4)
Canada Goose – 0 (13)
Greylag Goose – 0 (16)
Teal – 5 (32)
Mallard – 16 (29)
Pochard – 4 (29)
Tufted Duck – 10 (29)
Goldeneye – 6 (26)
Red-breasted Merganser – 0 (2)
Goosander – 2 (0)
Coot – 0 (11)
Cormorant – 2 (1)
Great Crested Grebe – 1 (4)
Little Grebe – 0 (5)
plus 5 Snipe.

At 8.15am the sun finally climbs above the Skelwith horizon and by the time I return to the village there is a renewed sense of purpose among Sparrows and Robins as warmth as well as light envelops the village. Chaffinches sing, Greenfinches wheeze, the Dunnock pipes from his shrubby perch – the day looks very good!

10 February

1.30pm – A glorious soft afternoon with light northerly airs after a night of hard frost. With the daily increase in sunlight and warmth, it's high time Buzzards were starting to soar above their territories, so I'm off to Fletcher's Wood hoping to see our local pair showing signs of behaving as such! In the village all the usual birds sing – it's only by consciously and daily making a note of which birds are singing that absentees

150

are registered; like migrant arrivals and departures, the former eagerly noted, the latter hardly register unless those present are monitored. The new ice on the tarns tells of the heavy frosts these past two or three nights. Although it's quite warm in the sun, the wood will be shadowed until I finally emerge at the little upland pastures overlooking Little Langdale. The quiet larches look fine, reaching up into tall reticulated spaces made by the spiky intersections of branches against the sky, their upper parts caught in a honey-glow from the sun and singing against the blue. This north-facing aspect of the wood is still quite frozen and where there is exposed damp black soil extruded ice-crystals some two or so inches long grow, ridged and cusped like giant transparent rodent molars.

High in this wood is where I photographed my Buzzards in 1972, although the site is barely recognisable now with so much more ground cover – brackens, moss and a thicket of young birch poles. It's very restful here, and one could be lulled into thinking that in this silence nothing lives or moves, but gradually the ears become tuned to one of those groups of mixed tits that wander the winter crowns, and you're either where one is or you're not as it moves around, leaving gaps of silence in its wake. Suddenly a pair of Buzzards appears, circling high in that patch of blue immediately above the clearing, the sun gleaming on each swung underwing as they revolve the light in their counter-soaring turns. One rides rather above the other – often, but not necessarily, the male because of his lesser wing-loading – in the first proper counter-soaring I've seen this year, the start of the long, two-month annual pre-breeding ritual prior to egg-laying in – usually, up here – mid-April. It is well worth searching quite high for counter-soaring Buzzards, particularly on days of high or rising atmospheric pressure, otherwise it is perfectly possible to walk through 'Buzzard country' without seeing any evidence of Buzzards whatsoever. (With x12 binoculars Buzzards are identifiable up to *c*.0.4 miles, becoming dots at *c*. 0.7 miles and invisible at *c*.1 mile.) Flying so high above the vertical territorial limit suggests that these first flights are strongly sexual rather than territorial.

Counter-soaring is the first step in establishing a bond before the birds actually touch each other – perching together, mutual preening, these come after they have learned to accept physical closeness in the air. In this crucial flight mode the two birds circle about each other as they soar, calling fairly continually. This is truly a magic circle, the crucible of their developing relationships. Distance is crucial at this stage – any lack of judgement in this respect, any infringement of what is felt to be an acceptable distance – too close or too far apart – results in the pattern becoming unstable and one of the birds will exit by means of a dive before counter-soaring resumes. This is a world of tilting planes and swinging horizons and the mechanics of these slow revolving turns are quite wonderful. One of Solomon's great mysteries was "the way of an eagle in the air". This "way" is totally involuntary – in purely aero-dynamic terms the 'way' is purely a matter of how a particular structure and design of wing and feathers react to the medium in which they move. Aerodynamics, however, doesn't account for the poetry! It doesn't dispel the mystery, but enhances it, surely.

The mellow warmth of the declining afternoon sun makes a little paradise of the delectable high pastures which overlook Little Langdale. Time spent here enjoying the lofty interface between wood and pasture, searching, as ever, for Buzzards, is time well spent. An old wall skirts the Blackwood to the very top of the watershed, its camstones grizzly with the true alpine Woolly-hair Moss – *Rhacomitirium* – found on many of the mountain tops. A long projecting through-stone has all the requirements for the perfect seat– sheltered, sunny, giving an open prospect of mixed habitats whilst allowing one to remain unobtrusive – a place to spend half an hour or so doing nothing in particular, entering a kind of blissful doze in which all the senses are fully awake and alert – body relaxed, consciousness enhanced. From here there's a view right down the length of Little Langdale and its surrounding fells. The valley is a swathe of intersecting undulating rhythms of sunshine and shadow with little copses of quiet dark trees, drifts of smoke from the farms and homesteads. There's very little sound here – a Green Woodpecker down in the valley, the occasional sheep bleating, a Chaffinch song in the wood behind – all so perfectly slotted in that they serve only to enhance rather than disturb this sense of solitude and silence. The walk back across the marshy top of the watershed reveals the great horseshoe of Fairfield and Dollywaggon Pike glowing in the late afternoon sun. Between the tops of two adjacent larches rests the nearly full moon, looking very pale but comfortable in its high nest whilst at the opposite end of the sky the sun is about to perch on the summit hump of Wetherlam before rolling off the edge of the world. I move and the moon balloons up into the sky as if a child has let go its string. Despite the sun's warmth the ground is still frozen hard beneath the just softened surface and it's getting colder by the minute.

3.50pm – In the lane-side hazels a couple of Coal Tits engage in much wing-flicking, like Dunnocks, as they communicate with very high-pitched calls. One of them perches on the highest twig and alternately calls – a sort of ticking sound – and sings a couple of piped notes exactly a third apart (upper G–B), accompanied by wing-flicking, not always by both wings simultaneously, and not always to the same degree of stretch above his back. How little I know about the astonishing vocabulary range of some of these small birds.

14 February
3.00pm – It's been a strange afternoon; rain all day yesterday, and torrential rain this morning clearing out bright and shiny with a brisk wind shoving the world always towards the east. I

hadn't planned on coming to Baysbrown Tarn but was led here by the always irresistible call of a Buzzard. He was fairly high and in full 'roller-coaster' mode, executing a vigorous figure of eight on a horizontal axis – steep undulating dives with wings shut, slowing to the apex where the wings opened to see him over the top prior to the next dive:

This powerful display represents significant points in his developing pair-bond, his demonstration of territory and, later, may mark the excitement generated by nest completion, egg laying, hatching and so on. A second, unseen, Buzzard responded to his call and he immediately embarked on another series of vigorous roller-coasting undulations before pulling in his wings and executing a stupendous, approximately 45 degree power-dive down to the trees on the rocky copse overlooking the tarn and calling continuously, whilst another Buzzard followed close behind, and then it too made an almost identical power-dive down to where the first bird (presumed male) had landed.

The fellside birches are acquiring that special plumb-bloom – the alders darker still with the faintest tinge of bronze. Add to these the subtle green of the hazel catkins on their dusty-pale stalks and the larches' pale umbers, the patches where remnant oak and beech leaves rustle – all set among variegated tones of dead bracken and ochre-tinted grey rock, and altogether it's one of the optimum times of year for colour. A Mistle Thrush song, disembodied, floats up from the valley below. This wind-borne music, together with the almost Samuel Palmer-like feel of these little pastures and their quiet sheep communicates an almost mythic quality as if something ancient, lost, but engaging the membrane, was enlivening the surrounding air.

15 February

8.00am – after another very wet night the river is once more roaring under the bridge. A tinge of yellow to the overcast denotes yet more wind to come. It is good to hear the increasing vocal output from all the current small songsters, along with that of the Wren, which has gradually assumed greater dominance. His song seems to come fully formed without preparatory explorations, except, perhaps, for that abbreviated, non-territorial song addressed to the female. Grey, describing this tiny bird's astonishing voice refers to the "shattering Wren." and it is another very welcome addition to the now gathering vocal momentum well away from human habitation. Goldfinches, too, have begun singing, their liquid bubbling, almost an inevitable development from the tinkle of their daily calls. Grey thought the song rather trivial, but this assessment ignores the fact that this is a bird in which song, behaviour and appearance are inseparable, bringing together both lightness and grace to the air around him. The collective noun for Goldfinches – 'charm' – really applies more to its song than to the general attractiveness of its combined voice and behaviour, for what was the Middle English 'charme' if not a magic, a spell, an enchantment in its original meaning?

Once both thrush species – Song and Mistle – start singing their special resonance lends different dimensions of key, tonality and amplitude, and with a seasoning of cautious optimism we may, perhaps, begin to anticipate the diversity and volume of what is yet to come. After the winter months during which practically all bird sound and movement has been centered around the village gardens, there's now the definite beginnings of a diaspora away from that centre, although the village seems as full of birds as ever. This surge of vocal activity away from the village is accompanied by a

155

corresponding increase in observable bustle – those almost furtive-seeming, quicksilver movements about the winter thickets and tangled trees – sharp calls on the ends of small dashing pursuits; the erratic movement of a party of Long-tailed Tits about the alder tops; the Blackbirds caught in the corner of an eye on low, urgent-seeming missions.

The sun's just rising above the Tanglewood, illuminating the meadows and the trees with that revelatory first flush of pristine sunshine, once only and for a mere few seconds and the visual impact, from one second to another, as long gentle shadows reach up the meadow, the trees washed with the softest of butter-lights, is always breathtaking. Four Crows forage among the riverside shillets, strutting and poking. It all looks very casual, but as they walk forwards, beaks angled down, their stare is intent, the eyes aimed straight down the ridge of the bill, focussed on a point on the ground beneath. One decides to take a bath, but it is nominal only, just a few wing-splashes over its back, a bit of a shake and he's off. Several rounded grey stones among the shillets suddenly move, resolve into three or four Mallard drakes, inching forward, dabbling quietly, unobtrusive, concentrated, self-absorbed, the grey flowing over them as the surface of a stone flows.

A pair of Crows has just flapped raggedly up from the bottom of Low Wood, gaining height rapidly. One bird maintains constant position relative to the other, acting as a kind of 'magnet', a focus, from and to which the other moves away and back. The 'focus' bird wheels in tight circles maintaining 'her' (the female?) function as a centre of attention and activity. They fly closely together for a while until the bird with the 'roving' function (the male?) separates away and out into a much wider circle around 'her' until 'he' decides it's time to work inwards, once more resuming their close flight before repeating the whole sequence two or three times. This ebb and flow of distance between them with the same bird remaining constant as the focus of activity is, in its own way, every bit as ritualised a sexually orientated exercise as the counter-soaring of Buzzards but without the added territorial component of the Buzzard flights. It is, truly, a sky-dance.

17 February

After a day's rain it's a bright morning and there's snow above 2,000 feet on the hills, the ridge from Great End to Scafell Pike looking splendidly alpine. All up and down the lane cock Blackbirds are sitting in those bushes from which I've been hearing sub-song. This morning there's no sub-song; some males are accompanied by females, but mostly they're all just sitting perfectly still, silent, self-absorbed, surrounded by all the usual morning song, almost as if they're listening – waiting perhaps for some other bird to make that first flute-like announcement which will stimulate each to respond?

2.30pm – Above Oak Bank rises the never-trodden little ridge of Yew Crags. Structurally like a miniature Yosemite Half Dome, the west-facing sheer of the quarry falls almost vertically about 150 feet. The quarry itself sweeps round in a huge horseshoe, its arms curving away into great slabs of multi-coloured rock – coppery greens, light reds, greenish-greys of all shades, ochres, sea-greens and pinks, all variously and wonderfully algaed. The whole has been worked slowly over the years into an intersecting series of levels and ledges which spiral down into dubs of brown water in the bottom. Behind the quarry, on a moonscape of stacked stone and detritus stand the slate processing sheds with their huge, massive-wheeled bulldozers and stone-wagons which stand idle today, like Tonka Toys abandoned where a boy ended his play. The setting of this chaotic scene is the natural order of the hills – from the westwards curve of Lingmoor to the ridge descending eastwards from Sergeant Man towards Loughrigg, the whole is aesthetically most satisfying, with the Pikes at the apex of this huge horseshoe within which fits the lesser, reversed curve of the quarry. A high Raven kronking towards Lingmoor emphasises the empty quarry's resonant silence.

Away from the quarry edge the ridge becomes a broad, upland stretch of brackens, grasses and many rocky outcrops, splendid sitting stones from which to watch and listen. Eventually the ridge falls away to a steep little crag dressed with small, hard-grown oaks overlooking a long narrow pool where a Heron walks slowly between stances of concentrated stillness and attention. There's not likely to be much up here yet, frogs in a few days' time, perhaps, tadpoles later, but other than insect larvae this is a stagnant lifeless pool. The Heron comes to the same conclusion, flies off, demonstrating its surprising agility in negotiating the obstacle course of close-grown birch poles between it and open space – tilting, folding, continually adjusting his position as if it's done this many times before and has its own well-tried route mapped out – it doesn't even vary its speed. The far end of the ridge, flanking Sawrey's Wood, is a delightful area with little heathered rocky outcrops and stands of elegant birch growing from mixed mosses, grass, bracken and fragrant bog myrtle – always a prime Woodcock site.

The sun sinks to the accompaniment of glorious Mistle Thrush music, rich and rolling out with a supremely confident fluency and maturity of voice, his utterance like slow, blue smoke rising into a blue-gold evening – serene and in-domitable. Not many phrases are repeated. It's like an impromptu speech, the phrases uttered each after a slight pause as if delivered with thought and consideration for content and manner – wonderful to hear on an afternoon like this – the sound of the river still in half-flood rushing beneath, the wind in the trees bowling great clouds down the valley from the west, the blue of the sky rinsed and shining after all that rain – as if uttered by some quite indisputable avian authority delivering the ultimate wisdom from a high, unassailable vantage point, at times a rallying cry as well as a meditation.

At 4.15pm the singing Mistle suddenly leaves his perch and flies in long, unhurried undulations to a tall, nearby fir, immediately followed by two more, the third, however, most unwelcome and emphatically driven away with much harsh, grating sound. Gilbert White notes, in respect of the Mistle Thrush's fierce territoriality:

> "The missel-thrush is, while breeding, fierce and pugnacious, driving such birds as approach its nest, with great fury, to a distance. The Welsh call it *pen y llwyn* – the head, or master of the coppice."
> (*The Natural History of Selborne*, Part II, Letter XXII)

Macpherson, too, in his note on the missel thrush (sic) – giving it the alternative, archaic name of 'Shrite' – refers to its courage (*The Vertebrate Fauna of Lakeland*, 1892).

Hazel leaf-buds are ripe and full, the scales on some pushed apart by the developing leaves within, so that these even show as segments of green between the scales. The catkins, however, are now fully expanded, the almost orange anthers hidden deep inside, but a jolt mists out a dust of yellow pollen. The female flowers, tiny maroon-red tufted filaments, barely a quarter of an inch long, are relatively inconspicuous, despite their fine, rich colour – little, inextinguishable female flames nestling within which, when touched by pollen from the male catkins, the nuts will form.

19 February

7.00am – A very cold morning with the moon just over half-full, hanging lustrous over Hullett's Nest. Robins were already singing at 6.40am when I opened the door to a frozen morning, every leaf, blade, twig thick and prickly with rime but not frozen enough to dumb the Song Thrush in the wilderness garden. Up the lane the same two Blackbirds noted above (17th) still sit dark and hunched within their silent mystery, listening to the world opening up around them as the thrushes, predominantly, give voice.

7.15am – Looking eastwards from the crown of Kitty Hall copse, there's a feeling of expansion, of opening, as fields and lake broaden out to either side. After the sense of enclosed, close horizons, often produced by the narrow confines of the valley, there is a shift in perspective from a vertical to a more horizontal emphasis, expanding outwards from Fletcher, the meadows and the tarn on the one side, towards Loughrigg on the other. A kind of geographical metaphor for a quickening consciousness – in those four most mysterious and potent of Wordsworth's words, "felt along the heart" – that inspired "along" a curiously physiological preposition which conveys the long, pumping passage of blood and life to and from every part of the body – felt throughout the living, breathing organism.

The resident Mute Swans register as flat gleaming presences on the dark waters of the lake over which, flying high due west and straight out of the sunrise glow comes a skein of about 60 geese, their conversation quiet with only an occasional louder call. They continually change their positions within the chevron, a shiver passing down each line as every bird adjusts to the slipstream of the preceding bird. They wheel northwards for a moment, resume their west-bound flight straight up the valley, receding into dots and flecks and are gone, leaving a powerful imprint of their passage on the morning air.

7.30am – The moon rests quietly between two larches on the crest of Fletcher; a very slim brilliant crescent on her east-facing rim reflecting the as yet unseen sun. Suddenly a little whisp of four Snipe springs from the frozen rushes, jinks up over the lakeside and with a single harsh alarm follows the lake shore until they vanish, as a whisp should, both coming and going. Two cock Pheasants drum and crow in rival call and answer from the neighbouring fields. Unfortunately, no matter

1. Elterwater Village and the Langdale Pikes

2. Elterwater – Middle Tarn

3. Greylags at Ashes Point

4. Ready to Go – Whoopers on Elterwater

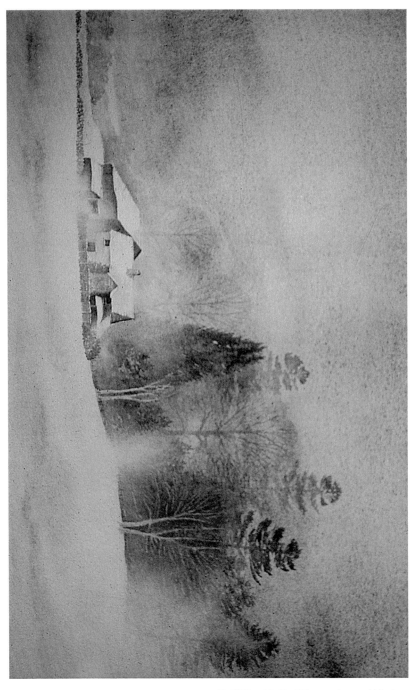

5. Kitty Hall, Elterwater – Winter.

6. Heron in Winter – Bottom Tarn

7. Bardsea Morning – with Waders

8. Canadas, Elterwater.

9. Mickleden Nightfall

10. Billy's Farm, Ullet's Nest, Winter.

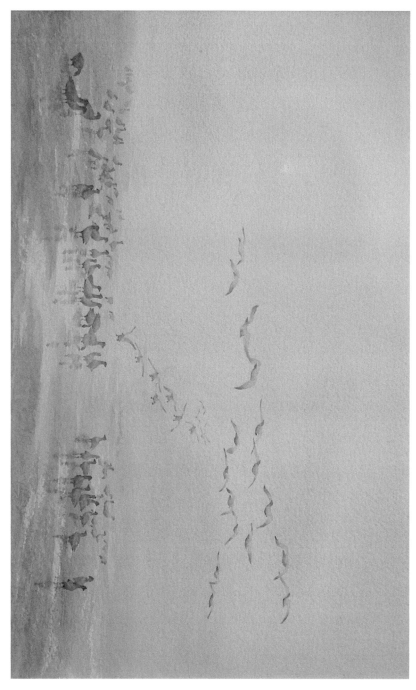

11. Estuary Dawn

12. Barnacles, Caerlaverock

13. The Old Boathouse, Elterwater, Top Tarn

14. Piel Island and Castle, from Foulney

15. Morgenschön – May Meadows, Langdale.

16. Billy's Field, Ullet's Nest, Haytime.

how much they strut and crow and drum, prospective females are not much impressed by all this plumage splendour and macho posturing. Apparently it's the extent to which the male's red wattles swell and inflate that determines the hen's selection of mate – size clearly matters when assessing the male's testosterone levels! Among a party of mixed tits feeding among the alder catkins at Ashes Point, a party of eight Long Tails zips towards the lakeside willows in a fragile wavering line, their little crochet shapes like an unplayed melody passing before the eyes. Two Canada Geese swim slowly up the now steaming lake, reaming the dark water with silver wakes. One stops for a minimal bath, merely plunging its head and swiping it wet over the mantle, using its head as a cat licks its paw to wash its face and scattering droplets as it does so. It shakes, rises, stretching from the water for a couple of flaps – shaking off the excess drops – and starts to preen. Two pairs of Tufted Ducks ride the slow revolving currents in Dead Sheep Bay, whilst three male and two female Goldeneyes emerge from the reeds by Rob Rash: one of the males bobs his head at a female but takes the display no further. There's the chime of Teal-talk.

A solitary Greylag heads down the golden sky towards the tarn calling continuously with a voice insistent like the groan of iron as if hoping for some response, but finding none it flies on. The first light touches the heavily frosted alders and at the stroke of a single second they're silver-sprayed, brilliant against the darkness of Park Fell, itself no longer merely dark but as if a transparent veil of light were thrown across its western aspect giving its darks a softly velvet appearance.

At the Tanglewood edge two couples of Woodcock spring up and out, turning on a wing tip and slant away towards the tarn. Somewhere from within this shadowy black tangle comes that clear double pipe – the second syllable like a far-off echo of the first – of a Bullfinch:

"A mournful note, a crying note
A single tin-whistle half-note…
Again and again – and the echo prompt.
Bullfinch is melancholy."
(Ted Hughes, from *A Primer of Birds*, 1981. *Collected Poems*, Faber, 2003)

8.00am – A Water Rail sharms in the reeds by the top tarn coppice – a sound mentally noted as missing earlier this morning. Up past the Snipe-feeding ground the whole world glitters, the tall rushes in a mist of shine against the sun with scatterings everywhere of small, shining, rainbow-coloured crystals – each a miniature prism – chips of spectrum which require only the slightest shift of head in relation to the sun and it's as if a multitude of tiny lights have been switched on. There are many Long-tailed Tit parties – family parties, still, I suppose – their small voices constant in the lake-edge alder carr and girdling the tarn in this sparkling sunshine with a continuous chiming belt of small birds.

20 February
3.00pm – A fine, brisk afternoon, the wind strong from the north-west. A group of Whooper Swans has arrived, and I've come down to renew a long-standing connection with these charismatic birds which were so instrumental in bonding me to Elterwater over fifty years ago. Elterwater derives its name from the Old Norse, 'Elpt-Vatn', meaning literally 'Swan Water', so their arrival is an Event! Magnificent birds, they bring with them a sense of northern wilderness in the way, when suspicious or nervous, their necks seem to stiffen erect, leaning into the wind – their taut Arctic awareness a complete contrast to those comfortable, luscious curves of our resident swans. When Linnaeus named them *Cygnus cygnus* he dipped into a reservoir of ancient mythology which inevitably accompanies the presence of these birds, for he named them

after Cygnus, the beautiful son of Apollo who was changed into a swan after leaping into a lake and, like so many ancients, is com-memorated by a constellation which bears his name. Aristotle wrote that the swans are "musical and sing at the approach of death", hence their English name 'Whooper', 'Singschwan' in German and 'Sångsvan' in Swedish. Both Whooper and Bewick's Swans have long, convoluted windpipes which enable the birds to produce far-reaching and resonant sounds used mainly for group and family communication.

There are twelve swans. Our resident Mutes seem unconcerned, maintaining a very close partnership on the water as if reinforcing each other in the presence of a superior number of visiting birds. They are certainly aware of the Whoopers – a small group splits off, swims by the Mutes and the cob raises his sails with assertive intent, but just as suddenly backs off, apparently without interest in the visitors as long as they preserve a proper distance. The twelve Whoopers group together, brilliant in the low sun like a great white flower on the darkening water. One or two swim, others, very relaxed, gyrate gently in the slow-moving eddies and currents generated by the river's flow into the lake; some stand on the little gravel island, preening, others still tuck their heads back and rest. It's quite impossible for me to look upon these "brilliant creatures" without thinking of Yeats at Coole with his "nine-and-fifty" swans paddling "in the cold/Companion-able streams...". Whether "unwearied" or not I don't know, but they're certainly resting, muttering quietly together on the dark water. Sometimes they come down like this, rest up and go at first light. Perhaps they'll go tomorrow morning. Winter-long residence on the lake has not occurred since 1990 when nine birds stayed a long time (the number augmented in late March by the grand spectacle of fifty overnighters), and it is thought that perhaps the attractions of being both secure and fed – to the north at Caerlaverock and to the south at Martin

163

Mere – may have contributed to this change of habit, for it's not only Elterwater that has lost its swans but also, over the last half-century, several other regularly visited lakes and tarns. It's an ever-changing scene as the swans drift apart – "lover by lover", perhaps, for they are all adult birds – and come to-gether over the endless modulating mottle and streak wrought by sun and wind over the water surface. Whatever individuals may be doing – preening, feeding, wing-stretching, dozing – there's always one or two with head up, alert. It's getting darker, colder, wetter. The Swans will not fly tonight, I think. Leaving, I wish them well as they "...drift on the still water,/Mysterious, beautiful;" (W.B. Yeats, *The Wild Swans at Coole*).

21 February

7.15am – A bitterly cold morning down by the lake, with a stinging north-east wind whipping up the water where there are still twelve Whoopers, close in against the reedbeds and under the eaves of the trees – probably the most sheltered place on this exposed bottom tarn.

The two Mutes fly, wings moaning, from the exposure of South Bay up to the shelter of the reedbeds. Canada Geese clamour somewhere on the middle tarn. A pied-patterned male Goldeneye blends well into the dark and light rise and fall of the wind-driven chop, appearing and disappearing like some sort of magic trick. A little group of five Tufteds ventures out from the reeds with a couple of Little Grebes, one well into his pre-breeding moult, dark with a flush of chestnut-red across his cheeks and throat, the other still quite pale. A Mallard duck swims with a vigorously head-bobbing drake on to either side. One grabs her by the nape of the neck and treads her ruthlessly. He dismounts and both bathe vigorously before preening – all this displacement activity is necessary to dispose of surplus post-coital sexual energy. The other drake merely observes.

164

From within the wood where the wind is much less abrasive, the Whoopers are now visible through a black tangle of branches, their shapes utterly fragmented as if they'd suddenly become disjointed pieces of some huge jig-saw. The wind shakes the tangle of willow carr, rattling the branches like a witch doctor's threat, rubbing, squeaking, moaning, yet beyond this strangely surreal, almost menacing strip of carr lies a new gold and blue of sun and sky and reedbed and the pieces of white puzzle waiting to be assembled into meaning, a weird sense of dichotomy between where I am and where they are.

8.20am – The swans begin to call, more oboe-like than trumpet. Sibelius famously recorded in his diary the passage of sixteen Whooper Swans over his property in Ainola, enthusiastically describing this event as one of the greatest experiences of his life, their calls eventually and inspirationally transformed into the final theme of the 5th Symphony.

Having crept through the reeds for a couple of record photographs without disturbing the birds, the return to the exposure of the lake shore renews awareness of just how bitter the wind is, with cold bones rattling to the same tune as the knocking trees!

As I leave, a magnificent rainbow arches over the bottom tarn and my last sight of the swans is to see them sail out from the shelter of Rob Rash towards the middle tarn, under the arc of the rainbow as if entering in under their own heaven of lost Celtic dreams and legends. Yeats returns to these great legendary birds in his wonderful sonnet *Leda and the Swan* in which Zeus in the guise of a wild swan raped Leda, one of the results of which was the birth of Helen of Troy, and a heroic sequence of events which culminated in

"The broken wall, the burning roof and tower
And Agamemnon dead."

Blake wrote, "Nature is imagination", the corollary of which being that our personal involvement with nature deserves, demands, an imaginative response and the visit of these wonderful, great birds emphasises that necessity. For a swan is not necessarily always a swan – it may also be Zeus, or a guardian of the Finnish underworld, a constellation or a symphonic poem, or a lost soul – whatever resonates in the imagination, as it resonated thousands of years ago when, via mythology and folklore, the first attempts to define some valid expression of man's kinship with the natural world were made. The current alienation of *Homo sapiens* from his natural birth-cradle would indicate that we need a re-evaluation of this vital relationship, away from the destructive mind-dominated homocentricity in all things.

24 February

1.30pm – The Whoopers left early Thursday morning. It's been a week of bitter north-east winds blowing great opaque showers across the hills, each bringing another layer of snow, whipped off by the wind in long, winding banners or great smoky swirls like the blown spume off an Atlantic breaker-crest – it's no weather for lingering long anywhere! I set out for a walk round Oak Howe. The wind roars among the trees on Yew Crags and the sun bursts into an unexpected blaze of cold, brilliant light which fades immediately as curtains of snow-laden cloud scourge fell and dale. The effect of this brilliant evanescent light on the birches makes them flash and fade continually – tall stands of scraped white bone. In Bayes-brown Wood nothing stirs, nothing utters – a reminder that we're only past the middle of February and where we were, possibly at the beginning of spring, we're right back now in the middle of winter. Here and now all is sleep and silence.

This wood is very like parts of Fletcher, an ancient wood-and once divided into lots, now only discernible by mossy, tumbledown walls, old trackways leading to long defunct quarries and pit steads – for charcoal was burnt here – and drovers' roads linking up with Hullet's Nest and Little Langdale. Once near Baysbrown Farm the high crags of Pavy Ark swing into view, skimmed with snow, remote and bleak. This is a magnificent stretch of valley with broad flat meadows reaching across its greatest width – here about half a mile – fine pastures stretching from Oak Howe to just below Baysbrown Tarn. In its heyday – literally its hay days – these meadows were rich with wild flowers but most of these have been lost to the less sympathetic regime of silage cropping, and large areas have been allowed to become degraded to a 'mono-culture' of extensive soft rush. Just before Oak Howe these flat meadows drop down to a rough marshy level supporting clumps of Sweet Gale, the rich, deep, bronzy aubergine which really sings against the faded golds and pale tans of the Molinia, and soft rush growing from the huge bed of Spaghnum beneath.

3.10pm – A Raven calls once from high on Oak Howe Crag. Viewed from near Oak Howe the massive bulk of Lingmoor appears remarkably zoned. Below the heathery ridge tumbles a length of shattered, broken crag, heather-ledged, beneath which a clearly demarcated zone of dwarf juniper gives way to brackens and grasses sweeping down to the valley floor. Dividing this mass are elegant broad-based fans of scree in a series of inverted 'V's' so that the whole presents an appearance of informal order and symmetry modified over the millennia by its geology and vegetation. These scree-fans are particularly pleasing, no two the same size or length but all conforming to the same rules as applied to slope, angle and gravity. There's no sound now except the constant abrasion of changing wind currents and vortices among the high crags against whatever surface it can find to rub itself. Silence is a wonderful vehicle for time-travel. Scientists talk about the 'space/time continuum'. Certainly, sitting here looking at this fellside, ignoring the occasional broken wall or stump of felled tree, it's not too difficult to be present at any time over the past 10,000 years wrapped in exactly the same silence. All sorts of changes will have taken place, of course – rocks shattered and fallen, temperature and vegetation changes from the ice onwards, the introduction of sheep, muir-burn. The silence, however, is the silence of 'light years' in which the consciousness has room to flower open in the same continuum – what Plato called, "A moving image of eternity" – for the beginning and the end of silence is never the same place – but this is heady stuff and the silence of the here and now is good enough for the here and now!

3.45 – Not far downstream from the confluence of Baysbrown Pool and the river, the latter has carved a series of 'S' bends narrowing between steep tilted slabs to form a long pool, several feet deep, the water so transparent that the slabby rocks glow a strange pale green as they plunge into the water. An enormous oak has fallen across the path and river bank – I can walk under its arched branches as a mouse under a twig! – a huge tree, yet the root scar in the bank reveals it to have been surprisingly shallow-rooted on a thin bed of gravely soil over rock. It has obviously compensated for its lack of vertical hold by the horizontal spread of its roots which bind together boulders, small stones, gravel and peat in a massive wedge covering about 180 square feet!

The local Dipper has just dived head-first into the rapids upstream of the footbridge, allowing itself to be swept downstream a couple of yards before turning to force a passage upstream – a matter of three steps backwards for every one forwards! It's extraordinarily tenacious in this upstream struggle against the fiercely broken water, using its wings as both oars and stabilisers. What's fascinating is the equation between energy lost and food found – on the face of it it would seem to be losing far more than it's gaining, without any kind of balance, considering also the bird's evolutionary economics of fitness for purpose.

28 February

6.30am – After a frozen, starlit night, morning breaks clear-skied. In the faint cold glow of the south-east sky a planet hangs in the most bitter north-east wind we've yet had, having brought fresh snow well down onto the hills.

6.40am – The official sunrise is 7.03, but as yet there's no pre-sunrise flush of colour on the hills, and the landscape is as hard and cold as the wind. The long meadows to either side of the river are empty – even of sheep this morning – and something about the light in this wind brings out the yellow in everything so that the meadows emphasise their dead tans and pale ochres rather than the as yet lifeless greens. The fields feel scoured down to their base by this flashing yellow wind, frozen from fresh high fell snows. I've met this strange, bladed yellow-flashing light in this wind from the north-east on the high fells, but only rarely in the valley.

6.42am – The repeated phrases of a Mistle Thrush penetrate the roaring of the trees. He sounds glorious out here in this bitter wind, perched on a tree top in the middle of the meadows, surrounded by emptiness and neither sheep nor other bird in sight. The freezing wind pours down the valley, flashing in the eye with its strange, unearthly yellow light. He sings in the midst of all this bitter emptiness, brandishing his right to ownership, flaunting his warmth of blood out over the flashing fields. He hasn't an extensive repertoire but compensates for this by a purity of tone clear as his own bright eye. He's joined in song by a Dipper – what a contrast! – the one out-flowing over the wind, the other an intimate babbled converse with water-voices which this morning sound warmer even than the scoured fields. I think this is quite the coldest early morning so far this winter. Down at the sitting stones the river is dull silver like shadowed mercury. The Pikes in their coat of new-fallen snow are hard-edged and arctic-looking, remote even, unlit as they are against the paling grey-indigo sky. A Robin sings, his voice full of heart, cutting as the wind, a hot wire through the ear, needling through barriers of white sound, the permanent background of wind-rush. A pair of Goosanders snorkel on the pool, the light not yet bright enough to reveal the drake's subtle beauty, the dull silver of the water too bright to see them as much more than moving shapes, the eye moving between these two perceptions with strange ease.

7.15am – In the valley here there is light but no illumination, whereas the entire high crest of the Pikes catches the sun, an irregularly castellated ridge warming, with so much yellow in the wind, to a soft, pale honey-glow. Further along, the ridge of Sergeant Man arches up against a dark cloud mass but he, being white, looks full of omen, menacing almost, the whites so very cold as if a shroud were laid over him. Two Ravens fly high overhead towards Lingmoor, wing tip to wing tip in their bonding synchro-flight. Suddenly one tilts away, loosening the flight-bond, whiffling goose-like down to tree-top level in a breath-taking aerobatic display. No sooner had one started than the other followed – two Ravens in sheer bond ex-hilaration in this hard, bright, bitter morning wind. Wanting to perch and settle in the shelter of Rob Rash, a Crow is flung across the small space of sky overhead. It turns into the wind – as it must, of course – hanging above its elected tree, letting itself down gradually if suspended from a gossamer, landing light as thistledown on the topmost twig of a lashing birch, bending it – a demonstration of the perfect relationship be-tween structure and aerodynamics. Perched on this topmost arched twig facing into the wind, its wings are outstretched, holding the wind, so that it's perfectly balanced both on the twig and in the wind. Held only by its feet, like a kite held by its string or a balloon in a child's hand, it sways for a minute then simply uncurls its toes – it needs do nothing else – and lifts off as lightly as it let itself down – magic!

7.30am – Blue Tits forage among the alder catkins, not remaining still for very long, creeping along the branches,

170

hugging them close like little coloured mice and everywhere Blackbirds, as always enveloped within their aura of mystery, are still busy with their obscure errands. The as yet unrisen sun illuminates the canopy of the pines by the top tarn, so that they flare like fiery torches. But it is the big wind that has dominated the morning, very noisy and bitterly cold. This sense of elemental turmoil is not only external – it flashes along the blood-stream, bounces off the skull's lining, buffeting the consciousness.

7.43am – The sun has pushed a brilliant sliver above the crest of Little Loughrigg, and quickly comes pulsing over the hill, shuddering out wave after wave of white light, until fully revealed, 42 minutes later than the official sunrise, and I'm standing in new sunshine for the first time this morning. There's just a hint of warmth in the sun – out of the wind! – and by 8am the village rings with song.

March

2 March
Caerlaverock (WWT) – Midday on a bright, cold morning, the Solway coast of Dumfries and the sound of Whoopers Swans – 236 at the last count. The setting is superb – much of the pond is frozen and the surrounding willows, seen against the dark greens of the conifers behind, are fired up to the tips with an extraordinary ochre-orange glow. There's only a narrow strip of water, pied in places with Tufteds and brilliant with the lit crowns of Wigeons whistling against a constant murmur of swan-sound, rather like a huge orchestra of deep-toned oboes tuning up for a concert. Way across the fields beyond the Whooper and Teal ponds is the flood ground covered by what appears to be a pied and blue-grey mosaic – thousands of Barnacle Geese. In the lane Yellowhammers flash like bolts of pure sunshine among the fine silvery velvet pile of the willows buds, while smart swart-headed Reed Buntings flash their white outer tail feathers at the many females, themselves enhanced by this glorious light, showing off their chestnut-buff, black-tipped secondaries.

The Whoopers generate a tension of expectation as they await their 2pm feed. Some doze in the sunshine on the bank. Some are more particular in respect of their personal space than others, and the unwanted presence of the 'wrong' bird stimulates an aggressive peck. Others preen, wing-stretch –

always impressive – others still simply swim about creating patterned abstract shapes as moving forests of white columns intersect and mingle in an ever-changing kaleidoscope of movement. The restless perpetuum mobile of the birds already assembled is disturbed even further as others fly in from the outlying fields, splash-down, raking the water, barging in unceremoniously and met with blares of indignant trumpeting, like wedges of brass fugue driven strident into the muted, muttered woodwind background. Gradually all resettles.

The Avenue tower permits extensive viewing, from the frozen flood ground to the merse – the rough grasslands bordering the Solway itself. The current estimated total of Barnacle Geese assembled below us is around 4,500, but there are often more than 12,000! Most of these delightful, little, neat-faced pied geese graze peacefully, but they are becoming increasingly restless as some birds fly in and others take off in whirling counter-circling groups. Elsewhere large numbers walk in solemn procession like a drift of grey, black and white mosaic tiles across the field, presenting enormous changes of tone as they move in and out of the sun. Feeding at the edge of the rushes behind the Barnacles' grazing area, three or four Roe Deer move about the rank vegetation, appearing and disappearing like unpredictable shadows almost before the eye registers their corporeal presence, the mind a name.

Beyond merse and Firth range the glistening snow-capped summits of the Lake District and the more distant Pennines. The Solway is blue-streaked, with yellow-ochre bars and strands gleaming behind the dark clumps of juniper and gorse studding the foreground merse. A small group of Pink Feet stir after their doze, walk solemnly down towards a little pond for a drink. In the sun they're very warm-looking against the cooler pied patterning of the little Barnacles. Suddenly hundreds of Barnacles take off towards the Solway with a huge clatter and an incredible shout as successive waves unpeel from the ground from the front backwards, thus giving clear air-space to the birds behind.

The Salcot Merse Observatory overlooks the merse – a huge expanse of salt marsh and wet tussocky grassland bordering the Firth shores, full of little meres delicately rippled by the bitter wind and all backed by the looming bulk of Criffel. There is a wonderful healing air in the space-time silence generated by this exposed vastness – a sense of remote wilderness enhanced by the passage of clamouring geese and it's the big scene which really claims the attention. The bird detail is merely a part of the big scene, their names irrelevant, interposing the glass of classification between man and bird in this unpredictable setting of the vast equations of time, space and silence. As the light wanes, the Solway colours slowly change – the mud-bank purples, the horizontal, silver-edged channels cutting through them – mud and water all the way to the horizon. A little group of Golden Plovers paddles about the wetlands. These little flocks have been restless all afternoon, wreathing and weaving above the merse, alternating variants of olive-brown with flashes of silvery white as they twist and turn into and out of the light.

The evening is extraordinarily lovely along the Solway and up the Nith valley – the receding tide leaves purple-shining mud, the last of the sun from over the shoulder of Criffel reflected across its multi-textured wet surface, gold and deep plum. Curlews and Redshanks make black silhouettes on the shining mud, whilst the air is full of gulls making their way down from their feeding fields to the safety of the estuary at night.

3 March

A brisk sunny morning. West from Southerness Point on the Solway coast is the Mersehead reserve. A Kestrel sits in an old wind-blown thorn eating prey, the sun catching the russet on her back. A line of dunes drops down to a long crescent of wet

174

sand, and along the shore-line frost and wind have carved a wide swathe of frozen tide froth into fantastic flakes, eccentric curves and arabesques. The sun, due south, glints cold on the wet, rippled surfaces of the blue-purple mudflats, the estuary itself just a glitter of light, a dazzling knife-slash beyond which rise the white-capped, remote-looking Cumbrian hills. The tide flows very fast here – a relentless creeping ripple of wavelets at speed as the mudflats of only a few minutes ago are now totally submerged. Among the sea-washed timber along the tideline there's a huge bleached branch, wave-smoothed, slightly curved along its length with a gnarly ball rounding off one end, like a gigantic femur – Henry Moore would have enjoyed that! Little groups of Dunlin and Ringed Plover lift off and re-settle a few yards on like small piles of leaves lifted and let drop in a restless autumn wind. Whereas the Plovers are in breeding plumage, the Dunlin stand hunched in winter wear, pale in the light with wet black bills as though freshly varnished.

Behind the shore, a shelterbelt and a small frozen mere overlooked by a hide. The high-pitched nasal yapping of hundreds of Barnacles and Pink Feet form a non-stop audio background. On the water itself – a long narrow channel surrounding the large frozen central area – is a wonderful collection of waterfowl: Shelduck, Mallard, Teal, Pintail and Shoveller and a few Gadwall, Pochard and Goosanders, with one or two Snipe feeding closer in around the mere's vegetated margins. A large – falcon – Peregrine has put down on the middle of the ice. She stands solid, imperious, lovely in her slate grey and white, looks around. She causes no panic among the assembled birds. The waterfowl continue to circle round her on their band of dark water, like colourful, respectable citizens taking a social perambulation around the local square. She remains an utterly dominating presence simply by being there, solid and implacable. She leaves the ice, burns her way up to the top of a dead tree on the edge of the pool – among all this wintry stuff she seems fuelled with an alien fire. Once more she sits and stares around with the imperious in-difference of death and only a talon-touch away from be-stowing it. All the Barnacles, yelping loudly, and most of the Pink Feet, swirl up and round, snaking lines across the skyline, shape-shifting as they go. Most of the ducks down on the water feed on quite unconcernedly, the Pintails elegantly up-tails-all – how could they possibly be less than elegant in all they do! A yelping crescendo announces the Barnacles' return, circling around each side of the dead tree and surrounding the Peregrine which stares intently, leaning forwards slightly and following with bobbing turns of the head. Yeats's line, "Cast a cold eye on life, on death…" comes unbidden to mind – it seems to fit her perfectly despite the different context.

3.00pm – Reports of heavy snow in Cumbria force an early departure. In the fading light at 6.15pm a Blackbird sings above Windermere, not with the full strength of his song, rather as if he's emerged from the shadowed secrecy of his sub-song and practice and has his song ready for dress rehearsal – in the weird yellow pointillism of a street-light seen through driving snow that's a truly wonderful sound.

5 March

8.30am – A fine morning after a hard frost, but with a bitter north-west wind. Much of the snow has gone, but the meadows are still white and frost still grips. The river is very shallow, hypnotically dappled by sunshine and shadow. A pair of Mallards cruises slowly downstream as if deliberately choosing to link the sunlit passages. The duck daintily scoops water from the very skin of the river into her lower mandible without spilling – a single pendant drop glitters, trembling from the tip of her bill. She is breathtakingly beautiful. Foraging tits call – in flight they become merely opaque hazed flickerings as pale, semi-transparent wings flutter open against the backlight of brilliant low sun with, apparently, no attach-

176

ment to any bird whatsoever. Across the river the open, exposed meadows are hard frozen and still largely snow-covered – but this is an exposed place and it's still very much winter down here. The back-lit tarn is a brilliant gleam of ice, fading outwards to dulled silver. On the dark band of open water in the middle of the lake a female Goldeneye is attended by two vigorously displaying males. A pair of Mallards arrives, shattering the dark glassy calm, light shards flying, breaking and spreading like cracks across a mirror. The Goldeneyes leave, wings whistling, looking disproportionately large-headed as they go, demonstrating the appropriateness of their scientific name, the generic 'Bucephala' – cheek-headed (from the Latin bucco for cheek) descriptive of the large, spot-emphasised cheek area – and the specific 'clangula' – sonorous, referring to the sibilance of its wings in flight.

The Tanglewood colours are strikingly vivid this morning – the silver wands of birches with their smudged plum/aubergine bud halo against the honey-lit ash twigs and the bronzy orange-greens of the alders. This, the end of February and the beginning of March, is a prime time for rich subtle colours. There's a fresh fox trail along the river bank, the tracks evenly spaced, one in front of the other along the line of his destination and typical of a fox when he trots with some purpose. Only occasionally are there signs of tail drag. When he comes to an obstacle – a matted tangle of fallen branches or a tree trunk – neither step nor stride falter, so familiar is he with his trod. The lake is so low that it's possible to walk out to the little, vegetated shingle bar – a sanctuary island for most of the year. Where the warmth of birds' feet have rested on the surface of the marginal ice there are clearly defined depressions – many Mallard imprints, the smaller, neat marks where Crows have strutted and several little trails where small birds have walked, stopping and starting, wandering randomly, telling of bewilderment. A couple of Greylags swing up from the bottom tarn, 'aaungh…aaungh!'. They circle, follow the river down, 'talking' continuously, their wings' leading edges flashing like blades against this brilliant morning light.

9.55pm – Back at Kitty Hall copse it's much more sheltered. I flush up an always unexpected, quietly sunbathing Woodcock from a patch of dead brackens under a rock. Its broad wings flicker away like a trail of dead leaves whisped off the ground by the wind. This area is full of Long-tailed Tits flickering about the tree tops, weaving fragile webs of small sound, not pausing anywhere, but two linger, calling, high in a tree. In the village there's very little song – on the ground beneath his 'skulking' bush the male Blackbird sits quietly enjoying the sun, unbothered by my near presence – perhaps by now he recognises me as his morning currant-donor! He remains silent.

8 March

7.15am – After nearly three days of rain, with fell top snow a fairly fresh morning. The river has lost yesterday's very cold viridian, the colour of snow melt. Among Blackbirds physical confrontations are becoming more frequent. Two males face each other with a still, stiff intensity each side of a garden gate, until suddenly both fly off in different directions without the need for any exchange of obvious signals, each clearly recognising the boundary marker for what it was. Up in the village a mature male Blackbird sits hunched on the bowling-green wall. He runs along the top with rapid bursts of little mincing steps. Both, his hunched posture, giving him a very bulky appearance, and the out-thrust jut of his head and bright bill as he runs forward, look impressively assertive as a second Blackbird lands on the same wall. They face each other, hunched and mincing about with little steps and bills thrust forwards until the newcomer flies off and the original Blackbird struts along the wall top in an unmistakeable and impressive gesture of ownership – implying both right and might – before flying down into the depths of a shrub by the side of the bowling green. Mysterious encounters are the order

178

of the day – a couple of yards away a Song Thrush drops down onto the village green and is immediately joined by another. After another tense, silent and enigmatic confrontation both fly off suddenly in opposite directions.

Walking through the village is a journey through different zones. The lane, from the cottage to the shop, is dominated numerically by Robins and Chaffinches with, in decreasing frequency, Greenfinches, Goldfinches and Dunnocks, although musically by Thrushes and Blackbirds. This is an area of large diverse gardens with mixed collections of native and exotic trees and shrubs to either side of the lane. The village centre, consisting of bowling green, village green, pub, shop and a few other buildings – lacks large gardens, and bird sound is dominated by Jackdaws and Chaffinches. From the bridge down the road out of the village past the Youth Hostel there's an area of small gardens and a diversity of large native trees, all bordered to one side by the meadows running down to Kitty Hall and the lake. Here the dominant sound is that of the Tits, Nuthatch, one Mistle and one Song thrush and, of course, the two birds linking all these habitats – the ubiquitous Chaffinch and Great Tit.

A Robin on a nearby wall combines his song with an extraordinary display. He utters a short burst of song and then shivers his whole body, fluffs himself right out, shivers again, flicks his wings and his tail and repeats the whole sequence three times before flying off. As far as I can determine there's no other Robin within both visual and audible range. His beak does not open simultaneously with the uttering of song. He opens it prior to the emergence of song, in preparation, as it were, keeping it open for an equally brief moment after completion.

A Wren sings, way out of sight up on Yew Crags. This diminutive bird has played a major role in various folk traditions throughout Britain and Europe and one of the curious facts is that, although it has become the King of Birds

179

in many folk tales, it has also attracted a considerable number of female names varying from Our Lady's Hen, Chitty, Kitty, Titmeg to Jenny – the latter particularly in the north of England. We all recognise the amazing power of the Wren's territorial song when performed full out to the very end, but it takes a keen, attuned ear to detect one of his least-known song modes. That keen-eyed Cumbrian, William Wordsworth, close ob-server of nature that he was, describing in great detail the setting of a Wren's nest overhanging a brook, writes:

"There to the brooding bird her mate
Warbles by fits his low, clear song."
(*The Wren's Nest*, 1833)

Here Wordsworth refers to yet another, rarely heard voice of the Wren described by Eric Simms as a "whispered song" between male and female. I can also hear what I've really been listening for – that unmistakeable golden phrase, distant, blown down the faint breeze – a first Blackbird.

11 March

2.00pm – Drizzling after a grey morning and further rain. Down at the bridge a female Goosander dives, works her way across the current to the tree-shaded bank where she disturbs a pair of Mallards. She's very handsome with her barred flanks, white speculum and a superb head with its gleaming swept-back spiky crest. Sometimes she dives smoothly, at other, in shallower water, she kicks vigorously with a powerful splash. Despite all this effort she has little reward and makes her way slowly upstream. The Mallard drake resents her presence, interposes himself between her and his phlegmatic mate who ignores the whole situation. Her darting head snakes among the underwater boulders and eventually she catches a small trout, promptly upending it in her bill and swallowing it down.

Up by Andrew's Field on the track to the watershed the ambient silence is charged with that sort of tension which presages a considerable change in atmospheric pressure, registering on the consciousness as if everything is holding its breath waiting for something to happen. The few scattered call notes are like flying sparks, alive and gone. In one of the tall, coppice-growth hazels by the path side a Coal Tit sings his clear, repetitive little song whilst simultaneously preening vigorously. He sings with his bill almost buried to the hilt in a puffed-up fluff of feathers, like an air-filled ball. He sings two or three phrases, digs under his wing, sings, digs under his tail, among his primaries, ferrets about among his contour feathers, tail cocked up. He's having a really good clean-up, letting the air in among all his feathers. He decides it's time to feed, resumes his normal sleek appearance and picks among the catkin scales high in the tree, singing non-stop.

From the top of the watershed Wetherlam looks dark against a grey sky, and the great comb of Greenburn is dense with atmosphere. As it starts to rain, the clean, the clear note of a Buzzard rings out from near Bield Crag, overlooking Little Langdale. A Green Woodpecker calls from high on Howe Banks where the upper outliers of Baysbrown Wood end abruptly at a crag end bouldered by masses of fallen blocks. His call is fragmented – snatches, yelped syllables only – driving hard wedges through the silence, which then draws itself even more tightly around their conclusion, sealing them. The secret of probing such a silence for remnant whisps of sound is to draw it inwards, avoiding the tension born of concentration, then, as you relax, breathing into it, everything falls into its rightful place, the powers of listening and observation both intensified. So much depends on becoming yet another animal part of the landscape, forgetting cerebral processes, the dreaded human will, and just receiving sensations as they come, absorbing the enormous non-human quality of life, not emotionally but as pure essences.

Back home the 'skulking' Blackbird maintains an intent, felt silence in one of his habitual 'skulking' bushes.

14 March

The premonitionary tensions of the 11th were well justified – the next day we had a heavy snowfall and winter continues with the coldest March for many years. Yesterday afternoon we had more heavy snow. We enjoyed a brief feeding visit by a brilliant male Yellowhammer whose bright lemon-yellow face and underparts picked up reflected light from the snow, making him, with his streaked back, much more conspicuous than when seen in a bush. The same applies to seeing a Yellowhammer against pale stone. Seen against the very pale, glacially smoothed rock on the edge of the Common on a very bright day, the male can appear extraordinarily brilliant. The effect of light on a bird's plumage can be extreme, and I have found that it pays not to rely too much on photographs as definitive guides to identification. By 5pm it was snowing hard, piling snow on snow. Nevertheless, a distant Blackbird sang!

This morning we woke to another six inches of snow and still snowing, but the birds are singing – half way through March and the gonadal urge will not be subdued. I walked up the lane in the snow – 'my' Blackbird was no longer in his 'skulking' bush but on top and singing! From now on he has but a few months of song, so every utterance is valuable. Each Blackbird is quite individual in his song, although there are components common to all, particularly the pause-linked phrase structure. The variety comes with the relative musicality of different birds. In the best songs the phrases are melodic and richly fluted, linked by silent pauses which always seem impregnated with an inaudible aftermath of the preceding phrase, thus giving the song – whilst retaining all its territorial and sexual connotations – an emotive quality touching some deep, resonating core within us, perceived intimations of that intimacy which is a characteristic of almost all Blackbird vocalisations. Even that first soft warning 'chuck...chuck' is uttered as a recognition between you and the bird directly and compels your personal attention.

We had a very special but fleeting visitor today. All the feeding birds suddenly dispersed, flung away together like spray from a wave top. There, coursing low over the Common, well below the level of the mist shrouding the hills, flicker-winged, dark and black-and-white-masked against the snow, a Peregrine, forced into a low-level marauding hunt for lack of clear airspace. More than any other bird, possibly anywhere in the world, the aura of danger vibrating from a Peregrine expands outwards, charges the air with a lethal voltage and the imminence of death. He swept up from low over the brackens hurtling along his corridor of dread, his intensity scorching the air behind. He loomed over the house, and his presence seemed to fill the sky. Peregrines are not uncommon visitors to the lower reaches of the valley, from their crags only two or three miles further up. Usually they fly much higher, circling, 'waiting-on', but this was different, dramatic, dangerous, lingering on the retina as a slow-motion aftermath, to be replayed on the screen of memory.

15 March

8.00am – The first morning for several days when it's neither raining nor snowing. Today we can see the ridge – the first time for some days – it's a strange thing, the security of horizons, of knowing one's place within the landscape. This is claimed to be the hardest March for over twenty years and despite the slow thaw and the snow-ploughed lanes the village still looks very bleak, very black and white. But there is a ring of bird music all around. The river is another scene of stark contrasts: its boulders – heavily mushroomed with snow – and river bank tussocks are merely round white shapes, stark against the dark water. Below the bridge a Dipper swims under deep and fast-flowing water. He surges up onto a snowy boulder. When he turns his back, dark, slightly hunched and rounded, he becomes an extension of the boulder. When facing, he's just another blob of snow on a boulder among

183

other snow-blobbed boulders! He stands there bobbing and blinking, looking around, and then begins to sing very, very quietly, just the faintest thin, warbled sound. He breaks off to preen, scans the sky and resumes his small song as he preens, as if quietly humming to himself, before flying off up-stream under the bridge and out of sight.

The sky begins to break as a bitter wind from the east blows straight up the meadows. It shreds the grey, revealing strips and patches of blue, lightening the landscape, shadowing its features and peeling the low cloud from its stasis over the Common like a revelation after so many days without horizons. Suddenly, above Chapel Stile, a brilliant shaft of sunlight illuminates a lofty arc of slowly emerging snow-bound ridge, gleaming white against blue when all else around is grey and shadowed. It is that vision tempting us.

"Always a little further; it may be
Beyond that last blue mountain barred with snow."
(*Hassan*, James Elroy Flecker)

16 March

After five days' snow the landscape still looks very arctic. It thaws slowly during the day, freezes hard at night. There's still about eight inches over the Common, the fells, the fields and in the woods. Today the wind is a bitter easterly but with bursts of glorious sunshine, the first for several days. It remains, nevertheless, the middle of winter. Hitting a bright, joyous note, a Siskin sings – a bright, lively tinkling little song, with a sharp tang entirely appropriate to the brilliant lemon yellow of the male's plumage, full of light and zest and air, high-pitched with a chime like little bells – the noun 'tintinnabulation' comes readily to mind.

Up the lane between Sawrey's Wood and Yew Crags a pair of minuscule Goldcrests flits about a substantial pine branch broken off by the weight of snow. The more vivid male, with his bright slash of crest orange, flies out onto the snow exploring the dead bracken fronds, acrobatic as any tit and very Wren-like in his movements. They look round, fit and well-fed, but they must find a large percentage of their bodyweight in fat/energy in order to survive another night like last night – they weigh only about five grams (lighter than a Coal Tit, Wren and even a Long-tailed Tit which weighs about eight grams!) and keeping so small a body warm presents difficulties. Many of these very small birds have the ability to lower their metabolic rates in order to cope with such severe conditions. The shelter afforded by densely foliaged conifers must be a critical factor in their choice of preferred habitats.

Up in the wood any thaw is very slow. The snow has smoothed out all the boulders and mossy hummocks into a bland grey and white surface. The plantations of tall, silent conifers in Baysbrown look more like the boreal taiga than temperate woodland, the effect enhanced by the resonant call of an unseen Raven overhead. On the far side of the valley, seen through the trees, sunlight and shadow play along the ridge towards the Pikes, swept by successive snow-showers. What little wind there is in the wood is a bitter easterly. It causes a sustained background of quiet wind-rub susurration over which trickles the babble of many little snow-melt streams. Adding just that small element of sound – the babble of running water – changes everything, verifies a law-abiding planetary motion – spring thaw follows winter snows, one of those annual natural rhythms so easily taken for granted but so potent in its healing potential. Underfoot the snow has softened and frozen so many times that the crystalline, granulated sugar surface glitters with a texture of tiny, brilliant glass beads reflecting the sun. Since that one Raven, the more remote parts of the wood, with their untended hazel thickets, birch, pole oaks and conifers, have maintained a dark, silent, almost oppressive stillness.

185

Opening out from the wood, the valley is a wide, white wilderness terminally blocked by the forbidding craggy mass of Pavey Ark. It's an interesting phenomenon that when snow falls heavily on trees that were previously emblematic of solidity and security they become so filigreed with snow-trails laced among branches that they assume an almost vulnerable fragility – as if they might break or shatter into the air; whereas when snow falls on mountain rock its subtlety of structure and its alien vertical surge, and solidity are revealed as if anew, emphasising forgotten, dark potentials for danger and death.

Once out of the shelter of Hag Wood, the weather smites. The ridge dissolves in a fury of driven snow slanting across the valley, and there's almost a complete white-out over the Pikes. But there is a Buzzard winding silently over the edge of Hag Wood in tightly controlled narrow circles. Despite the fury of the wind down the valley, there, under Lingmoor, there's relatively little – he has to flap on the turns in order to maintain airspeed. He's very pale beneath. He drops his legs, mutes forcefully, its trail as he voids it is clearly visible. The snow thickens as he circles, not much above tree height, out over the valley and away up the fell towards the top of the wood, a pallid pointillistic apparition in the driving snow, merging and re-materialising, streaming the element from his paleness. The ridge-top is claimed by the sky – the fellside falls from it dizzily into up-swept swirls of snow, shredding like opaque milky banners. Another Buzzard drifts across the flank of Lingmoor below the crags near the Needle. He's much darker and hard to follow, not breaking the skyline, dark against the snow but lost against rock. Quartering the fellside almost like a Barn Owl, he circles low, looking for a sheep carcass or other carrion among the boulders beneath the crags – obviously an experienced and successful bird. He gains height, swings up to break the skyline above the Needle, holds himself hanging head to wind for a long breathless moment and drops down the far side of the ridge.

2.30am – At Oak Howe. The Pikes have vanished. The valley winds blindly into a vortex of spinning snow. Over Lingmoor the sky shatters open and shafts of brilliant light illuminate the hill, cloud shadows sliding like predatory amoebae across the fellside. Time passes. The skyline, that vital but fragile edge, repository of the known, hoped-to-endure, becomes visible once more with less black now down in the east. To the west the faintest shadows of summitless mountain walls, huge dim pillars, pale grey ghosts of veiled snow and crag rear up forever into infinite sky greys.

18 March

It's a beautiful day but with a biting north-east wind. Much snow lingers on the lower fells and fields, whilst the higher fells remain quite alpine. Many small birds feed about the village gardens, but the Common is empty. A Buzzard sails very low past Oaks Farm towards Loughrigg with the sun directly behind him. He picks up reflected light from the snow, making him look so very pale that he appears and disappears in his passage across the landscape according to his tilt into or away from the light. From the farm comes the chatter of Jackdaws and a solitary Robin song jumps across the shadowy tarn like a hot spark. The water is very dark until facing the sun, when the glitter blinds with glare like the birth of a world. Water birds wishing to remain unobtrusive couldn't find a better place today than the centre of the tarn, a magic place where the merely corporeal dissolves into incandescence.

Hazel catkins, having lost their pollen-laden gold-green, look grey-ochre, spent, streaming in the wind like little prayer-flags, lacking vitality, but some sycamores are flushing and small daffodils spear up into the sunshine in sheltered spots, the first of the imminent orgy of yellows – primroses, celandines, coltsfoot, dandelions – celebrating the welcome return of the sun, a merely predicted tilt of the universe now seen to be actually happening – always a matter of some relief.

187

Walking round the tarn changes the angle of eye to light and now, clearly visible once deprived of their magic dust, three Goosanders and one Tufted Duck occupy the common water of the tarn.

Upstream from Skelwith the river flows very dark between the snow-laden fields. For the first time for several days a Song Thrush sings up on Birk Rigg Park, answered by another from Neaum Crag, the songs carrying clear to each other across the valley from points of almost equal altitude. They sing alternately, each listening before replying, their listening clearly audible until, some point being mutually made, recognised and acknowledged, each is enabled to sing continuously without reference to the other.

The meadows look flat and virginal under their layers of snow. There are no footprints, no sheep; no grass shows through and the sun – lowering now between Fletcher and Lingmoor – casts long blue-grey tree shadows which emphasise the restfulness latent in all horizontals.

19 March

1.30pm – Down to the tarns. The north wind has brought a fast thaw, renewing song and activity everywhere. Up the lane all the village birds sing. A Green Woodpecker yaffles down near the tarn. A Woodpigeon crashes out of the riverside trees by Kitty Hall copse where a Nuthatch bursts into furious alarm. A flock of about 30 Redwings seen only as silhouettes sprays out from the tree tops and heads towards Fletcher. In a crag-end holly a Blackbird sings very quietly his proper, full song, but privately, softly to himself. There remains, however, a wide margin of ice all around the western edges of the tarn. The pines look very dark today against the still snow-clad fields and fells.

For the naturalist such an expanse of apparently un-trodden snow is an adventure waiting to happen, but not without pause for thought. A virgin snowfield is a potent vehicle for time travel, for a return to the integrity of wilderness before the advent of man, the land purified as if millennia of use and abuse were recovered, and a reminder that in our earth walk we should be careful of the kind of footprint we leave. The snow-bound meadows present a broad expanse of featureless white with small irregular patches of marginal grass picked at by four wandering Greylags. The glare off this expanse of white meadow causes an unrelieved numbing of the retinal receptors so that concentrating on the snow, searching for footprints, takes the colour out of everything else, darkening it with a strange, dislocating optical effect.

The snow shows where a Heron had landed, and the strong imprint of his stride indicates a long, slow, careful stalk across the field to the ditch where the frogspawn. Now there are goose tracks, two birds side by side, about a yard apart; one shows a clear set of footprints; the other tends to trail its right middle toe slightly. Two Greylags come low off the tarn. The snow glare is picked up by the forewing coverts both above and under the wing, the white stern and ventral region gleaming with reflected light. Crossing the white expanse in front of the dark wood, they shine incredibly pale and beautiful with reflected snow-light. Nobody has walked down here since the snow first came. After the passage of the geese the air settles once more and the landscape, freed of wings, subsides into that silent heaviness of withdrawal that only unrelieved snow under a grey sky can bring. Geese and swans have left their prints on the snow at Ashes Point, and there are many crow-probed goose droppings where they've come to graze at the grassy edge of the lake. All the tonal subtleties of the bright ochre reedy lake margins with their dark tree reflections are enhanced by the stark light of the surrounding snow. An unexpected Snipe breaks cover; he flicker-jinks away over the willows and is gone. High overhead an unseen single Curlew calls. Eventually a solitary bird, calling continually as he circles ever lower over the meadows and tarns, glides round and

189

down – the first Curlew of the year, a male, prospecting, returned from Ireland, perhaps, where many of our birds overwinter. Curlews bred for the last time in these very meadows in 1977. This Curlew's calls are unanswered; he heads off to the south east and I wish him luck.

3.00pm – It's darkening early this afternoon and to go down into the Tanglewood in these conditions would create a needless disturbance, particularly for any sheltering deer whose only escape is a cold plunge into the river! The white quiet of the afternoon is occasionally punctuated by restrained Goose conversation – there must be a dozen down here now – but along the river bank there's no evidence of anything having made any sign, track, trail or mark, not even the fox which trots along here in the early mornings. The village, however, full of Sunday walkers, Jackdaw chatter and bird song is a different world, removed from the austere, purged and frozen silences down at the tarn.

21 March

Afternoon, blowing a bitter nor'-easterly. The Spring Equinox, first day of spring, marks, as ever, a significant point in the tilt of our earth walk. We are told that this is the coldest spring for at least ten years, and these last two weeks have seen a reversal to winter with a vengeance. However, it is thawing now, the wind burning snow off rapidly from the Common and the lower fells. There are one or two little promises of spring – the thaw has revealed the border of yellowed-green budded daffodils all around the village bowling green, and on the big larches near Elterwater Hall the female flowers characteristic of European larch are just opening, showing little spiky recurved shaving brushes sprouting purplish-crimson out of a green 'crown'. Over the Common a party of some 50 or 60 Jackdaws wheels about a solitary soaring female Sparrowhawk, the axis of this whirling column. I've not seen such an interaction between Sparrowhawk and Jackdaws before, but in summer, up on the Common, it is not unusual to see quite large numbers of hirundines spiralling about a Sparrowhawk or a Peregrine.

22 March

The morning is brilliant, but bitter after a night of brilliant stars and heavy frost.

10.00am – Forsaking my usual very local preferences, I'm enjoying a glorious morning beside Bassenthwaite. Around the smooth, slightly greenish-grey of the sun-washed beeches diffuse-edged shadows curl softly as if cherishing them. The birches gleam like polished bone against the intense blue sky. Skiddaw, immense and serene, looks superb this morning, white-crowned, high gleaming, his almost perfectly coned summit rears blindingly pure against the blue. Wordsworth wrote of Skiddaw as equalling Parnassus:

> "What was the great Parnassus' self to Thee,
> Mount Skiddaw? In his natural sovereignty
> Our British Hill is nobler far… "
> (*Miscellaneous Sonnets*, Part 1, No. V, 1801)

The serene symmetry and perfection of his cone and satellites in these conditions bring to mind Hokusai's *Fugaku Hyakkei - One Hundred Views of Mt. Fuji* – Skiddaw this morning might well qualify as a hundred and first! The lake surface is large and spacious, studded with dozens of birds dozing and gyring to the rhythm of underwater currents – Tufted, Pochard, Goldeneye, Goosanders, Mallard, Teal, small parties of Pintails, Moorhen, Coots, one or two Cormorants and full-plumaged Little Grebes whose pursuit skitterings across the water leave brilliant silver reams as if Turner's sharp knife had been scratched over a dark watercolour wash – a graffito of light droplets and spray. A Buzzard sits in the top of a dead tree in the marginal reeds, unmoving, taking the sun on its back, unbothered as yet by Crows in the area.

191

11.00am – A superbly camouflaged Bittern has emerged through the shorter vegetation fronting the great banks of Phragmites. He stalks, elongated, so that, like a Water Rail, he slides narrowly through the vegetation, predatory as a tiger, head parting the grasses, sliding his body through after peering intently into the marginal water and marshy pools. Suddenly his posture changes – neck outstretched, sun-pointing with the whole length of bill, head and neck, wings half open to his sides soaking up the sunshine, he slowly assumes the classic Bittern pose, bolt upright, his paler, buff-streaked underparts shining in the sun, exactly the same colour as the massed froth of spent Phragmites seed heads. He's very restless, though, and moves on, his tread regular and measured, and feet meticulously placed. His reflected image wobbles, Whistler-like, a long way down the sunlit water.

According to the visitors' log book, the last recorded sighting of an Otter was February 12th 2006, but there he is, swimming rather further along the same shore length as that used by the Bittern. His porpoising passage silvers the water, whilst he gleams like shone pewter as successive bits of him catch the light. He seems to be enjoying himself, almost leaping out of the water, arching up and over, leaving behind him a ream of short-lived glittering bubbles which betray his underwater progress. Again he heaves out and over in a stupendous display of porpoising. When he swims along the surface the large, powerful dog Otter head is very obvious. He lands near a little tree and disappears. A Heron stands on the far shore absorbing the sunshine, sun-pointing with bill and neck, but his wings are opened only from the carpal joint exposing the underwing coverts to the sun. By midday most of the birds are dozing, Otter, Heron and Bittern have withdrawn, and I'll follow their example.

1.30pm – Swirls, Thirlmere, walking the Red Squirrel trail to look at the recently installed hide. Despite the sun, the wind is still very cold. The sunlight slanting through this dense conifer forest is very dramatic, illuminating the lower branches with a pale glow varying from yellow to a rich russet cast from the bark of the spruce poles. The forest beyond is in deep shadow, the trees rising up in an endless perspective of poles, pillars and columns supporting all this textured contrast of light and dark. It's totally silent as if in a vast empty cathedral. From high up in this part of the forest one can look down on the dark indigos and near blacks of Thirlmere far below. Up here there is a small willow-wand hide, an open wicker igloo which does not permit standing. Its reticulated structure should break up its outlines and the 'planted' willow wands will themselves leaf and blend. A Red Squirrel feeder is installed on a tree in the clearing overlooked by the hide. The snow is deep and the wood is utterly silent, lovely in the sunlight – dense shadows, brilliant highlights, the upper trunks of the pines a vivid light red. I've been watching a little Short-tailed Field Vole stumbling about the snowy hummocks covering boulders, clumps of moss and grassy tussocks. Fortunately for him the snow crust is quite hard. It's surprising how high into the hills these bottom-of-the-food-chain mammals live.

Far below on the lake, the distant clang of Canada Geese; overhead, a bouncy group of Siskins, their flight calls light, bright, tangy chimes as zestful as their colour against the dark pine canopy. Preferring more open spaces, it's a while since I've been into the deep heart of a large, mature, well-maintained conifer forest and I'd forgotten that exquisite sensation of solitary remoteness to be found in such places, particularly with much snow still quite deep on the ground. The silence resonates, is so deep that if one sits perfectly quiet and still for long enough the forest's finest sounds become audible – even the very faint crackle of a seed husk being split open high in the canopy. Here one senses the pervading, profound mystery of non-human life, organic and earth-rooted.

At 3.30pm there's the crunch of approaching, intruding footsteps. The couple approaching is obviously very disappointed to see the hide occupied, but I'm already leaving, not wanting disruptive conversation. I don't think they'll be here long; it's getting very cold now and already freezing out of the sun.

24 March

The last 'timetabled' review of the daily morning's events was a month ago. These often small 'events' passing unnoted in the greater scheme of things are the building blocks from which the lives of our common birds are built. They have their own intrinsic interest as well as providing data about local bird distribution and populations. The snow has gone completely from the Common and the lower fells, but much remains above 1,000 feet. It's still bitterly cold, not a morning for hanging about!

6.00am – A grey featureless morning. Predictably a Robin is the first bird to sing. In the lane Chaffinches, Greenfinches and a Woodpigeon lay down foreground sound against the more distant, maintained crowing of a Pheasant.

6.10 – Dunnock sings. Blackbirds perch, silent, withdrawn-looking almost, on trees and bush-tops. They look as if they intend to sing, but do not.

6.15 – Nuthatch calls from near the bridge.

6.18 – Great Tit sings. Nuthatches call from near the Hall.

6.20 – Blue Tit sings. Wren sings behind the Youth Hostel where also a single Goldcrest flits about.

6.21 – A Green Woodpecker yaffles from beyond Kitty Hall.

6.25 – Great Spotted Woodpecker drums in the trees up behind the Youth Hostel, is answered by one from Kitty Hall copse. I've not yet heard a Blackbird or either of the Thrushes.

All this sounds as if there's a lot of song, but it's not so much a chorus as a thin choir of soloists, lacking the depth and fullness of early morning song. Despite the bitter wind there's a tension in the air – the probability of rain is high. Based on the evidence of these last wintry weeks, the question arises of whether such a very cold spell positively inhibits song in some species, quite apart from the question of mortalities. Both Song and Mistle Thrushes were singing gloriously, uninhibited, throughout the day only two or three weeks ago, becoming almost silent during these last wintry weeks. The Blackbird was only starting his song and there have been periods of 'private' singing between long periods of skulking silence.

By contrast, the meadows on both sides of the river seem devoid of life and the river has remained low despite the enormous quantity of thawed snow, testifying to the efficiency of a bitter wind with east in it to burn it off into the atmosphere.

6.35am – At last, in the distance, pure on the wind, a Blackbird song. The power of this song is astonishing; not necessarily dominating by volume as here and now, but purely because of some quality and frequency. A pair of Goosanders paddles slowly up a quiet stretch of water, ignoring my presence on the river bank. Downstream a Dipper bobs on a stone, his song carrying clear above the babbled flow of water over shillets, but somehow withheld from full, so that even if the river were quiet it would still be a restrained song. An ominous milky-blue haze begins to gather up the valley and over the still Arctic-looking mountains adding to the acute sense of unease already in the air this morning. It's too cold to stand still for long and I move on.

7.00am – There, at last, is a Mistle Thrush, very distant, over by Low Wood and answered by an even more distant bird. His song, caught up in the wind, reaches me only in snatches – lost and found – weaving his music through a gusting wind, giving this bird's glorious song its special sense of flaunt and challenge, justifying its old country name,

Stormcock, a tribute to its "exultant and ringing song" (Coward, 1950).

7.05am – A Song Thrush forages among the path side debris. She tilts her body forward in order to concentrate the focus of her eye – whilst keeping the other cocked on her surroundings and the sky. She alternates between our two concepts of thrush as she moves – the 'sleek, attent' thrush, focussed, aimed totally down the line of eye and beak, ruthlessly predatory as she runs forward for the stab; and the more familiar childhood image of the thrush on the lawn, head cocked to one side – as if 'listening for worms'. She's both these images, as traditional fancy blends with biological imperative.

7.15am – The Dipper has been singing quietly to himself for nearly 40 minutes! A Wren sings from a wall by the top tarn meadows. A Mistle Thrush rings out from the top of the Common. These flying sparks of song seem somehow to ratchet up the pressure of atmospheric tension numbing the surrounding landscape. The strange milky haze now enveloping the whole valley brings with it an ever-deepening, tense hush, increasing the sense of unease in the air.

By 9am it's raining, a hard, cold rain, like driven nails, the first proper rain for nearly three weeks! The barometer has plummeted. It rains all day.

25 March

1.00pm – After a very wet morning the afternoon is fine and mild, almost springlike, but the wind is backing – not a good sign. The gardens all along the lane seem resurrected with song and if ever there was an afternoon when Buzzards should be flying this is it – pressure rising, acres of blue sky, towering cumulus – after all, only another month and they'll be on eggs. The snow is going fast from the south- and east-facing slopes of the Pikes, but the north face of Wetherlam remains gloriously and severely alpine, looking much higher than his 2,502 feet, with the cloud brushing his summit and a soft blue haze over his crags and gullies. Nevertheless, to stand on the Common among the freshly revealed vegetation, to hear snatches of song brought from all quarters of the wind is a great therapeutic release from the oppressive atmospheric tension which has been building so relentlessly over these past few days, reaching its climax yesterday. Suddenly, the combination of the rise in temperature (to 11°C), a change in the wind and the upward surge in pressure has stimulated more song in terms of both quantity and quality.

Low Wood looks superb today – there's very little wind and nothing stirs. The soft tans and muted russets of the leaf-strewn mossy floor, the different textures and colours of the oak, birch and hazel coppice, the still wet ash poles, glistening golden ochre, the tall European larches scraping the clouds – all this lit so that every colour and subtle change of tone sings its true song – recedes in a kind of magic perspective to a dense, columnar mosaic. Shadows, almost erotic in the sunshine, curl and cling, sensuously soft, ghosting up the trees and winding diffused around stems and branches in searching spirals. The sunshine, like the rainbow, 'comes and goes'. Suddenly, only 20 yards away is a beautiful and totally unaware young Roe buck in prime condition – still in grey pelage of course – grazing small mosses and the spiky grass shoots growing through. He's a second year, and his antlers are still in velvet surrounded by a fuzz of halo in the sunlight. Despite my stillness, he lifts his head, suddenly aware, wary of the rank human taint – surprised, he bounds away down the wood.

2.20pm – From the top road I take the track up onto Hammerscar. Up here it's very windy; another front is blowing in fast from the south, building an ominous veil of blue-grey light. What a superb viewpoint this is – the three basins of Elterwater and its little village looking like a toy lay-out among trees. Beyond Loughrigg shines the long, crook'd level of Windermere and its distant hills. Nearer, the alpine magnificence of Wetherlam, and the final craggy tops of the long Coniston fells ridge curving down to Wetside Edge, enclosing the misty-blue bowl of Greenburn; behind Lingmoor the serrated ridge of Crinkle Crags and Bowfell – and then the Pikes and the long broad ridge forming the northern boundary of the valley.

3.00pm – This relatively humble ridge with its attractive little craggy summits was made for lingering. From its perched terminal crag one overlooks the dark waters of Grasmere towards the generally more rounded slopes of the fells, from the great soar of Helvellyn to the north down to Fairfield frowning over the glacial scoop of Grizedale Hause, rumoured to contain the crown of Dunmail, Cumbria's last king. However, my gaze is always drawn to the west and points south, to the craggy ramparts of my own valley – the Pikes, Bowfell and the Crinkles down to the icy, alpine glory of Wetherlam as he is this afternoon.

3.30pm – In one of the pools on the Common there's frogspawn, the first of the year and fresh as if laid last night, whilst from the dense tangles of snow-flattened brackens darts that most unobtrusive of small brown birds – the Meadow Pipit, found all over the upland landscapes of the Lake District, its Commons and moorlands. Described by Macpherson (1892, *The Vertebrate Fauna of Lakeland*) as the "commonest of birds on our hills during the summer-time", it was identified as long ago as 1544 by that founding father of British ornithology, William Turner. At one time this was very much a bird of the heather, as its old Westmorland names testify – Heather Lintie and Ling Bird – and as such became the favoured prey of that dashing little moorland falcon, the Merlin. Following the destruction of much upland heath by sheep grazing, the pipit has settled for more diverse habitats and has become the most favoured target on the Cuckoo's parasitic hit-list. Its life, therefore, is fraught with dangers of one kind or another, and the readiness with which it is disturbed reflects its wary and anxious outlook on life. His

198

display flight, a rapidly fluttered vertical ascent over his territory – accompanied by piping call notes – from the apex of which he 'parachutes' gently back to earth with a variety of call notes and trills, is pleasing to both eye and ear. Some males are beginning to explore their first seasonal song-flights over the Common, bringing with them a renewed vitality to the huge expanses of tangled, snow-flattened bracken.

By 5pm there's a drenching mist of mild soft rain. From the wilderness garden next door a Song Thrush sings – a most welcome return! It's been a good day – the return of song, the flight song of the pipits, fresh frogspawn – all on the same day – not quite the first day of spring, but after nearly a month of winter near enough!

28 March

After two days of continuous rain and higher temperatures the wintry spell is surely over. The valley is inundated, the lake flooding over into the Tanglewood on both sides of the river, all forming one continuous sheet of water! However, today is bright, fresh and washed, rinsed by the rain, blown crisp and clean by the brisk south-west wind. Today sees one of the year's highest tides, and I was particularly keen to come out to Walney and Foulney whilst there are still numbers of waders before they leave for their breeding destinations in the far north.

11.30am – Snab Point, South Walney, where there are some inland lagoons with marshy areas and much whin. The air here vibrates with the sound of two contrasting voices creating a curious counterpoint – on the rising curve the 'silver chime' of the many towering Skylarks, invisible against the sky-glare, beneath which droop the long melancholy notes of the Redshank. The rough pastures, bristling in places with brilliant whins, have had a large fall of Meadow Pipits restless as blown leaves after their recent arrival. As if by magic, the tip of one of the whins sprouts the unmistakable black head, white neck-patches and rusty breast of a male Stonechat – he looks very handsome in full colour on the yellow whins against a blue sky – what colour singing! Unfortunately, his own little song is not really adequate to his surroundings – little bursts of rather scratchy piping – a cheerful sound nevertheless, perky as befits his trim appearance.

Some 300 Curlews wait out the high tide around the banks of a rushy pool where a Little Egret makes a brilliant white statement. Over the last few years this elegant bird has been steadily increasing its range both westwards and northwards and can now be seen in both spring and autumn at various sites around the Cumbrian coast. Whatever its future in Cumbria, its purity of whiteness and exotic elegance have the power to invest its immediate surroundings with an almost Mediterranean air, most cheering on a dull day around our northern estuaries. It springs from the rushes, its black legs and yellow feet – strangely incongruous, looking as if fresh-painted this morning – trailing out behind. Its wing strokes are steady and completely unhurried, as befits members of the Heron tribe. It lands near the Curlews, preens its plumes for a few minutes before settling into that hunched, folded umbrella stance which so well expresses the limitless patience of all the heron kind.

1.00pm – The Foulney parking area is a spit of rough grassland and shingle, occupied at the moment by a couple of Golden Plovers, gold and black spangled but not quite moulted into full breeding plumage beneath. They potter about on their rather short legs, poking here and there before settling into a hunched passivity. Nearby is a pair of Wheatears fresh from their long flight from Sub-Saharan Africa – dropped-in this morning I'm told. The male looks immaculate in his blue-grey crown, nape and mantle, pink-flushed buff breast – all set off by the black 'trim' of wings, tail and broad eye-stripe. They are very content to sit quietly among the grasses in the sun. The ebbing tide is roaring across the Foulney causeway in a white seething curve of dire warning and at the far side of the breakwater, all around the broad shingled shelf of Foulney embankment, is a mass of roosting Curlews. Everything shines here today under the hard blue sky and unaccustomed sunshine and, as if to express a proper reward for such a sparkling day, a spanking new Small Tortoiseshell butterfly flickers across the sward with that characteristic blind-seeming apparent lack of control, yet stubborn beyond its fragility, making way against the wind – another first for this day. I sit munching my sandwiches in the sun watching the Wheatears and Golden Plovers until the causeway clears and foot passage can be made to Foulney. Once off the shingle and onto the short turf, there are more newly arrived restless Wheatears showing that 'white arse' which gives them their name. The rounded hummocks that were the bunched Curlews have resolved into an irregular sequence of bird-shaped silhouettes against the skyline which shatters as I approach, for there's no cover here.

Further out, the curved shingle horn of Slitch Ridge is whitely peppered with dozens of Eiders waiting for the ebb to create the current which will sweep them round the island's southern point in a grand marine procession – one of the great attractions of Eider-watching here. The drakes are busily displaying with much head-tossing and foot-splashing accompanied by what, to us, sounds like expressions of amazed delight – 'oo-OOO-ooo' on a rising and falling curve. Once swept round the point, most of the drakes are content to raft on the gently rocking tide, dozing in the sun, preening. Unmated females, however, very much in the minority, are pursued by strings of competitive, testosterone-fuelled males – there's one such now, the target of about fifteen displaying males. Eventually she submits, flattening herself out on the water whilst the successful suitor mounts, mates and then escorts her ashore where he leaves her. His job is done; he will take no further part in this year's breeding cycle.

There are also nearly 50 Dark-bellied Brents out here – small, neat, dark geese, dipping into the tide edge, picking about in the mass of floating weed. Some of these are beginning to feel a bit 'edgy', and it won't be long before they fly back to their breeding grounds in Arctic Russia. Some swim in water just shallow enough for dabbling on the bottom, flashing their white under-rumps as they forage among the submerged weed. Others move about the weed-strewn shillets and mussels of the shore line. This is a strangely isolated group of Brents, as may be deduced from their usual wintering destinations. The Dark-bellied Geese (*Branta bernicla bernicla*) from arctic Russia winters in large numbers along our south-east and southern shores, whereas the Canadian/Greenland subspecific population of Pale-bellied (*B. b. hrota*) winters mainly in Ireland, whilst the Svalbard population winters in north-east England. This little local population was first noted in the late 1970s when it was observed that "a small family group" (Hutcheson, M., 1986) had wintered in the Walney/Foulney area. They have been steadily increasing ever since.

Small groups of Oystercatchers with Redshanks and a few Turnstones also feed along the now fast-receding tideline. The busy Turnstones look very resplendent in their breeding – plumage. It might be thought that their bold, pied patterns on head and chest together with the rich black and brick-red plumage of their wings and back would make them very conspicuous – an impression heightened by their updated name 'Ruddy Turnstone' – but they are excellently camouflaged among the wrack where they find small crustaceans, worms and molluscs, flicking over the stones with as much ease and indifference as a Blackbird overturning leaves in winter. Unlike some of our other waders, they are almost exclusively a coastal species. Those that winter with us breed around the coasts of Greenland and as far afield as arctic Canada. Others come to us on passage from wintering on the coasts of tropical Africa – these will go up to the high Scandinavian tundra to breed.

It is lark song, however, that fills the air. It is appropriate here to spend a little time considering the Skylark, this nondescript, little bird which, nevertheless, has been one of the most charismatic presences throughout the long history of our agriculture and countryside, widely celebrated in folklore, poetry and music. Shakespeare called it the "ploughman's bird", placing it firmly not only in a time and a place but also within a long-held rural tradition. The song from Act 2 of *Cymbeline* reflects its primacy as a significant dawn presence:

"Hark, hark! the lark at heaven's gate sings
And Phoebus 'gins arise…"

It was what the song signified, however, that occupied the sensibilities of the Romantic poets, and it was, indeed, a native Cumbrian, addressed by Shelley as "Poet of Nature" who saw more clearly "into the heart of things". Wordsworth made that essential naturalist's link between the song and what it represented on earth below:

"Dost thou despise the earth where cares abound?
Or, while the wings aspire, are heart and eye
Both with thy nest upon the dewy ground?"
(*To a Skylark*)

Later in the same poem there is an extraordinary, wonderful line – "A privacy of glorious light is thine", emphasising that profound biological link between song and territory ownership – the essential natural history expressed with both accuracy and profound, illuminating imagination – the essential key to 'knowing' nature.

Unlike the more structured songs of, say, Chaffinch or Willow Warbler, the Skylark's has no predictably repeated pattern. It is largely a free-form composition in which certain phrases recur, often in variation form, sung from the summit of a column of air instead of the tree top favoured by many of our song birds. Some have claimed that the Skylark's song has nothing special to commend it. We tend to forget, however, that what we hear may bear little or no resemblance to what another Skylark hears.

The hearing of birds is tuned to detailed resolutions of complex sound way beyond the limits of human capability, so that, although we may try to define notes as a 'trill' or a 'warble', it will be heard by another Skylark in much greater detail, revealing structures and patterns only available to us by the use of sophisticated technologies which enable us to record and replay that song in slow motion. It has been shown that two or three dozen syllables may be condensed into a second's worth of utterance, making it into a kind of code to which only other Skylarks have the key. That's the technology – what we hear is something transformed by the imagination into a deep personal response.

More recently Vaughan William has given us an equally illuminating musical image, his romance for violin and small orchestra inspired and prefaced by George Meredith's poem, *Lark Ascending*, reflecting a sensitivity for the herald of rural England up to the end of the Second World War when the countryside still rang to the sound of lark music.

For all the tradition, joy and inspiration the Skylark has given countless generations over hundreds of years we have repaid him very badly. The dramatic post-war change from the time-honoured spring-sowing of cereal crops – for the Skylark was essentially a bird of arable farmland – to winter-sown deprived it of its traditional, essential winter stubble foraging grounds with devastating effects on its ecology and population. Here in Cumbria, instead of its former status as the characteristic bird of our agricultural lowlands, it is now found more up in moorland habitats and around the coast.

3.15pm – As I walk back, the tide-washed mud gleams so wet that it has no colour of its own, expanding into the sky, mirroring its colours perfectly and all across this huge expanse of shine are feeding birds, mainly Redshanks, Curlews and

Oystercatchers. The shingle patches occasionally meta-morphose into Ringed Plovers, their outlines disrupted by their pied patterning. Curlews call; occasionally the full-blooded song drifts down the wind, bubble-linked, rising and falling, beyond description. On the Piel Island side the water is all a-glitter, the island and castle looking very dark, menacing al-most, in the shadow of the advancing cloud. Paired Oyster-catchers are everywhere, their reflections smudged down into the shining mud. The males are very assertive about their mates and resent any over-close approach by any other bird. Brents, Eiders, Oystercatchers – all demonstrating similar assertive behaviour now and then as the gonadal urge becomes daily more strong, more commanding.

30 March

2.00pm – A bright, warm afternoon following a very wet night and morning. The tarn is still flooded, right out over the meadows and into the woods on both sides of the river, so that from this huge sheet of water rise the twisty, fallen stems of the Tanglewood, more like a mangrove swamp than a bit of Cumbria. Over the meadows flashes of iridescent blue steel and white underparts mark the passage of House Martins as they flake off the wind with unpredictable changes of speed and direction, curves drawn on the sky with exquisite geo-metric precision.

The surface of the middle tarn is alive with the dark flickerings of hundreds of Martins. This is an annual event which will last a few days while the birds re-fuel before moving on, the Sand Martins either towards the coast or up into the Eden and Lune valleys. Most of the House Martins will disperse, but some will remain to nest locally within the valley. There is a continual pin-point flicker of light – a sun-dazzle into and out of which the birds materialise and disappear like shooting sparks which glow and fade within seconds.

Whilst watching all these hirundines at their manoeuvres, a stately Buzzard pale and beautiful against a pure blue sky, circling directly overhead, draws its wings slightly in and back gliding against the wind towards Fletcher with a slow, poised, indifferent mastery. Down by the river an elegant male Grey Wagtail in prime livery pulls vigorously at boulder moss. His black bib, hard-edged, sets off the brilliance of his lemon-yellows, blue-grey cap and mantle. There are also the other bits of 'trim' – the white coverts and scapulars against the black primaries and the neat white-striped slight curves of super-cilium and, below the eye, the moustachial, cut against the immaculate line of the black bib. In the sunlight against the yellow-green moss he's not so vivid, but lit against a dark shadow he's truly spectacular.

A Blackbird sits on the lane wall listening to another, unseen male. He sings a phrase then listens, his head cocked as if in concentration. He flies, still singing, onto the top of a telegraph pole where he's more challenging. He listens again, head cocked for all of half a minute, but this time there's no response. This particular Blackbird has a way of defining the perimeter of his territory by moving from perch to perch, singing a phrase here, another there, as well as his use of important perching stations from which to declaim his full song. There's a mass of dark cloud behind him, highlighting his bill which gleams like a chip off the sun. The lack of response relaxes him and he flies down into the garden.

I reach home at 4pm – two hours to walk the mere mile or so down to the sitting stones and back – a bit of a record even for me!

April

1 April

2.00pm – Clear and bright after a clashy morning with heavy showers – a typical April afternoon. April has had a long and variable poetic history from Chaucer to the present day. Unfortunately we've had anything but a "droghte of March" and at the moment we can do without "Aprille with his shoures soote"! Browning's ex-pat bit of fluffy nostalgia (*Home Thoughts, from Abroad*) does at least contain the identifying feature of the Song Thrush's song – "he sings each song twice over" – but I much prefer the uncomfortable direct honesty of Eliot's challenging lines reminding us that spring, the season of natural renewal, is a hard landscape for the flowerings of personal renewal:

> "April is the cruellest month, breeding
> Lilacs out of the dead land, mixing
> Memory and desire, stirring
> Dull roots with spring rain…"
> (*The Waste Land*, 1922)

Down in the Tanglewood is exactly what I'd hoped to hear today – the unmistakeable song of a Chiffchaff, two notes so simple yet so welcome, flying in the air like chips from a woodcutter's axe. Until relatively recently the Chiffchaff was regarded as a fairly marginal species in Cumbria, its fluctuating annual numbers reflecting periods of drought in its Saharan and sub-Saharan winter quarters, but over more recent years both its distribution and population have greatly increased. It has a distinct preference for valley and hanging woodland in which mature, oak-dominated woodland form a semi-open canopy over dense ground vegetation suitable for nesting. This suits the male Chiffchaff very well, for once his song has done its job – defined territory and attracted a mate – he takes no further part in the breeding cycle, migrating up to the high canopy to sing and feed whilst the much more secretive female uses the dense under-storey to rear 'their' family on her own. Nevertheless, the song of the first *Phylloscopus* leaf warbler is always an event to be marked, as if some threshold is passed and others will be on their way.

Much frogspawn has been deposited in the traditional path-side spawning ditch – 'dollops' of various sizes from dribbles to where there has evidently been a communal spawning – one patch covering about a square yard, densely packed, domed up in the middle by pressure from beneath, where there'd obviously been a multi-ranid orgy!

3 April

6.15am – A fine, fresh morning after rain. Down towards the lake from Silverthwaite the wood is very quiet – an occasional Robin only at the moment. A couple of Greylags approach wing tip to wing tip very low over the lake; they look pale and beautiful in the early morning light. A sky-wandering Curlew high above, unseen, projects his song-bubbles down the wind.

6.47 – Wrens everywhere are shattering into song. A Blackbird sings. This bird is a master singer. He sings one way and with great deliberation, turns round on his perch and sings in the opposite direction, dominating by a combination of volume, frequency and sheer musical quality.

7.10 –The first sun on the Pikes casts a hard, cold light, the pale rock only just tinted a grey tone of yellow-ochre, the grasses washed out to desiccated tans and sere straw, whereas on Lingmoor to one side and the ridge to the other, the bracken-clad slopes glow deep warm rose. It's all in the wind. If the wind contains a touch of east, the actual colour of that wind is often a cold bleached yellow flashing like a twisting blade through the meadows and along the fell-grasses, casting this particular cold dawn light on everything it touches.

7.29am – A single Greylag comes flying low, following the bends in the river, circling the tarn and calling continuously. The increasing number of Greylags is becoming a regular and attractive feature of the meadows, grazing among the sheep and Woodpigeons – a splendid, majestic sight in the mornings when they come in low, the light flashing on their wings. Silently a Buzzard sails over from the top of Rob Rash to Low Wood in a long slow glide behind the trees. Rob Rash, too, is silent save for a brief snatch of Chiffchaff song, a very few notes only. It's as if, suddenly, after all this morning's song someone's simply turned a switch and it's extinguished, as if what had been real a few moments ago was illusion, the air sealed, quite, behind it, forgotten, denied. On the bottom tarn two Goldeneyes huddle and bob in the lee of the Nab. Even Wetherlam, so glowing warm in the first light, has been touched by this bitter, yellow-flashing wind.

(Later – Out of this bitter wind came a drenching rain, falling as snow above 2,000 feet on the hills.)

5 April

8.15am – A fine morning but with a bitter wind from the north. The one or two small Jacobs Sheep lambs in the meadow look very vulnerable in this cold wind. A couple of Woodpigeons feed in the top meadow – they've become a regular feature these last several days along with the Greylags which haven't yet arrived for their morning's grazing. Woodpigeons have been scarce this winter following last autumn's very poor seeding, but more and more pairs are dropping down to feed beside them in the meadows, responding to that flash of white on the neck which acts as a signal attracting the birds to flock in safety. They tend to be taken for granted, but like other 'pest' species – the Corvidae, for example – we give them unjustly scant regard. They are both visually and aurally fascinating. Their colour is so subtle, as if dusted on with a touch of iridescence about the upper breast and lower neck. Their 'coo'-ing, which fulfils the function of song, is a sound that repays much listening for it's not as soft and murmurous as one might think on first hearing. There are two aspects of the sound which reveal much about the meaning of this apparently soft, soothing 'song'. First, it is insistent, repetitive, ensuring that its message is received and understood. Second, it's not uttered on just one clear note softly enunciated – there is a distinct abrasive quality caused by the projection of one dominant sound synchronous with an undertone marginally, microtonally different. These two simultaneous notes rub together with the result that not only is the song insistent but also projects a harsh, almost grated 'edge' which belies that first apparent softness and emphasises its insistence. Its other, tri-syllabic call – a long, falling 'growly' note followed by two shorter notes is even more grating.

There's a pair of prime-condition Goosanders on the river, swimming slowly and snorkling for fish about the pools, foraging under the large stones which form the under-water foundations of the bank wall and finding small trout there. He looks particularly fine, quietly and continuously calling to his mate. The light emphasises the structural 'shot' silken greens in his head and picks out all the delicately marbled striations down his lower back and rump between the black scapulars – he looks splendid. They synchronise their movements, so that when one dives so immediately does the other.

A Buzzard swings low over Lane Ends; he has to flap on his turns to gain some initial height. He glides, turns and flaps, rising slowly, swinging downwind as he goes. Once over the

Common he gains height more easily, and it's obvious when he gets a sudden uplift because he actually 'levitates' as if caught up in an invisible lift. Over Low Wood he's joined by another flying very much higher. They soar together then split, each towards its own territory.

What song there is this morning is rather thin in this bitter, bladed wind. A Great Spotted Woodpecker drums intermittently. The Wrens occasionally let loose a tremendous volley of song, which when heard at close quarters, like that of the Sedge Warbler in season, drowns out everything else. It's essential to keep coming down here morning after morning, however briefly, just to keep an ear on what's going on because this is where I usually hear the first *Phylloscopus* warblers, the first Redstarts and Pied Flycatchers and, down in Rob Rash, the first Blackcaps and Garden Warblers – it has been so for years.

Suddenly, confounding this bitter wind, another glorious Blackbird perched, facing up-valley, in the top of an old ivy-covered ash. His whole song is broken by pauses that, rather than being heard as silences, should be heard as one hears Brucknerian pauses in which the preceding phrase is summarised and held within, filling up with whatever has gone before in preparation for whatever is to come… Unlike the pauses, which seem to me to be of almost identical length, the actual phrases are very variable. He seems to go through a period in which he builds up the quality of the actual song elements until he reaches an optimum and, although he continues singing the quality of these ensuing elements, subtly declines. Thus his song could be said to consist of a series of pause-linked phrases, each series with a rising and falling curve – a beginning, a middle and an end – with the very best song at the apex of the curve. What it teaches is that it's no good listening to a Blackbird casually en passant. One *must stop* and listen properly. Because their songs are so variable, it is necessary to listen to many Blackbirds in order to locate the master-singers – time well spent! That Blackbird sings me all the way up the path right to the bridge. It's nearly 10am – holiday walkers are appearing – time I was disappearing.

1.30pm – The bitter north-west wind continues. The big larches at the foot of the Hullet's Nest track are beginning to flush, with both male and female flowers now fully developed. The little female flowers, only about half an inch long with their purplish-crimson 'shaving-brush' bracts, are very attractive. The male flowers look like small, rather squashed green cushions, some slightly purple-tinged. Everywhere else on the tree the green buds are ready to flush, little fists holding bunches of concentrically arranged needles. On top of a hazel twig what I assume by its behaviour to be a female Coal Tit is engaged in a positive fever of high-speed twitching and twisting, vibrating her wings as if soliciting, seeking the male's attention either for courtship, feeding or mating. A male lands on the same perch, sings, with much high-speed tail and wing-flicking and twisting/swivelling actions until both fly off together. What a voltage of excitement generated by two such very small birds!

Wild strawberries and celandines flower among the first local primroses in the south-facing rim of Andrew's Field. On the hollies flower buds are bunched in the leaf axils, so small at the moment that they must be sought out rather than merely seen. These will unfold as clusters of small cruciform white, purple-tinged flowers towards the end of April. The male and female are on different trees so that berries can only appear when they grow close enough together. Hawthorn is well flushed in the hedge, a crisp fresh green against the darks of the hollies.

I'm heading off-track towards those 'delectable pastures' overlooking Little Langdale. Once removed from the lee influence of Lingmoor, this watershed pastureland becomes a grand, exposed expanse of landscape, open and windy and wide, enjoying a compass sweep of over 180 degree from the

212

Tilberthwaite fells to the long ridge which forms the northern wall of Great Langdale. Further, there's the snow-streaked summit of Helvellyn, brooding Dollywaggon and windswept Fairfield, all with rolling shadows sliding over fellside and crag, fitting snug around the contours in a constant movement of light and shade. Where the grass is lit it shines silver with soft pewter shadows or tan with almost blue shadows. It looks as if there might be the beginnings of grass growth on the fellsides – there's a greenish cast in this light where all winter long the fells have retained their shining ochres and tans which I much prefer, having a strong aesthetic objection to mountains wearing the same colours as the valleys whence they spring.

A Buzzard rises on the high wind out of Little Langdale. He ascends vertically, again as if lift-borne, between me and the sun, a dark shape continually re-adjusting all sorts of planes and horizons, swinging in the wind. He suddenly tilts onto his right wing, swings downwind with wings drawn in to slant across it arrowing at great speed towards Lingmoor, where he pulls steeply up and initiates a huge, exhilarating roller coaster display over the valley. Between me and Wetherlam now, back-lit against a very dark cloud, the sun strikes his back and he gleams like new ploughland or polished pewter with just a tinge of burnt umber, the light catching the grape-like bloom on his feathers rather than the colour of the feathers themselves. Along to the south the wind flashes silver blades across the fells, but here on the edge of the wood the only sound is the constant rub of wind in tree tops.

4.10am – Emerging from the dark stillness of Fletcher onto the marshy meadows around the head of the lake, the first thing I hear is a rather urgent Buzzard call; staccato, repeated, this particular call usually has intimate pair-bonding connotations, a female soliciting copulation perhaps. Buzzards, like every other British raptor from Little Owl to Golden Eagle, must copulate astonishingly frequently during the pre-lay period in order to ensure success at the right time. I once watched a pair of Buzzards go through the motions of copulation in two separate series of three matings, each within 45 minutes. Such frequency not only ensures the female's readiness when the time is right, but it is also an expression of the pair bond and which I've seen used, for example, as reinforcement after, say, a territorial dispute with other birds or some other disturbance within their territory. I couldn't pass by here without visiting the old boathouse – scene of many memories of paintings, boats, Barn Owls, Water Rails and long hours in hides. The recent heavy snow has brought down another segment of roof and the entire supporting structure is lurching – still in defiance of gravity, but not for much longer – it can't last this year out. A pair of Reed Buntings flies up into the hedge from a clump of rushes. I've always had a special fondness for this smart little black-headed, white-collared bird with his simple but cheery song, the best description of which is given, as usual, by Grey in an image which has remained vivid throughout a lifetime's bird watching:

> "It suggests to me the ascent of steps, the first two or three being mounted sedately and the last two taken trippingly."
> (*The Charm of Birds*)

At one time Reed Buntings sang their little step-song from the willow-carr all round the lake, and it was always deeply satisfying knowing that the lake was, then, ringed round with so many of these handsome little birds. He sits now fluffed out, with his mate, enjoying the sunshine, and I'm delighted to see them.

8 April
8.30am – Over the past couple of days there's been a considerable drop in pressure, the north-west wind driving a succession of blinding, wintry showers down the valley. Up the

valley, just visible through the murk, the dim shapes of the Pikes, bleak and inhospitable, swished across by great veils of snow, look like ghosts of themselves. I'm taking advantage of a relatively clear spell to walk down by the river. Unlike the wintry spell in March, the birds are not now put off their song, but we are approaching the middle of April and the biological necessity for territorial declaration whatever the weather is much more imperative, so that in the garden and up the lane all the local males are in full song.

There are eleven Greylags in the long meadow this morning, by now accustomed to the constant human traffic up and down the footpath only some fifteen to 20 yards away – they do look fine! and one or two are becoming quite aggressive, running with neck assertively outstretched towards any goose standing where it shouldn't – they seem to organise themselves into four well-defined couples and three 'others'. They are completely blotted out as curtains of wintry rain, hard and cold, sweep down the meadows, over the Common and across the face of Loughrigg.

9.05am – The ivied-ash Blackbird that sang with such mastery the other day is on the river bank under his singing tree, but singing softly as if to himself. He flies up into the tree, still singing quietly as, branch by branch he makes his way to the top and once there he opens out, full into the rain and sleet and the hard, cold wind, opening his syrinx to the elements as he does to the sun. A Treecreeper climbs, poking among the mosses on the same tree, working his way upwards in small jerky runs. It reaches a heavy growth of moss and pulls vigorously at it until shreds fly in all directions in its eagerness to find what it might conceal. The ferocity of the attack is totally unexpected in so small and mouse-like a bird, and very eloquent of the urgency of its survival instinct – such chance observations occur as revelations! It searches deep into the hole it's made, stabs and hammers at something it's found, then onwards and upwards, continually finding things between

215

the moss and the trunk and tucked away in cracks in the bark. There's another huge shower, but the Treecreeper works on the sheltered side, still pulling off moss as if its very life depended on it – which, of course, it does!

9.15am – The one or two sheep with very small lambs are clustered close in under the lee of the wall, the lambs mostly snug against the woolly bulk of their dams, although one or two remain exposed in mid-meadow, hunched, wet, cold and very vulnerable-looking in these, the very worst combination of conditions – beating rain and a bitter wind. By the time I get down to the sitting stones it's still howling down the valley and even the one or two Crows poking about the meadows are forced up and away to seek shelter, but I can still hear that Blackbird!.

9.30am – The rain still sluices down; Wrens and Chaffinches sing, joining the Blackbird – but no Chiffchaff today. At last the rain eases and the sun tries to break through. The Pikes look even more ghostly now, appearing only as slightly different changes of tone against the distant sky; no outlines, just dim smudges of rather paler grey, darker where the crags fall. The Blackbird at the bottom of the long meadow is still singing (half to three-quarters of an hour later!), still facing the weather at the top of his tree.

10.15am – The weather shows much more promise of clearing – the fells are visible once more. The eleven Greylags are exactly where I left them nearly two hours ago, but apart from me there's been no footpath traffic to disturb them. However, with the cessation of the rain and sleet, people are emerging from their cars, some already starting down the footpath – it's time I was going.

10 April

9.00am – A most beautiful morning after a very heavy frost. A pair of Grey Wagtails upstream of the bridge flits among the mossy boulders both in and beside the river, picking at moss, looking for insects. They arrive together onto the same stone, and the male assumes a straight bill to tail alignment, pointing up to the sky so that his line makes an angle of about 45° to the top of the stone. He bows, skypoints again, bows a second time eliciting a wing-shivering, soliciting response from the female, either to be fed as part of a bonding ritual or to be mated. He indicates his refusal by flying downstream to another boulder where he preens very thoroughly for several minutes and forages among the boulders there before rejoining her on another stone – they both fly off upstream.

2.00pm – In the marshy meadows below Kitty Hall, a couple of disturbed Snipe climb fast, jinking their way over the cottage and curving round towards the top tarn – spring arrivals, or lingering winter visitors? Meadow Pipits forage in the muddy patches between the rushes; a Nuthatch calls persistently, loudly, and a solitary Starling's song, blown downwind from the big oaks where Starlings have nested for years, suddenly becomes clearly audible, bubbling, wheezing and rattling, inserting bits of Buzzard, Blackbird and Curlew into his random, carefree babbles.

In the tarn-side meadows there are many new-born lambs basking in the sunshine. It's good to see the meadows greening up, providing that essential first new-growth bite for these vulnerable youngsters which have so far endured heavy rain and frost – this afternoon, however, they're making the most of the sunshine. Down in the rushy part of the meadow a sizeable lump of frogspawn has been left stranded on the grass after the little flood-pool where it had been laid had dried out. It's rather more solidified than aqueous now, set and dried just enough to retain the imprints of beak stab marks where a Crow has probed for the little black embryonic tadpoles, still curled up tight within the jelly. A Buzzard calls very high over the watershed, makes a long sloping accelerating dive down to the tree tops behind the skyline of Fletcher. It's very tempting on an afternoon like this, at this time of year in what is known

217

to be good Buzzard-country, to imagine that the area is totally devoid of Buzzards. They really have to be sought out high in the sky, where they may often be found as little more than revolving specks. At times, according to the angle they make relative to the sun, they gleam briefly and disappear as they make another turn on the opposite axis, emerging and fading like shining motes as they tilt and revolve their horizons in the sun.

The lake is all a-dazzle this afternoon, the water still flooding up into the surrounding vegetation. A pair of Goldeneyes comes noisily off the top tarn. As they circle round, the male comes close, between me and the sun, so that he moves in a whistling transparent web as the trailing edge of his pure white secondaries catch the light. Around the tarn edge some of the willows are coming into flower. The male flowers are like small golden brushes, their filaments terminating in golden anthers with their full pollen sacs, attracting small insects ready for the imminent arrival of the migratory warblers. A bumble bee drones closely by, quite filling the eye.

3.05pm – Suddenly there's another lot of Martins falling out of the clouds driven from the west, until there's a great twittering over the water, birds coming and going into and out of visibility according to whether they're flying in the shine or not, for the water is bright with glitter. Seven Teal spring out of the nearby reeds, and from the tangle of carr along the lake edge a Woodcock rattles out. Nothing quite prepares one for the sudden under-the-foot rocketing out and up of a Snipe or a Woodcock, remaining invisible until shocking out from almost underfoot. (Later – I've just been looking at the figures I collated in respect of waterfowl numbers on Elterwater from October 1989 to April 1990, when on some days in March and early April there were counts of over 100 birds in 12 species on the water. Elterwater, like Grasmere and Esthwaite, has suffered badly from eutrophication and virtually the whole food chain from aquatic insects to birds has suffered accordingly.)

3.15pm – It's very peaceful sitting here beside the lake with the glitter of rocking water in front and the tangled stillness of the dark wood behind, poised between the dark and the light. In front, the slow, silent sliding ripple of wavelets, little pools of reflected skylight, which wobble, link and unlink, appear and disappear, shape-changing constantly as they advance to-wards the shore, the reflected reeds giving a vertical balance to so many horizontals. High above, two Ravens glide wing tip to wing tip in that most perfect and moving of all flights – a bonded pair synchro-flying about the sky, contact maintained as if an unseen current sparks from one to the other. They loop about, separate and re-merge as if the tension between them will not stand further stretching, linked as if by invisible elastic.

4.15pm – The lake surface is now alive and spinning with Martins and Swallows, weaving intricate, flickering nets over the water, hawking the bounty of insects, maintaining a height of about one to two feet above the water, the prime insect zone. There's no twittering now, however – they're all silently intent on their feeding. A pair of Pied Wagtails on the shore at Ashes Point probes the gravel for the small insects dimpling the mud 'cement' which binds it all together where the lake tide laps.

As I come up from the silence of the tarns and meadows into the village, there's a sudden increase in song – Mistle Thrush, Chaffinch, Blue and Great Tits, Robin, Blackbird, Nuthatch, Dunnock and Woodpigeon. Down the lane they are joined by Greenfinch and Goldfinch whose chiming greets me home at 5pm.

11 April
Fine, mild and windless after a hard frost overnight.

9.30am – Arrive at Dungeon Ghyll for a Wheatear-count up Mickelden, the great glacial valley cutting up into the heart of the mountains beyond the road end. Mickelden Beck, the

219

main stream flowing down this valley, eventually becoming Great Langdale Beck, is one of the two main rivers feeding Elterwater and is itself fed by a multitude of small streams draining the high fellsides to either side of Rossett Ghyll which is the source water. One of the peculiarities of this valley is the dramatic difference in terrain from the north side of the beck to the south, given that the valley is quite narrow, so that they form two very contrasting habitats with corresponding differences in numbers and distribution of birds they contain.

The onward way towards Mickelden's terminal sheepfold is superb, the huge mass of the Pikes looming above to one side, with, to the other, the long ridge of the Band leading up onto Bowfell, past Bowfell Buttress and continuing on to Hanging Knotts overlooking Rossett Ghyll. Streaks and ribbons of snow linger among the high, north-facing crags and gullies. A Magpie flies off from the foot of Gimmer Crag, the blue of the sky so luminous and radiant it renders the flickering spread of its white primaries almost transparent, their dark tips totally invisible at this distance. Gimmer itself, towering above the glacially curved slopes of scree, grass and bracken, looks magnificent, its great rock wall bathed in light with subtle ochre undertones shining through the lit greys. A Buzzard takes to the air from the Band on the opposite side of the valley, sails grandly across the high blue, its underparts glowing like illuminated honey, and alights on a crag end beneath Gimmer.

The three most numerous species up the valley on the north side of the beck as far as the delectable waterfall pool have been Meadow Pipits, Wheatears and Pied Wagtails in that order. The pipits are quite hard to see in the dead tans and umbers of sheep-cropped grass and among the endless jumble of rocks, borrans and scree-clitter which, together with the grass, constitute this side of Mickelden Beck below the Pikes. This everywhere clutter of stone and vegetation from which birds appear and disappear just as rapidly means that to make

220

any sort of viable assessment of numbers care is needed, but this actual 'corridor' of suitable habitat along the valley bottom is not very wide. A disturbed bird gets up and shows itself, flushes another, and so on, in a sort of slow-motion chain reaction, so that some accuracy of count is possible. Fortunately, most of the smart male Wheatears are very prominent, often perched high on substantial boulders, many of them singing – not much of a song – a short, rather scratchy warble – but a song for all that. Occasionally there's a short 'song' flight, a thing of thin, piping calls and typically chat pebble-rattlings. Watching their use of ground and the distance covered by males from one song perch to another, I wonder if Wheatears do not, perhaps, occupy territories larger than one might think for a relatively small bird. The females tend to flit about after the males in short, ground-hugging flights, but they are harder to see, being coloured more to blend with rough fell vegetation and rock.

By 11am I'm directly under Pike o' Stickle. It's noticeable that, as one advances up the valley towards the further montane habitat, both the numbers and the distribution of birds tend to decrease, but Wrens continue to sing from any small, isolated pocket of juniper, rowan or thorn among the crag ends. The narrow habitat 'corridor' for Wheatears and Meadow Pipits, which exists almost entirely on the north side of the beck, gradually becomes increasingly barren and less favourable as habitat, as indeed is the entire south side which is totally different terrain. Glacial moraines flow both down and across the fellside from the valley terminus of Rossett Ghyll, forming large expanses of dry, coarse grass-covered mounds which offer very little in the way of protective cover. These gradually give way to an equally unappealing habitat – a large expanse of very acid marshy land holding many small pools with narrow, interlinking waterways and which extend down the valley nearly as far as the uppermost enclosed pastures of Stool End Farm.

The way continues up the north side of the beck towards its upper reaches where the main beck is fed by those tumbling down Rossett Ghyll and Stake Pass, flowing through a series of deep green, transparent rocky pools fed by sparkling cascades and shallow rapids, the flood force of which has, over the centuries, cut through both the meagre surface soil and the bedrock scouring out a series of delightful little craggy 'gorges' nowhere more than about eight or nine feet. All the way up this upper stretch of the valley as far as the fine terminal sheepfold, the path runs with the beck, closely following its 'banks' – a euphemism for the wilderness of stones and boulders through which the mainstream winds, enlivened here and there by little pools, with sun-dappled stones like green jewels emerging from its transparent water – and into which, during very dry spells, it may disappear altogether, because in places there is no fall to give the water the gravity fed impulse it needs to flow downstream. Despite the lack of any great fall, the water is always hurrying and full of the voices of water among stones. A Buzzard circles high over Stake Pass, is joined by another as they counter-soar in tight circles, evidently very well bonded, with egg-laying now only possibly a week or so away. They call excitedly over Mart Crag Moor, allowing the wind to drift them over towards the great fissured crags of Bowfell and its huge wedge of a buttress looming over the ever-narrowing valley. The sheepfold marks the end of the valley and a most suitable spot for coffee, a sandwich and a bask in the glorious noonday sunshine, dreaming of long by-gone exploits on the high crags above and listening to the Wheatears among the stones by the footbridge over the beck.

1.00pm – My way back down the south side of the beck now lies first among the moraines and then via the extensive marshy area below the Band to Stool End Farm. For many years Ring Ouzels have held a territory among the vegetated crag ends and stunted junipers high on the steep northern slopes of the Band. These magnificent dark thrushes, their breasts emblazoned with a white crescent are, together with Wheatears, among the earliest spring migrants to return to their upland breeding habitats. The last forty years, however, have seen a marked decline in the Cumbrian Ouzel breeding population to such an extent that they are now Red-listed, but it is still very far from clear what factors are involved in this decline.

Certainly the disturbance caused by the immense increase in human traffic on the fells must be one factor. The Ring Ouzel is also much shyer than his bold cousin the Blackbird, and it had, at one time, been suggested that the latter's gradual intrusion up into the montane habitats preferred by the Ring Ouzel may also have had an effect. However, it is much more likely that environmental factors – the possible effects of climate change on its overall breeding biology, for example, or problems in respect of its wintering grounds or migration – need close investigation. Nevertheless, despite their sad decline there are still one or two lingering outposts among the fells surrounding the head of our valley. I am lucky to hear his triple flutey call at this hour of the day, but now, in the still air within the cup of the valley, his song carries well – a joyous reminder that life is returning to the fells as well as to the valleys.

1.30pm – The day has suddenly changed, as it can do among the mountains. Bowfell is capped by cloud, which, due to some very localised thermo-dynamic magic, is also pouring down the Buttress gully, and suddenly the voice of the Ring Ouzel is completely muffled. There's no sign of life, no birds, not even frogspawn, among all the little pools and channels in the acid Sphagnum bog on the south side of the beck. These wind their tortuous way towards the main beck which gradually widens into a broad, shallow, pebbly pool above a substantial weir constructed as part of the valley's flood control measures. Just below the weir the large boulder-piers are all that remains of a former bridge which once carried the way round from Stool End to the main Mickelden footpath. At

223

Stool End the valley opens out into broad pasture with sheep grazing. Here one of the other main feeder streams, Oxendale Beck, cascades down into the valley via a series of little stepped weirs and levels between superbly made cobble embankments – more flood-control measures – until it joins Mickelden Beck somewhere about Middlefell, and the whole thing becomes Great Langdale beck in all its glory!

2.45pm – Arrive back at Dungeon Ghyll car park. Neither Peregrine nor Kestrel showed today, but I know they're there, and in a very short time Willow Warblers will be joining the Wrens and Robins among the scrubby crag ends with perhaps the occasional Cuckoo; Sandpipers and Grey Wagtails among the river shillets and boulders; Swallows, House Martins and Swifts based round Middlefell Farm and the Old Dungeon Ghyll Hotel hawking high and low for insects among the valley airs; and perhaps one or two Redstarts around Stool End. But today, this very excellent day, I've made a tally of 26 bird species, including the fell-end farm habitats – 14 within the valley beyond the farms, including a total of 19 Wheatears – not bad for an apparently barren mountain valley at the beginning of its spring!

14 April

8.45am – A very cool westerly breeze blowing a hint of drizzle. The bridge Blackbird flies down to the gravel beach, walks slowly into the water and steps out very sharply! It really doesn't look all that inviting, but he paddles in once more for his morning bath, splashing water up and over his back with vigorous, rapid wing-flicks. He bows, ducks and flicks, repeating this sequence several times until he steps up onto a mossy boulder, shakes himself and prepares to preen – first by wiping his bill clean on the moss and then by vigorous indirect scratching to right and left. He preens systematically attending to the same feather groups to left and right applying symmetry to his actions, then, when ready, flies up into his ash tree to sing – until suddenly in the middle of his full song he changes to something altogether more subdued with long, irregular gaps between each utterance. This suggests that even at this stage in the season he has two song modes – the proclamatory territorial song and a much quieter version, not exactly a sub-song, and sung to a quite different rhythm of phrase and pause – uttered as if singing for himself alone.

The meadow is full of new-born lambs, content just to lie there, sleeping or basking, safely in the lee of their dams' large woolly bodies. What a difference it makes to have so much life in the meadow, and all the usual river bank songs are augmented by the extrovert babble of a Starling on the wicket-gate wall. The rocky voices of Ravens up between Loughrigg and Hammerscar provide an almost continuous dark, sonorous background tone against which the songs and calls of smaller, closer birds seem to spark more lively. There's very little growing, but at last the first celandine is breaking bud on the path side by the Tanglewood where the Blackbird sings. The middle tarn is still alive with a host of hirundines – they don't venture far from water as they refuel on the first insect hatches.

2.00pm – A fine afternoon with plenty of blue sky and huge cumulus blown out of the south-west. I've been watching a Nuthatch on a slab of rock, vertical for about six feet and then set at a mossy incline of well over 45 degree out of which grows an old gnarled oak. Rock-climbing is not an activity one associates with Nuthatches! Over by the leat wall the local male Grey Wagtail is hunting insects, catching them in dashing mid-flight forays – at a distance of about 30 yards he's almost im-possible to see for all his bright colour, the yellows blending with the grasses, the greys with the slate stonework. Only his movement and the constant waving of his banner betray his presence. He's taken an acute interest in the stone wall where there's a particularly fascinating recessed hole, a classic Grey Wagtail site, but so far there's been no sign of the female who must approve, build the nest and incubate the eggs.

The glow of Lesser Celandines makes a golden aura over the sunlit river bank. This lovely spring flower has a very ancient connection with our migrant spring birds and the origins of its bright chiming name reach far back to the old Greek 'khelidonion' from 'khelidon', a Swallow. In Pliny the Elder's monumental and influential *Historia Naturalis* it is stated that Swallows used this plant as an aid to developing their nestlings' sight by a process of sympathetic transference – the celandine opens when the Swallow arrives, closes when it departs in autumn. We may, therefore, look at our celandines as we look at many other common plants which give so much pleasure over the year, across centuries of fascinating lore, some of which still lingers on in modern herbalism.

2.50pm – The air sustains a barely audible, softly droned undertone from the many bumble bees humming their way through a more dense general insect 'soup'. It's taken a long time to cover the few hundred yards as far as the footbridge at Chapel Stile – I never bother too much about destinations – the next step is destination enough and who knows what that may bring within the attention of one sense or another! At the big bend above the footbridge the backlit river appears as a molten stage of dancing glitter, whilst in the clear pools the shape and colour of every pebble and slate-chip is clearly visible. Lingmoor rears dark-shadowed behind, and beyond the scud of cumulus and blue sky. A Buzzard comes up from the bottom of Baysbrown, circles over the river bank gaining height. Each time he turns head to wind he pauses fractionally, allowing himself to be drifted gently down-wind. He comes into the wind slowly, very controlled, his outer primaries splayed wider than those on his inner turn, thus allowing an equal laminar flow of air over both aerofoil surfaces because the outer wing must, of course, travel faster than the inner, more pivotal wing.

Off the path and into the wood where hazels and larches are flushing. It looks like a wood of sleeping giants the way the huge, rounded backs of great, long-dormant mossy boulders have pulled a soft green moss blanket over their heads and shoulders until some apocalyptic day of awakening. In the angle of a great log a Peacock butterfly, perfectly sheltered from any breeze, basks full in the sun. The spot it's chosen is considerably warmer than the ambient temperature – does the butterfly find it by accident, or does some sensory awareness draw it there? Very little moves in the drowsing wood and, although it's so quiet, it's a totally different silence from that of midwinter – one doesn't feel that profundity of withdrawal – the sleepers are stirring. A nearby ancient alder attracts a Goldcrest, bustling about its branches stabbing at the moss and catkins, now dry and dead, falling apart almost to dry dust when picked. A close examination of these mossy branches reveals myriads of tiny midge-like insects, shining like dust-motes in the air above the disturbed moss. A Jay flies through the wood with a flash of white rump as he ground-hugs his way among the trees without making alarm. Baysbrown Tarn sleeps and rather than disturb its few drowsing waterfowl I'm drawn back up onto those fine little rounded sheep pastures above the tarn which command such a magnificent view, the valley smiling in sunshine, shadows sliding across the Pikes with an almost sensual, caressing intimacy of contact.

The second Buzzard of the afternoon rises out of the tarn copse, calling, circling over Baysbrown Farm. It's joined by another, and they begin a sequence of counter-soar and separation like some ancient courtly ritual dance. They glide off across the wind and are lost behind the riverside trees. There's suddenly a confusion of Buzzards as three more appear arriving as if peeled off the sky, flaking out of the light itself and there's a great deal of excited, even urgent calling. Two more appear above the Farm, one soaring faster and higher than the other. Aerodynamic theory argues that because of their lesser wing-loading the uppermost of a soaring pair is possibly the male. They're all very high against a deep blue sky, appearing and disappearing as they catch the light. It's been a rather hectic few minutes with at least six Buzzards active in the area at one time or another, but there's not a Buzzard in sight anywhere now.

3.50pm – Down by the river there's another Peacock butterfly basking in the warmth of a bed of dry bracken. Birch tops still look mainly purple against the blue but just beginning to show the very first little pricks of green in the first really spring-like afternoon we've had.

17 April

Cool and overcast after a wet night. It's good to see the Swallows sweeping over the meadows again, hawking low, catching and losing the sun shining on the tempered steel of their blue-black plumage. The two pairs of Swallows which nest annually in the village centre are perched on their respective telephone wires, looking very composed and settled. One of the males – with the longer tail streamers – sings his prolonged musical twitter to all points of the compass. Male Swallows show some variation in the length of their tail streamers, and it may be that this is yet another of those subtle signals to the female indicating fitness for purpose in the male – nothing is casual or accidental in nature. The meadows are white-peppered all the way down with sheep and shining white lambs; even more this morning as they are brought off the hill and down to these fields for a good green bite.

A female Grey Wagtail pauses briefly on the shillets by the bridge, superbly camouflaged among the washed-out greens and pale tans of last year's wood-rush and the mottled greys of the boulders and shillets. Wrens sing all the way down the river, and in the Tanglewood song increases in direct proportion to the amount of dense cover available. Dog's Mercury is in flower. The leaves of this mostly unnoticed plant are poisonous. The ancients expressed their disdain for it – as compared to the annual mercury used for medicinal and culinary purposes by applying the prefix 'dog's' for anything generally worthless and/or unclean. Nevertheless, you may be sure that where Dog's Mercury grows, so will ash, for which it is a prime indicator.

There, at last, is the song of a Willow Warbler – a rather whispy but very carrying song, with a downward-drifting cadence. Now I know it's here, the other warblers, flycatchers and the Redstarts will not be far behind. Of them all this is probably the most numerous and widespread, despite its name which implies – erroneously – a specific dependence on willows. 'Warbler' it is by taxonomy only, belonging to the genus *Phylloscopus* (from the Greek for 'leaf searching') – the leaf warblers, of which group we see the Chiffchaff, Willow and Wood Warblers. Once the warblers start arriving, it's time to brush up on your songs and calls, for they're either up in the canopy – the males, usually – or tucked away within dense vegetation, remaining mostly unseen. The Willow Warbler's song is one of the most important of all. Foraging among the trees, it sings continually and with a penetrative quality which makes it impossible to miss or ignore, heard as the default background, in aural perspective, to all other song. It is exactly this persistence of song that is assessed by the discriminating females when choosing a mate. The song itself is not so easy to define – a rather 'wistful' sequence of falling notes which to-gether make a single phrase that is then endlessly repeated. Grey likened it to a "cadence soft as summer rain". After recovering from his post-breeding midsummer moult silence, the Willow Warbler along with the Chiffchaff, will sing again, briefly, and one day they'll slip away on their first leg back to Africa, probably without notice, for one tends to notice and celebrate arrivals more than departures unless we make a definite point of noting what is singing and where every day.

229

At the south end of the bottom tarn are two Great Crested Grebes. I hope they might make some attempt to breed this year – the lake is suitable, a large area of clear open water with plenty of reed cover and no shortage of fish and they have bred here before. They are engaged in that part of display in which a sequence of looking off from each other is followed by side-touching and preening.

In Rob Rash the carpet of succulent Bluebell leaves and Ramsons is studded with tight Wood Anemone buds which will open as soon as the sun touches the wood. Once out into the open after the shelter of the wood the wind strikes cold. As yet there's no Sedge Warbler in the reeds below Rumple Crag, but there is a Reed Bunting. This little bird spends its vocal life climbing steps and tripping up the last one or two – a very unassuming song that has always given me much pleasure. He's singing from a willow bush on the far side of the river, catching the morning sunshine, his white moustache and collar shining against his black head and bib.

19 April

8.15am – A mild, damp mist after heavy rain over night. Everything that should be is singing. It's essential to register what is singing every day because only then can one become conscious not only of what might be an addition to the current state of song but also of what is not singing.

The year's first Redstart sings from Kitty Hall copse. It's not much of a song and rather variable, structured within a framework of separate linked phrases and is an important feature of the sound-scape of our Cumbrian oak woods. He is heard far more than seen, which is a pity, for of all our summer visitors the Redstart exhibits the most sexual dimorphism, the male being an arrestingly beautiful bird. In good light the blending of his white forehead with the grey head can invest him with an almost silvery appearance, his black masked head and throat making a vivid contrast with the

230

soft grey back and russet orange breast. But this is 'phaneric' colouration, a display plumage only, designed to be seen, and after breeding he reverts to a more cryptic plumage. Both sexes are distinguished by their bright orange-russet tails which they flick constantly and from which it takes its name, 'steort' being the Old English for tail, which the male fans constantly during his courtship display. Some of his old local names reflect this – 'Jenny Redtail', 'Redrump' from Yorkshire, and the one I like best, 'Fireflirt'. Between Kitty Hall knoll and the gateway I've heard four male Redstarts, each from his own quite separate group of oaks.

A Pied Wagtail trots along his wall-top at the bottom of the long meadow. His walk is rather exaggerated with a kind of ritualised head-turning and wing-flicking. He bows, straightens up showing his throat patch, still wing-flicking, repeating this sequence several times. Next he fluffs out his flank contour feathers, curling them round and over the alula and primary coverts, making himself as broad and impressive as possible. The object of all this attention – another male – emerges from behind wall-top stone. The displaying male advances towards the 'intruder' who responds first by lying down (!), then by walking away looking very submissive and finally by flying off the wall down into the meadow where he walks daintily and unconcernedly away through the dewy grass – an extraordinary encounter. I suspect the displaying male could well have a nest within the wall – a traditional site over very many years.

In the Tanglewood both Willow Warbler and Chiffchaff sing. It's fine to hear these two, with the Redstart now, taking their place in the morning song. Listening to the Willow Warblers is like listening to an unending cadence, each song picking up off the other so that there's a continual chain reaction of this delightful song rippling through the perspective of the landscape.

20 April

6.30am – Mild but overcast. Official sunrise was at 6am and dawn, of course, some time before that, so at the moment the birds are in feeding rather than singing mode. Many of the ground-feeding birds are back up in the trees, clearly having fed, for many are cleaning their bills and busily preening. A male Blackbird stands in frozen immobility on Kitty Hall driveway as if by sheer immobility he renders himself in-visible to some threat he thinks he's seen. Most predators are acutely eye-orientated – movement-awareness their speciality. Eventually he relaxes and once convinced that the perceived threat no longer exists he continues foraging – he's probably got a mate on eggs somewhere nearby and can't be too careful. Sometimes, as now, one hears a quite exceptional Mistle Thrush perched high in an oak in the Hall Woods. He repeats his favourite phrase frequently – 'girl-eee…girl-eee…girl-eee!' which, given that it is the nuptial season, seems particularly appropriate! A male Blackbird hotly pursued by a female Sparrowhawk swerves by with a great rush of wings, pale flash and dark shape, pursuer and pursued so locked into their different motivations that I am merely a shape to be avoided as they weave past, skim the wall and bolt into the wood, both birds silent save for the heard pressure of thrumming wind in wings stretched to maximum effort. I wish him luck, though it's really much more matter of speed and stamina than luck!

7.05am – It's a perfect morning for listening to birds, the grey, windless overcast providing a totally blank background which conducts individual sounds as if brightly etched on its surface, and up at the watershed track top gate I can still hear 'girl-eee…girl-eee…girl-eee!' This gateway and its large oak have been the territorial centre for generations of Redstarts, the current male incumbent singing high among the branches, with a flash of silvery white as he drops down through them. Hearing him and registering his return is one objective satisfied by coming up here this morning.

7.20am – It's just starting to rain, but return is impossible until either the presence or absence of Tree Pipits is determined. A Willow Warbler sings in the scrubby thorns high on the fellside – the first of the many which annually colonise it up to about 1,000 feet among the straggles of stunted hollies, birches, rowans and crag-end oaks.

7.30am – A lengthy stop at the watershed summit is always mandatory, and this morning there is indeed a Tree Pipit up on Howe Banks. Whereas the Meadow Pipit inhabits open moorland, rough grassland and Commons, our local Tree Pipits prefer rough upland grassland with the addition of a few scattered trees or the edge of a wood, both essential as song-posts. All our pipits are 'small brown jobs', subtle plumage differences not easily picked up in the field, so the surest guide to recognition is song. The Tree Pipit's song-display flight is particularly fine, an opinion endorsed by Grey who described it as a "very distinguished performance", but it is complex and difficult to describe. The birds whose glorious song-flights I watch up here are particularly attached to a very old thorn by the track-side and a large oak. The bird I'm watching is singing on top of the thorn – a kind of 'prelude' preceding take-off into his steeply climbing song-flight, a complex series of short phrases repeated until he reaches his flight apex when the volume is raised to a performance of calls, chirps and trills as he, more often than not, spirals down in 'parachute 'mode – wings and tail spread, the body held at a slight angle to the horizontal and floating rather than flying. His song ends with a penetrating 'zeea, zeea-zeea' or a more musical, rather wistful cadence, 'pioo…pioo…pioo'. This spiral descent glide is diagnostic of the Tree Pipit, whereas that of the Meadow Pipit is much more direct.

7.45am – It's now raining very hard and time to return to base – but I have achieved the three basic objectives of this morning's walk – to establish the arrival of Tree Pipits and Redstarts at their long-established territories and to determine whether Willow Warblers were spreading up the hill as well as along the valley.

23 April

7.00am – A cloudless sunlit sky. The Grey Wagtails are busy on the mossy river boulders below the leat wall, fluttering up in brief insect forays, almost tremulous in the brightly lit air. Further downstream in his old ash a Blackbird sings in full sky-pointing mode. Except for his bill he's motionless, almost as if in a trance of song, extraordinary and beautiful. I find it a source of continual amazement that such birds are not surrounded by people listening! A Starling perches close beside him, and the contrast between them reveals so much – the one a solid matt black save for the light-reflecting gloss of his primaries, the other shiny with oily iridescences which, as he turns in the sunlight, slide across him in gorgeous sheens of green, purple and black; the one so 'sheer' and aristocratically elegant, the other rather 'punk' and sparky about the head and bill, both yellow-billed, the one with the melodic wistfulness of a Schubert, perhaps, the other a street busker, and each equally enjoyable.

The willow flowers fuzzing the tops of the carr bordering the lake are very bright against the shadowed wood this morning, as if they've had tiny touches of very bright lemony green flecked on with pastel and left as small individual marks.

Other than the second-year Swan there's not a bird to be seen on the water. At the mouth of the little stream running into the lake half way down the north shore reedbeds it is very beautiful – surrounded by song, with Wetherlam clean and warm-looking in the sun and Lingmoor refreshed with new morning light. The lake, however, for all its privacy, reedbeds, riparian diversity, once so full of birds – winter and summer, is more often depressingly devoid of birds these days. Landscape beauty alone may be enough for some people, but this landscape is a complex interrelationship of sensitive living

234

habitats which assume less meaning as they become depleted of life. To some extent, therefore, this journal is both a lamentation for what was, for what we have destroyed in one way or another, as well as a celebration of what we still have whilst we have it.

Suddenly, however, a Sedge Warbler sings, rescuing me from a droop into despondency over the fate of this depleted bit of precious landscape. Where the river flows out into bright sunshine the reeds are brilliant with both light and the sound of his irrepressible song – a combination of chatter, warble, trill and pipe, each of these components capable of enormous variety – notes musical and harsh-jangled, grating, totally unpredictable in its contrast of animated and slow, restrained and excitable, full volume – all this and mimicry too! – its loudness and dominance designed to attract a mate. He remains well-hidden, very well camouflaged by his streaky plumage, moving about inside the reedbed without venturing onto the sunlit seed heads, his song flowing on and on.

> "…And sedge warblers, clinging so light
> To willow twigs, sang longer than the lark,
> Quick, shrill, or grating, a song to match the heat
> Of the strong sun, nor less the water's cool,
> Gushing through narrows, swirling in the pool.
> Their song that lacks all words, all melody,
> All sweetness almost, was dearer then to me
> Than sweetest voice that sings in tune sweet words.
> This was the best of May – the small brown birds
> Wisely re-iterating endlessly
> What no man learnt yet, in or out of school."
> (From the poem *Sedge Warblers*)

This detailed description of the Sedge Warbler's song by Edward Thomas is as penetratingly accurate to our aural sensibilities as is the work of John Clare to our visual imaginations.

The ash by the lake is just coming into male flower, at the moment tight little aubergine-coloured buttons which grow laterally and terminally from last year's shoots. Ash is interesting because on some trees at one time or another there may be purely male or purely female flowers or even hermaphrodite flowers embodying both male and female. Like many tree flowers, they tend to be overlooked, but as these ash flowers gradually unfold they repay close attention.

8.25am – A Nuthatch calls as it forages about the trees. I'm always taken aback by the shattering volume produced by so small a bird as the Wren, until I hear a Nuthatch at full strength. He's a very vocal little bird, and among his various calls the long, shrill, unmusical trill is, perhaps, what lingers in the memory – intentionally, for this is his territorial announcement. Except for the Nuthatch, a few Willow Warblers and the Tanglewood Blackbird, most of the woodland birds here are now engaged in silent, post dawn-song activities – feeding themselves, their mates and young, feather care. In the field oaks near the footpath, however, Redstarts still sing and they will continue to do so until they attract one of the rather later arriving females. A Great Spotted Woodpecker has just flown up into a nearby tree where it immediately scuttles round to the opposite under the illusion of remaining unseen. But this is a large, wide oak offering good opportunities to watch him at work, climbing in a series of short, sharp jerks, investigating the bark cracks as he goes – a very charismatic bird, exuding an air of ferocious concentration in all he does. The wind has backed right round to the north, and a very cold north it is!

1.30pm – Destination, Loughrigg Tarn – still a bitter wind but warm in the sun. The Common is very quiet – its jungles of rank brackens flattened down to a layer of litter and forests of sharp, jagged stems. In High Close Wood a Blackcap sings from a dense thicket of rhododendrons. The Blackcap and the Garden Warbler enrich the woodland canopy and shrub layer with perhaps the most richly musical songs of all our visiting

236

warblers (discounting the Wood Warbler for the moment), and because of their shared habitat, the similarity of their songs and the fact that for most of their stay they will sing unseen, they really deserve to be considered together. They belong to the group of *Sylvia* warblers in which the males tend to be rather brighter than the females, but marked sexual dimorphism – among our warblers – is restricted to the Blackcap, the name descriptive of the male only. Now, before full leaf-flush, is the only time available to identify visually which bird – Blackcap or Garden Warbler – is singing which song. Both enrich their habitats with wonderful melodic outpourings. The Blackcap's delivery, however, is richer and fuller, perhaps even a little slower, developing slight pauses in its phrasing, but as if to compensate for this rich variety the Garden Warbler's bursts are more sustained.

The first violets unobtrusively enjoy the dappled shade of a small holly bush. This modest, often unnoticed little flower is truly one of the gems of the earth. With a very human yet visionary eye on his botany Wordsworth compares Lucy – who "dwelt among the untrodden ways/ Beside the springs of Dove" – to that most simple and modest of beauties – "a violet by a mossy stone/ Half hidden from the eye". These are dog violets. The taxonomists have created for us a confusion of violet species which didn't exist when Zeus named it 'Ion' (the Greek name for violets) after the poor mortal Io whom he so disastrously loved – they were just violets – there was no 'dog violet'. Later, mediaeval herbalists applied the title 'dog' to this particular violet in a mood of somewhat peevish distaste, for unlike *Viola odorata*, the sweet violet, it has no scent, thus justifying the derogatory term 'dog'.

Down at Skelwith Bridge there's a Garden Warbler. It may be fair to say that this little bird is noteworthy for its total lack of any distinguishing marks, being without speckles, streaks, spots, eyestripes or wing bars, yet here is this undistinguished little bird pouring out his seemingly endless song among the leaves and he's no longer unremarkable. The song is generally regarded as being somewhat inferior to that of the Blackcap, being less rhythmically phrased and lacking that depth of rich musicality which is at the core of the Blackcap's song. However, it is more sustained and with fewer pauses – a characteristic which sometimes earns it the entirely undeserved epithet, the 'garbled warbler'. There's also a Willow Warbler feeding at the end of a branch, an excellent view of a bird mostly hidden by foliage. The sun illuminates the merest hint of dorsal green and a promise of palest primrose-yellow suffuses his face, supercilium and upper breast. When his breeding cycle is completed he'll stop singing and retire for the moult from which he will emerge in a spanking new plumage, as if his former plumage had been washed over with a transparent glaze of lemon-yellows – an almost totally different-looking bird.

In the meadow up-river from the Force the blackthorns are opening – their as yet dark, leafless bushes studded with galaxies of delicate, almost white flowers, their long, yellow-tipped stamens giving their massed blooms a lacy, almost fragile appearance. Compared with the hawthorn, the blackthorn's is a very cold white, but we won't be seeing the hawthorn's flowers until after leaf flush, usually in May, giving rise to that ancient country saying, "Ne'er cast a clout till the May is out."

25 April

1.30pm – After a wet morning, an afternoon stroll up the valley in bright sunshine. This period from noon onwards is the beginning of 'lull-time' and, as spring advances into summer, will develop into an almost oppressive, silent, midday somnolence.

Just below Baysbrown there's a snatch of Pied Flycatcher song from the sparse oak wood by the New Bridge – a regular Pied Flycatcher site for as long as I can remember. This fascinating bird, like the Redstart, is a bird of oak-dominated deciduous woodland in mainly upland areas and in our Cumbrian valleys where you find one, you'll probably find the other. Macpherson (1892) gives a first record in 1793 on the river Kent, and its subsequent spread and breeding performance has very much depended on the availability of the right food at the right time and the availability of the right kind of tree holes. The tremendous increase – 39% since the 1968-1972 Census (new *Atlas*) – is due in no small measure to the provision of nest boxes which they accept very readily, even in gardens. Like the Redstart, the Pied Flycatcher is strongly dimorphic, only the breeding male being strongly marked black and white. After the post-breeding moult he much more resembles the less striking female. Despite his bold, pied breeding plumage however, he's more often heard than seen, particularly early in the season when the males first arrive to select a nest site a week or so in advance of the females. This is when his song is at its very best for once he has attracted a mate his song declines because, although he defends his nest site, he does not defend a territory. He has a very appealing, sweet-sounding but small song – simple variations on a syncopated trochaic rhythm, and for which, my mnemonic is approximately, 'Pretty boy – who's a pretty pretty boy!' – appropriate to singing for a mate! It's a very pleasant little song, with a certain bright jauntiness which never fails to clear the air around him and one of my annual regrets is that we hear so little of him, particularly once he gets settled with a mate and nest. As his name suggests, he specialises in catching his food on the wing and cuts a striking figure as he flickers up from his perch in a flurry of black and white. Like Redstarts, Pied Flycatchers also take large numbers of oak-defoliating caterpillars, such as the Oak-leaf Roller Moth which, like both these birds, plays such an important part in the overall ecology of the sessile oak woods of western Britain. When there is an excess of females male polygamy is regularly practised. Once

239

he has a mate tied down to incubating eggs, the male may go off visiting one or more other females, temporarily deserting his first-chosen until the subsequent females have also laid. He then returns to his first mate and helps to rear her brood only. Any secondary broods, therefore, cannot be so successful without a male to assist in the feeding and rearing.

Oak Howe Bridge is a good place to stop and contemplate the Pikes, for they can differ from one day to another according to circumstances. Some days the combination of lighting and atmosphere endows them with a truly awesome monumentality, a towering, looming presence felt all down the valley. Today, however, under the sun's benign smile and bland sky the rough edges appear smoothed, the fall of crags blurred into a pervading tonality through which Mill Gill, a white mare's tail of a cascade, tumbles lace-like down the rocks from Stickle Tarn. The curve of the river forms the ideal 'picturesque' compositional lead to the Pikes, situated perfectly in the 'V' between the spur of Lingmoor which comes down to Side House and the spur of White Ghyll on the other side of the valley. I find such a theoretically perfect composition disturbing. Such symmetry, even within a 'naturally' formed conjunction of components, somehow frees it of the necessary elements of chaos inherent – even if only implied – in mountain landscape. It erodes the sublime, smacks almost of organisation with an eye to please, and the huge pleasure people find in such a landscape and its tourist representations perhaps says more about the human condition and its needs than the landscape itself.

28 April

1.30am – Up Hullet's Nest. Blue sky, warm westerly breeze – time to listen for Wood Warblers. Through the lower levels of Sawrey's Wood the hazels are now beginning to form delicious misty fume like a drift of tender green smoke from within which Willow Warblers, Wrens and Redstarts sing. The sun is bright and warm, and it's very pleasant just to walk a few yards, stop awhile to look and listen, walk another few yards and so on. It makes for gloriously slow progress and one of the reasons why I prefer my own company! The primroses along the amphitheatre rim this afternoon look particularly fine, folded back and laid right out to the sun. Reaffirming the perfection of this afternoon for leaning on a gate and doing absolutely nothing but listening to birds, a Blackbird sings in the bottom of Fletcher, his voice resonating around the superbly dished amphitheatre of the field as with complete assurance and confidence he pours all his future into his song.

Between Andrew's Field and the gate is a long-standing Wood Warbler territory – the males could well have arrived by now, and this is the real object of my expedition this afternoon. The Wood Warbler is the only one of our breeding birds to have two quite distinct songs, either of which would stop even Keats, spellbound, in his tracks! It is the largest of our three *Phylloscopus* warblers, sturdier in build and brighter in colour, but is, however, by far the least common of the three leaf warblers, favouring the kind of closed-canopy, mature oakwoods without much undergrowth found mainly along the length of western Britain. Its taxonomic history takes us right back to the seventeenth century origins of British ornithology. To Gilbert White goes the honour of being the first to clearly differentiate our three leaf warblers, initially by song. He called them

a) The Smallest Willow Wren (Chiffchaff)

b) The Middle Willow Wren, with its "joyous, easy, laughing note" (Willow warbler)

c) The Largest Willow Wren with its "sibilous shivering noise in the tops of tall woods" (Wood Warbler) – hence its proper name *P. sibilatrix.*

In his letter XIX of August 17th 1768, in which he discusses these differences, White refers to the founding father of British natural history when, talking of these three warblers and of the Wood Warbler in particular, he concludes by saying:

"This last haunts only the tops of trees in high beechen woods, and makes a sibilous grasshopper-like noise, now and then, at short intervals, shivering a little with its wings when it sings; and is, I make no doubt now, the *regulus non cristatus* of Ray, which he says "*cantat voce stridulâ locustae.*"

Yet this great ornithologist never suspected that there were three species.

The 'great ornithologist' so revered by White was the Cambridge cleric John Ray (1627-1705), a somewhat controversial natural philosopher and all-round naturalist who published seminal works on both the plant and animal kingdoms and is now credited as the 'father' of English natural history. Via its song/s, therefore, this one remarkable little bird takes us back to the founding heart of British ornithology. But what of this song? The Wood Warbler is so committed to its song that it seems almost careless of being watched.

Sitting on the wall here where I have so often sat and listened, I can hear Nuthatch, Chaffinches, Great Tits and one or two Tree Pipits. As the sky opens up and the sun begins to penetrate the wood, a Pied Flycatcher sings – so far I've passed three singing males. All these sounds are registered when suddenly – for I'd almost given up hope – comes a rather melancholy piping note, very pure but with implied minor harmonies, 'Pew... pew... pew... pew'. There's something so plaintive about these repeated, downward-curved notes that I defy anyone hearing them to pass them by unheeding, unmoved even. Inevitably the second song is not far behind, the bird as yet unseen, a sibilant tremolo starting fairly slowly, accelerating to a quicksilver, shivering trill. Both songs are quite random in their mutual association, sometimes sung separately, sometimes alternately. My ears have never registered this as a grasshopper-like stridulation, a rubbing sound – it is all syrinx, all voice. Here he comes now, a Wood Warbler, this beautiful leaf explorer, dropping down from the canopy, almost in 'parachuting' mode, to perch on a branch half way up an old oak. He bursts into his long shimmering trill once more. As he sings he lifts his head, his wings droop slightly, and so physically powerful is the utterance of this shivering trill that he vibrates visibly all the way from throat to wing tips. W.H. Hudson referred to it as "long and passionate, the woodland sound which is like no other", and Grey in *The Charm of Birds* wrote:

> "The song that is most frequent is the shivering or sibilant sound …When this has been watched and remembered the song will always suggest a little ecstasy whether the bird is seen or not."

Of all our migrant warblers the Wood Warbler, however, is the most habitat dependent and therefore least widespread; my own experience has indicated a sad local decline over the past few years.

3.30pm – It's taken just over two hours to climb to the top of the watershed, a walk normally achieved by sturdy, destination-conscious walkers in a quarter of that time! There's a mild westerly breeze and it's pleasantly warm in the sunshine – time for a prolonged sit! A Peacock butterfly has just flown past, over the top of the watershed, flying – in so far as a butterfly can in a westerly wind in an exposed place – with considerable directional determination, vigorously, as if governed by some destination awareness somewhere within his mysterious being. Behind the abrasion of wind on skin, behind the birds' singing, holding the seeds of future generations in their songs, behind the drift of clouds – behind all these things there is a stillness palpable to the 'affections' – generations of silence felt all along the hidden landscape of which the visible is merely a temporary surface skin.

A Buzzard has just appeared above Fletcher; it finds airspace very rapidly and is followed by another at which the presumed male stoops in a tremendous, almost vertical dive before they counter-soar together, calling excitedly. They're joined by a third appearing, as they so often do, from nowhere, slipping through some unseen space in the sky, but by now they're so high they're probably all well above the vertical territorial limit in free and open, communal airspace where there's no need for aggression. The higher they spiral they play lost and found as they change position relative to the light and the sky, eventually streaming off at great speed over the top of Fletcher. One re-appears briefly, tumbles over and over in the high air and simply disappears as if fallen through one of those strange spaces in the sky whence he came, where sky and light and sun and bird become a blazing unity.

4.15pm – I've been lying on this daisy-studded, sunny bank for over half an hour and reluctantly decide to move on, across and up the flanks of Howe Banks, aiming for the jumble of cliff, old quarry and fallen rock separating the top of Baysbrown Wood from the eastern end of the Lingmoor ridge. A Tree Pipit parachutes down into the old thorn with a wistful shivering trill. It's astonishing how fast the parachuting phase actually is – the mind tends to replay it in slow motion and because it is so savoured it is made to last longer! The remembered pleasure deceives!

The far side of the col gives a prospect down over the green marshes and great broad meadows of Great Langdale, with the Pikes blue beyond. The vegetation here is dominated by stunted junipers which twist closely round and over all the rocky outcrops. They are hard-grown, gnarly with that kind of demented twist and distortion as if they'd escaped from a Van Gogh painting. A very steep slope leads down into the top of Baysbrown Wood which is now an extensive tangle of fallen rock and old, lichened, windblown trunks overgrown by brackens. Robins flit secretively over the brackens to little, secret caves within the depths of its dark litter. Small bits of bracken litter flake off, metamorphosing into sun-basked Small Tortoiseshell butterflies fluttering away to another warm resting place. I take the old drover's road back through my Wood Warbler territory to the track by Andrew's Field. From the distant recesses of Sawrey's Wood float two Tawny Owl hoots, rounding out the hidden silences beyond. A Pied Flycatcher sings from a tree half way down the field, sitting upright in typical flycatcher posture. He tilts up his head when singing, but between phrases he looks around with sharp head movements. His white breast shines and the small white spots on his forehead gleam against the dark crown like little twin headlamps. He sits mostly with his wings drooped below the level of his tail. Another sings close by in Sawrey's Wood and every now and then, in a rather charming gesture, he tilts his head to one side as if listening closely to the message coded within the song after which he straightens up and sends his reply. He flies off and is lost behind the trunk of a large oak, very old and in places dead enough, perhaps, to contain the nest hole he's been seeking.

May

1 May

1.30pm – A beautiful afternoon, but the wind retains a cool, northerly edge. The Cuckoo has been calling from the Common and Low Wood area ever since the sun warmed things up earlier this morning, so that's my target for this afternoon. A pause for listening – lambs bleating in the meadows, pipit trills, Willow Warblers, Chaffinches and Wrens. Peacock butterflies are everywhere. Two Ravens 'kronk' urgently over the valley, maintaining a powerful directional flight towards a Buzzard spiralling high between the river and the Common. One of the most remarkable things about raptors is the way other birds are drawn to them like filings to magnets, from all corners of earth and air – but he's sublimely indifferent to them. They turn and head back across the valley in perfect synchronised flight, croaking continuously, reinforcing the pair-bond in the face of a recognised predator – until one launches into a steeply undulating flight-mode and I lose them all, Ravens and Buzzard in the dazzling sun-glow where they fly. Several minutes pass; a third Raven flies over and all emerge from the dazzle in a different arc of the sky as three more join them, all flying together with much mock diving, turning, twisting, half-spins and upside-down flips until they return to the ridge-top cliffs. They are obviously a family, the parents demonstrating the age-old instinctive protective reflex at the proximity of a recognised predator, reinforcing their pair-bond and finally releasing superfluous adrenalin in a boisterous family 'celebration'.

The approach to High Close wood is very pleasant with its little stream meandering through carpets of celandines and anemones under a light birch dapple, particularly after the Common where everything is so openly declared. Here the sense is of melting through a subtle interface to a changed, quite other reality – walking slowly through secrets and touching the immensity of non-human life. Something about bird calls reaching inwards from unseen corners of the wood emphasises its aura of veiled reservation. You hear the continuum of bird calls, are aware of their ceaseless activity, but even their heard, unseen presence tells of ever more remote, darker secrets – the powerful magic at the depths of a wood. The canopy is high here; the birches are green, their leaves just flushing. The ash flowers are fully open up in the crowns – little sprays of purple and green, like reef creatures reaching for light; a green haze begins to spread right through the wood. The woodland floor is very clearly zoned, Bluebells giving way to a densely leaved area of Ramsons without any of the flowing of one into the other, beloved of gardeners. Further on the great beeches are flushing, the first leaves fragile and tender, transparent, silvery with down and exquisitely fringed with tiny delicate hairs. Beneath the beeches the ground layer is entirely of dead leaves.

A Cuckoo calls from way up in High Close wood. Macpherson (1892) talks of its "abundance …upon the moors of the Lake district" and comments further:

"Far up the mountain-side, where bird-life becomes scarce and little varied, you may generally hear the Cuckoo practising its song as it wanders in search of the caterpillars upon which it chiefly subsists."

247

Research has shown that changes in global weather patterns may already have begun to impose themselves on the abundance of their preferred food. There was a time when on a day like this you'd hear a succession of Cuckoos all along the open fellsides from here to Dungeon Ghyll, calling from scattered crags and thorns, hollies and rowans. The Cuckoo has become part of our mythology and has a long and honourable part to play in the history of our poetry and music – it would surely be tragic if this bird became lost to our springtime countryside.

The 'Cuckoo problem' has been a potent part of European folk-culture for centuries, attracting speculation among scientifically inclined ancients as far back even as Aristotle. The main puzzle had always been exactly how the egg was inserted into the nest of its chosen prey. The celebrated scientist, Edward Jenner (1740-1823) – of small-pox vaccination fame – was the first to undertake proper scientifically regulated, extensive field and laboratory studies in order to shed a fully explanatory light on this long-standing 'problem'. His results were published in the *Philosophical Transactions of the Royal Society* in 1788, earning him his Fellowship, but it was not until the twentieth century that Jenner's findings were confirmed, firstly by Edgar Chance, an ornithologist working with Reed Warblers between 1918 and 1921, and subsequent filmings by the well-known naturalist Oliver Pike, that the Cuckoo's full ways and means were finally revealed to a very much wider public.

The Cuckoo's ability to mimic its host's egg and the fact that she can only lay eggs of one type imposes on her a life-long dedication to one specific host, which here is predominantly Meadow Pipit, Dunnock or Robin. Once the host has been chosen – after much careful field-work – she must work quickly to extract the host egg and lay her own before being discovered. In this way she may lay as many as ten eggs in ten nests in one season. My 'quarry' today, how-ever, is a male Cuckoo.

As he moves up and down the margin of the wood calling from strategic positions from which to overlook both meadow and Common, I wait for nearly half an hour until he swoops down very fast on those narrow, pointed, falcon-like wings to a small tree where I have an unimpeded view of him. His whole appearance is very raptor-like, very alert, continually scanning all round his space. He preens – down his mantle, under his wings – patterns of light and shadow transforming his barred breast to more resembling a flaked outgrowth of lichen than feathers, emerging from which are two very small-looking zygodactylar feet, opposite toed, so that he perches with two toes forward and two back. When he calls his entire throat swells, rounding him out between bill and breast making visible the pulsed rhythm of the syrinx as he expels those two extraordinary carrying notes. He moves off at great speed with that rapid, dipping wing-flicker, very falcon-like in its sculling stroke. I lose him in the margin of the wood where there's suddenly much small bird-fret.

Downstream at the little clapper bridge near the bottom of the Common there's a clear stony pool. Jackdaws are bathing, enjoying the pleasure of a glorious afternoon's sunshine. After emerging, they shake their wet spiky feathers preparatory to a good preen. They're so involved, so full of their own pleasure, they totally ignore me, only six feet away! One jumps back into the stream; he bows and scoops the water up and over his back with vigorous wing-action until he's really wet, and for good reason, for he's discovered that he likes his bath so much he's reluctant to finish. Each time he comes out to shake and preen he jumps back in. I think he's done when he gives himself a good rousing shake and starts to preen; but he's joined by another and together they return to the pool which is obviously a favourite bathing place – these two are like re-luctant children at the end of the day, unwilling to leave their

249

pleasures behind. The other nine or ten have flown off, and eventually his 'partner' joins them as the bather sets about a really thorough preen. He faces the afternoon sun. First he cleans his beak, then under each wing, demonstrating some mysterious urge to symmetry. There's a great deal of shaking, of shuffling and re-shuffling feathers, of both direct and indirect scratching. All this activity in the warm sunshine releases body parasites so that he can reach them with his bill as they are forced to move out of their hidden, secret places. His final tasks are to preen down each wing, taking particular care over his coverts and scapulars, re-aligning them to perfection, and lastly a thorough beak-clean on the grass at his feet. He looks around. He's satisfied. He flies away. These few moments sitting by the little bridge listening to the stream and watching the Jackdaws at their water-play is time well spent. On an afternoon like this one senses strongly the gradual ripening of one season towards another. The Cuckoo continues to call from his branch at the edge of the wood, and I am well content to leave the last word to old John of Fornsete:

> "Sumer is icumen in
> Lhude sing cuccu!
> Groweþ sed and bloweþ med
> And springþ þe wude nu
> Sing cuccu…
> Wel singes þu cuccu
> Ne swik þu nauer nu!"

3 May
8.45am – Ashes Point. A fine spring morning after a cool night. The Great Crested Grebes have been more secretive than usual this year, active about the reedbeds but rarely showing on the open water. This morning, however, on the open water of the middle tarn, they are engaged in some of their formalised display routines – facing each other, head-

shaking, neck-dipping, side-preening, all accompanied by short sharp clicking grunts. Suddenly the formalised movements stop and the birds separate, submerge and swim away from each other. They surface and, with a sense of purpose so focussed it excludes everything except the drive of the current moment, swim towards each other at speed, neck, head and dagger-bill extended to nearly full length just above the water surface until there is nowhere to go but to rear up, gleaming white breast to breast, paddling furiously to hold the pose for a few seconds, ruff and tippets fully fanned and expanded, both heads shaking, one with a great beakful of weed. For a few moments these are the only two birds in the world, but the intensity and excitement of this exclusive commitment cannot be sustained and both birds subside into the water, turn and float away from each other until about eight feet apart. They look at each other, turn away, as if still in a dream of ritual, and start to preen. Backlit, they look wonderful in the flush of their mature breeding plumage, their ruffs all fringed round with a halo of light as if singled out this morning under the sun for this particular purpose.

After the fully charged adrenaline rush of display the birds settle to a prolonged preening session, a necessary 'winding down'. A female Goldeneye approaches too close; they drive her away. Wherever they are together on the lake is their space of the moment, surrounded by an invisible boundary defined only by their lack of tolerance to intrusion. They gradually become engaged in a much slower, but no less formalised cycle of activities – approaching each other with much head-shaking, as if flashing signals, followed by a strangely stiff, almost balletic, looking-off from each other and side-touching with the tips of their beaks, the whole repeated – separate, approach, head-shake and preen. When separate, involved in preening, they revolve slowly in obedience to unseen currents, the random and the ritualised in an ongoing, stately pas de deux, its exclusivity moving and beautiful. This particular display, known as the 'Penguin Display', was first described by the naturalist Julian Huxley in a 1914 paper – in which the word 'ritual' was used for the first time in this context – for the *Zoological Society Proceedings* and later expanded into the now classic work *The Courtship Habits of the Great Crested Grebe* (Cape, 1968).

Their fine feathers were very nearly their undoing. According to Macpherson (1892), "the species is quite unaccountably scarce, even as a winter visitant." This is hardly surprising when one considers the slaughter inflicted on it from the mid-nineteenth century for the millinery trade, until by 1860 the entire English population was reduced to a mere 40-odd birds. The concern of the then 'Fur, Fin and Feather Society' led to the formation of the RSPB and its legislated protection.

9.30am – It's very warm. There's not much song and very little movement in the water. The grebes have split up, one bird having disappeared into the reeds, whilst the other stations itself off a specific area of reedbed and gradually relaxes, head and neck hunched down along and into dorsal plumage, and this withdrawal of the bright pillar of his neck renders him almost invisible, so well does he merge with the cast reflections. The little Tufteds, on the other hand, are never still – diving and foraging – in complete contrast to the placid serenity of this lovely grebe, utterly relaxed now, quite unmoving save for a slow drift and turn in obedience to the influence of whatever current stirs beneath him.

11.30am – He wakes from his doze, dives, and suddenly everything changes for when he surfaces there are two birds on the water, and the ritualised movements resume, the birds swimming together and moving apart, head-waving, looking off and side-touching until, facing each other, both dive. Once more the voltage crackles between the two needs of physical proximity, space and time apart and, although they separate, the occasional flicked, directional head movement betrays a remaining, mutual awareness and unresolved charge, until, almost inevitably, the dance resumes – head-shaking, looking off, mock side-preening, together, apart, the unseen elastic between them pulling them back and back again should they separate too far. Their bond reaffirmed they swim out into the open water, face each other and rear up breast to breast, head-shaking vigorously, crest and tippets flared, paddling furiously, water churning, to maintain contact. Once again the climax and their strongly communicated sense of exclusivity are too strong to be sustained for long, and once again they subside, settle to prolonged and thorough preening, separate individuals within their bond and re-established in the great noon-day life-complexity of their water world.

4 May

Certain repeated happenings in the huge cyclism of natural events carry with them the infinitely comforting and reassuring knowledge that at least the basic physics of the solar system are still in place however much we may have threatened and destroyed, and one of these, for me, is the return of the Swifts in May. For many years, and with astonishing regularity, May 9th was Elterwater Swift Day. Gradually, however, that date has crept forward until this year a single bird, like a black spark skittering across a dark cloud, arrived here in Elterwater yesterday.

This morning, in a brisk south-west wind, more arrived, flinging themselves down through holes in the radiant sky with brief flashes of their hard-polished wings touched by the sun. Elterwater has always attracted numbers of Swifts (its name, Swift, derives from the OE *switan* – to move fast) and where we lived in 1987 – a large detached house opposite one of their favoured breeding walls – formed a sort of tower around which they would circle and scream and chase, particularly in the long summer evenings. The old Westmorland name for this furious wild invasion is 'Deviling' as they scythe and sheer about the village sky, screaming down the lanes. When they arrive they are indeed very dark, but as summer progresses a certain bleaching due to their continuous exposure to the elements takes place.

The Swift is no ordinary bird – it is an avian mystery, a non-conformist, a bird totally unlike any other, for other than the scrappy, stuck-together bits of grass and feather – gathered in the air, moreover – with which it makes its nest under the eaves of the local, stone-built houses, it is in all other ways – sleeping, feeding, preening – bound to the skies for life, even, amazingly, mating at high speed on the wing, which that redoubtable observer Gilbert White describes in *The Natural History of Selborne*:

> "If any person would watch these birds on a fine morning in May, as they are sailing around, at great height from the ground, he would see, every now and then, one drop on the back of another, and both of them sink down together for many fathoms, with a loud piercing shriek. This I take to be the juncture when the business of generation is carrying on."
> (Op cit, Letter XXI, Sept 28th, 1774)

Its extraordinary aerial manoeuverability is due to the bow, length and position of its scimitar-like wings which are very often held at an angle below the horizontal axis of the body – the 'anhedral' position, giving the bird a much greater ability to twist and turn at high speeds. This bird really is a dark projectile, its large eyes sunk into the sides of its head for streamlining and protection against air-blast whilst flying at speed. It has been estimated that in any one Swift-lifetime, living, perhaps, up to 15 years, a Swift may fly in the region of two million miles. One aspect of its flight worth listening for is the exciting wing-'thrum' caused by separating the first two primaries, thus allowing the air to rush through at great speed, particularly during morning and evening group pursuit flights, vibrating the first primary, analogous to the Snipe's 'drumming' through his outer tail feathers. Classified among the Apodidae, literally 'without feet', the Swift's rudimentary extremities preclude perching – indeed they are quite helpless if grounded – another adaptation to a completely airborne life. The classic, must-read account of the life of Swifts is *Swifts in a Tower* by Dr. David Lack (1973) which follows and describes the life of a colony of Swifts living in the tower of Oxford University Museum.

1.30pm – For once the top tarn is actually a picture-postcard blue, reflecting the rather bland sky above, and the background hills are gradually retiring behind that veil in which they sleep the afternoon away. Under a dapple of willow among the reeds on the far side of the tarn a Mute pen is curled up on her bulky fortress of a nest. The scene is rather that of a Japanese print, viewed, as this is, through a screen of pale, rattling phragmytes stems. She dozes, preens occasionally and spends much time attending to her nest – moving stems about, replacing them with great care, with clear intent and purpose; just stems which to her, at this time, are simply in the wrong place. One is tempted to think that over her very long (five week) incubation duty this gives her 'something to do', raising questions about aspects of non-human consciousness we know nothing about – such little gestures, but its im-plications are matters of mystery and endless fascination.

Most of the northern shores of the top and middle tarns are bordered with extensive areas of large, tussock-forming sedge (*Carex paniculata*), very difficult to negotiate on foot, the spaces between tussocks being filled with puddles of varying and unknown depths – traps for the unwary! In some of these the first Marigolds have opened, their gold so brilliant in this overhead sunshine that each flower seems to vibrate within its own aura. Two Greylags accompanied by three three-week-old goslings emerge from the shelter of the tussocks and take to the water, adults fore and aft, the goslings bobbing between them. This tarn-side meadow has had a sad history in terms of its declining bird life for Curlew and Snipe regularly nested here up to the mid-1970s when the new riverside footpath brought an increase in human traffic which trespassed upon the birds' territory and tolerance limits. Yellow Wagtails, too, always at least two pairs, bred here until the change from hay cropping to silage – my records show that the last pair to rear young here was in 1992.

Ashes Point – A Buzzard spirals up from the wooded hill across the lake, owning the entire sky until suddenly, with that ability of air-borne raptors to act as 'magnets', the empty air is full of high-flying Swifts swinging about him, towering up and 'buzzing' him on the downward swoop. And, as suddenly as the Swifts appeared, the Buzzard himself, now very high, is re-absorbed in to the same blaze of sky-light from which the Swifts emerged. By now there must be 50 or 60 Swifts over-head, their feathers so hard and polished that they gleam as they tilt towards the sun, borrowing its light like stiff, black crescent moons scudding above the tarn at just above tree height and scorching the air as they go.

4.30pm – As I walk back through the village, there's no a sign of Swifts – they're all over the water and we won't see them again until tomorrow morning. They will simply tower up through the evening into the night, sleeping on the wing, scything black shapes cutting blind curves through the un-navigable dark. Only when morning comes will they know where they are, re-orientate themselves and head back for home.

7 May

7.15pm – Ashes Point. A very beautiful still evening. I come down here regularly to listen to the evening settle and watch the Pikes as they slowly metamorphose from milky, soft-hazed bluish shapes to stark indigo panthers crouched sleeping at the head of the valley. The water shimmers with the non-stop gyrations of hatching gnats and midges, dazzling as if particles of silvery-golden light were falling star-like upon the water and splashing up a sudden blinding incandescence, and then gone – gone and replaced a million times a second. A Sandpiper calls from a little, willow-fringed bay. These little waders impart a restlessness to the air around them, piercing their way ahead with needle-sharp calls, their speed and manoeuverability achieved with a minimum of sharp-flickered wing beats followed by glides in which the wings are held in such a negative, dihedral position that their tips almost touch the water. If they embody all that's ephemeral in such an evening, the Mute Swan floating serenely by in the dark-smudged reflections lends a sense of placid permanence, that not quite everything is due to explode into flight, metamorphose into endless flux and incandescence.

7.30pm – The sun, a glare of white light, hangs an inch or so above the summit of Lingmoor, and nothing's visible in its reflected glitter. A few Mallards and a little flotilla of seven week-old Greylag goslings with adults fore and aft hug this shore. A nearby Reed Bunting steps up his little song and a Sedge Warble begins his 'performance' in the reeds fringing the Nab. Away in the distance a Snipe drums. The air is thick with an insect soup within which Swallows hawk, sometimes sweeping down and across the surface with only about six inches to spare. The white smudge of their reflected under-surface keeps pace with them as they traverse the water, making them easy to follow. One pair of Swallows is courtship feeding, twisting and twirling about each other over the lake, towering up into the air trying to maintain bill contact, followed by a twisting, tumbling flight in which food is passed from bill to bill at speed.

A female Mallard quacks quietly, continuously, as her seven tiny, very recently hatched ducklings maintain a tightly controlled huddle around her, as if held in close body contact by little feathered magnets pulling them close in should they exceed a regulation distance! The Sandpipers' thin flight call announces their arrival, visible only in silhouette, on the gravelly shore of Ashes Point.

7.50pm – A fine Blackbird starts his evening song from the top-tarn pines, his voice carrying loud and clear through the calm evening air accompanying the sun as he drops gently down onto the top of Lingmoor. At 7.55 exactly, the very last sliver of sun falls off the edge of the world from the summit of Lingmoor into a wash of golden radiance grading up into a very soft blue, becoming increasingly saturated as the eye travels up and over towards the east. Strangely enough, coincidence or not, the pine-top Blackbird stopped singing the moment the sun fell off the ridge, as if the gold of his bill needed the sun to touch it off. Chaffinch and Willow Warbler still sing and always, behind everything, there's the call of sheep and the bleat of lambs.

The sun's final descent brings almost immediate results – it's suddenly much cooler and the shadows deepen rapidly. The trees overlooking the lake begin to close in, the breeze drops and despite the constant insect-dimpling of the water surface a sense of restfulness begins to pervade the atmosphere. The Swallows have retired and, though the indefatigueable Willow Warblers and one very persistent Chaffinch still sing, the former sense of surround sound is weakening. In the west a spread of gold suffuses outwards from that centre where the sun fell off the world. It grades very softly up through the palest of golds, seeping into the blue, so that within this expanding golden glow the Pikes gradually darken, never becoming totally black – more an opaque density of the deepest indigo.

8.10pm – A solitary, late Buzzard flies across the tarn towards the Common. This bird has started the wing moult with the inner primary in one wing.

8.20pm – A drumming Snipe joins the few birds still singing. A few Swallows hawk high over the tarn making no effort to come down to the water, and one or two Swifts, like sweeping slivers of black moons, slice through the sky.

8.45pm – A Cuckoo calls persistently from Loughrigg, joined by another high up on the edges of Fletcher. These two are involved in a call and answer session over what must be well over 1.5 miles of valley air. The Sandpipers call once more from the gravelly edge of the point. A solitary Crow flies high, eastwards down the length of the tarn.

9.00pm – The first Tawny Owl hoots – a well-rounded, quavering, full hoot – a doorway allowing a passage through from one time to another. A clattering Woodpigeon shatters the expanding ripples of his hoot. Together with the Snipe's drumming these sounds seem so to fill the ambient air that identifying their points of origin is quite impossible. As the glow behind the Pikes fades and their indigo cloak intensifies and darkens, so, at last, the encircling Willow Warbler song begins to fade.

9.30pm – It's beginning to get very chilly as well as darkening rapidly and I need the little remaining light to negotiate the river crossing pausing to watch low-hawking Pipistrelles, the few expanding ripple-rings evidence of a dipped wing tip perhaps or a larger insect snatched from the river surface. There's a pronounced late evening scent as the dew forms on the heated grass and the new sappy foliage.

8 May

2.25pm – After some rain this morning it has cleared to a fine, warm afternoon with a cloudless sky. It's not far from the Old Hotel at Dungeon Ghyll to the New Hotel, but it must be among the finest of valley miles, passing beneath a vertiginous profusion of crag and scree, its rocky building blocks so piled one upon another that a summit cannot yet be seen, remote to the eye, perhaps, yet not to an imagination displacing layers of memory and time back to the Neolithic Age when men up on Pike o' Stickle chipped out axe-heads from the vein of greenstone, volcanic tuff running all round the head of the valley at a height of about 2,000 feet. It is a hard, unforgiving landscape, but spring and summer soften some of its edges – brackens, wood-rush, grass and sedge, the crag-end floral succession form the vegetative bases for stunted thorns, hollies and rowans from which Robin and Wren, the occasional Willow Warbler, Chaffinch, Tree Pipit and even Blackbird now sing where once, in much less populous days, Ring Ouzels might be heard. From beneath Raven Crag and Middlefell Buttress looming above the Old Hotel, the path winds among boulders and scree until it crosses Dungeon Ghyll somewhat below its re-emergence into the light after its passage down the huge rocky, but richly vegetated gully cleaving the fellside just below Thorn Crag. It culminates in the impressive rocky chasm which gives the stream its name, a visit to which Wordsworth, in his most admirable *Guide to the Lakes,* strongly recommends the tourist "if there be time".

Past Dungeon Ghyll's often tumultuous, boulderstrewn, rowan-decorated tumble down to Great Langdale Beck, the path winds beneath lofty Pike How and Miller Crag until it reaches the equally turbulent lower reaches of Mill Gill in its fall from Stickle Tarn below the remotely ethereal Pavey Ark. Once one reaches Stickle Cottage and the New Hotel, with its attendant trees, shrubberies and gardens, everything changes as at a desert oasis and one doesn't even have to try to hear the surround sound of Willow Warblers, accompanied by Wood-pigeons, Chiffchaff, Blackcap, Redstart, Blackbird, Mistle Thrush, Chaffinch, House Sparrows, displaying Siskins and Wren, in addition to which I count seven Swifts, four Swallows, one Buzzard soaring high over Pike How and a couple of Ravens flying over from White Ghyll.

Once onto the Old Road, the perspective changes and the fellside can be appreciated from its grassy intakes to high, radiant summits all the way round from Loft Crag and Harrison Stickle to Pavey Ark, the rock almost tinged with pink in the afternoon sunshine, the shadows a warm blue, and the huge amphitheatre held fast between Thorn Crag and Tarn Crag, drained by Stickle Ghyll. The walk down the Old Road to Robinson Place is dominated by the sunlit slopes of the soaring ridge forming the northern boundary of the valley and is best taken slowly and with many stops, for it is full of interest; its farmsteads, holdings and great, broad meadows are among the best-known in Lakeland, celebrated in photo-archives of farmers and their work in the fields, the Pikes ever-present as background to their long, hard days. These pictorial records are full of nostalgia for what were, literally, the hay-days of this great valley. At one time there were over two dozen such farms and holdings in the valley, but times and methods have changed – the land, flocks and work now divided between the seven or eight remaining working farms. All these fields had names, of course, some descriptive of their character – Thorny Intake, Wet Parrock, Broad Meadow, Straight Meadow, Stoney Close; others identifying them by location – Across Ghyll, Behind House, Back o' Beck; others still related to their use – Cow Pasture, Horse Pasture, Calf Parrock, Corn Hinning; while yet another group is identified by names which may be personal to the long-gone folklore of a particular farm, but their origin is now lost – Fitzhead, Big Robsay, Matthew Meadow, Willie Wife Intake. These names do more than merely identify them – they invest them with a certain tradition of life and labour, points of reference within not only a particular landscape but also within the annual cycle, suggestive of the intimacy of relationship between man, land and landscape.

Butterflies are active – Peacocks, Small Tortoiseshells, Red Admirals, Orange Tips and whites – and a superb male Brimstone has just gone by, its brilliant sulphur-yellow like a flake of detached sun flickering among the track-side bushes and trees. A Cuckoo calls from the fell above Pye Howe and it's worth a stop here to seek out a path slanting away up and

261

across the fell towards the top of the far side ridge. Locals once used this as their regular way over the ridge to Grasmere. In March 1808 it was the scene of a tragedy which shocked the two valleys to their core. From their cottage at Blind Tarn overlooking Easedale on the Grasmere side of the ridge, George and Sarah Green set out one Saturday late in March to attend a farm sale and visit their eldest child (all the children were under 16) who was in service at a nearby Inn, before returning over the fell to their cottage and very young family of seven children, left in the care of one of their older daughters, Jane, aged 14. They were caught in a bewildering mixture of mist and snow among the higher crags, became hopelessly lost, and died on the fell. In mounting anxiety the children waited three days for news until it became apparent that something was seriously amiss, the alarm was raised and search teams from both valleys were roused until the bodies were found, after a six-day search, miserable and mangled, having been cut by the crags where they had fallen. The Wordsworth family was closely involved, already having employed the second youngest girl, Sarah, as a trainee housemaid. William commemorated the widespread grief and pity aroused by this incident in a poem of 1808 (publ. 1839) simply entitled *George and Sarah Green* and helped to organise a public subscription – reaching nearly £600 – to cater for the growing needs of the now parentless, destitute young children – homes, clothing, education – the subscription list reading like a *Who's Who* of the landed gentry, aristocracy and literary eminences both north and south of the border. Most of what we know of this dreadful affair was written by Dorothy Wordsworth in a meticulously detailed, yet warmly sympathetic account of 4th May 1808.

Oak Howe – known locally as Yak Howe – with its fine sentinel pines is one of the more ancient holdings in the valley. Records of its occupancy date back to the mid-sixteenth century, and vestiges of much more ancient walls, long tumbled and covered with vegetation, may be sought out from the path skirting the lower flanks of Lingmoor. Another of its claims to fame is an ancient plot where local victims of the plague were brought to be buried. Between Yak Howe and Bayesbrown the valley changes – the fields become fewer in number, but much bigger and broader, and the river between Oak Howe Bridge and the New Bridge has undergone extensive re-enforced embankment work to minimize flood damage. People still remember the great storm of August 1996 which did immense damage in both Borrowdale and Langdale when it was estimated that some 4 to 5 inches of rain per hour fell, with thunder-clouds centred over the Pikes towering to over six miles, unleashing a non-stop lightning display for many hours. Bridges were swept away, houses and farms flooded, stones shattered and swept from fellsides and the fields left mud-covered and boulder-strewn – quite useless for the rest of the year. Nothing so apocalyptic this afternoon, however, the river running straight and sweet, transparent over weed and stony bed, alternately placid-flowing and rapid, and where a few small trout may still be found.

On the far side of these great fields, under the shadow of Lingmoor, stands Baysbrown Farm, historically one of the most ancient and important farm holdings in the valley, once a manor dating back to the twelfth century, although the present building dates from the late seventeenth century. It figures in a fine novel by Ruskin's historian secretary, W.G. Collingwood, *The Bondwoman* (1896), which tells the story of two slave girls sold to the descendants of the first Viking settlers in the area, drawing a vivid picture of domestic life in Langdale when Christianity first appeared in the area. Collingwood's novels, the other being *Thorstein of the Mere – A Saga of the Norsemen in Lakeland* (1895), are beautifully written and meticulously researched. His guidebook, *The Lake Counties* (1902), cannot be bettered as a picture of the Lake District, its lore, natural and human history prior to the Second World War. The Editor of the 1938 edition points out that since its first publication in 1902, "Lakeland has, unhappily, suffered, in some degree, at the hands of the despoilers. The litter-fiend has not been deterred even by the grandeurs of the lakes and fells, commercial vandalism has caused advertisements to appear in places which should be sacred to natural beauty, petrol pumps have sprung up here and there like malignant growths...yet solitude may still be found both in the inner valleys and on the higher fells." Sixty years later other Lake District authors would write uttering the concern "that too many concessions to recreational requirements will change the character of the Lake District" and that an "unthinkable economic future for the Lake District is that it should become a playground..." (Pearsall & Pennington, 1973). I wonder what they would make of the vandalism wreaked today by bodies responsible for conservation and planning against precisely that unthinkable?!

It's long since anywhere in the Lake District, never mind Langdale, could be claimed as truly wild or, indeed, for having even a remote connection with any concept of 'wilderness'. Its fells retain many of its components, their dressings of boulder and scree and the surface intrusions of ancient, deep-rooted rocks from among its long-buried bones, yet even its most remote places are layered with the never-still whisperings of age-old ghosts.

11 May

Mornings should be celebrations of something new and forever unrepeatable in the procession of days along our earthwalk. Here in Elterwater, particularly down among its meadows and by the lake, we are gifted by nature with some morning celebrations, mainly in October and May, which are special beyond expression, gateways to regions hitherto unknown and cherished in the memory for that reason. There was quite a hard frost last night and this morning the meadows are heavily rimed, the grasses showing a pale, almost chrome-green undertone to their crystalline coats, and all seen in a constantly changing visibility modified by varying densities of cold, shape-shifting mists through which the grey sheep and monumental cattle move slowly, undefined, like huge boulders or standing stones moved gradually, shifting from one stance to the next only after aeons of some alien, thoughtful purpose buried deep beneath yet still connected to the surface sward. Here in Elterwater we never see the actual sun rise, so that by the time the Sun climbs above the shoulder of Loughrigg the solar disc is haloed with brilliant white gold pulsing up into the blue. Everything changes as the mist burns off, golden across the face of the fell, the trees in softly washed layers, blue-misted between. Then the first light on the ridge and a very special moment when the top-tarn pines stand like pale etchings in a blue-grey mist, briefly catching a light-blaze in their crowns before becoming actual common trees. The whole world is caught in a moment of becoming. There is no evolution, just a moment by moment nowness and newness and one's entire self expands into it, losing its petty self-consciousness so that the revelation of sun, mist, trees and hills are as much within as without in a kind of mutuality and correspondence by which the huge unity of life is realised anew.

Behind me, in the long meadow, hawking low for insects disturbed by the new morning sun and the movement of sheep are many Swallows. The perfection of their long, curved swoop and sheer trajectories are accompanied by non-stop twitterings as they break into short, liquid bursts of flight song which changes abruptly into a mass expression of hirundine outrage as a Peregrine appears at speed from out of the sun over Loughrigg, hurtling down into the meadow – a wing-flickering black death skimming the grasses among the outraged Swallows before casting up and disappearing over the wood behind Bessy Well. The inevitable tension relaxes, such is the charisma of danger communicated by this magnificent bird, but this time I think he was simply exhilarated by the morning, attracted perhaps by the pied flicker of the smaller birds, was just having a bit of fun – he can afford to do this – he's top bird, indomitable, untouchable.

The river is low and very clear. Already it is warm enough to have stimulated a large, peculiarly localised hatch of small dipterous flies in mating flight over the sitting stones' pool, which is so clear that fascinating shadows of surface 'events' are projected down onto and along the river's well-lit bed stones and boulders where they relate rather a different narrative, being both magnified and distorted by the water's passage along the irregularities of its bed. For the watcher this flowing stream of double events becomes almost hypnotic, for it is like witnessing in miniature the passage through time and space of one reality simultaneous with an alternative, parallel universe.

Up through the warm meadows glowing in the aura of massed celandines, past the thorny corner where for many years Yellowhammers have sung their song of summer and sunshine, and on to the little lane leading to the bottom gate of Low Wood. Nearby, the vegetated top of an old walled dyke forms a prime site for that most charming of unobtrusive plants, *Adoxa moschatellina*, the Moschatel. Among the tangle of grasses each plant towers up to perhaps three inches and bears at its top tiny, greeny-white flowers arranged as a four-sided clock face with a 'hat' on top. It is the only plant in its family, the word *adoxa* derived from the Greek for 'obscure', and together with the diminutive ending to its specific name we have the delightful 'obscure, little, musk-smelling plant'! So much charm hidden, indeed obscure, within such rigorous nomenclature!

All this ground from where the wood begins on the edge of the Common and along the wooded skirts of Loughrigg is prime Green Woodpecker country. Were it not for its very characteristic yaffling calls, however, few would notice its presence – its plumage of mainly greens and yellows blending perfectly with the dapple of woodland foliage. Leaning on the gate, watching the interface between wood and meadow, there's a sudden flash of yellow and green as a bird enters the wood. With its powerfully built dagger-bill and dark head leading, it seems more missile than bird, structured for penetration, and when seen at rest the combination of gleaming eye ring set within the dark head and the streamlining effect of its moustachial stripe produce that powerful sense of intense concentration and focussed purpose common to all our woodpeckers. Within the wood all's a-dapple, sunlight and shadow gliding, shape-changing over the woodland floor, a terrestrial mirror of the river and its reflecting bed, bestowing and withdrawing light randomly over the clear waxy whites of Ramsons, the clusters of stellar Stitchwort. The woodland floor is powdered pale ochre-green with the shed husks of sycamore flowers, the beds of darker moss spiking up through like dense forests of miniature conifers. Under an old ash lies a scattering of bark chippings, debris from a newly worked woodpecker hole much higher up, its owner, perhaps, the same bird seen entering the wood earlier.

I've come to see the Bluebells, now at their very best, vast swathes of them undulating over the woodland floor under the dapple of hazels and light shade cast by the still developing tree canopy. As cloud shadows slide their close embrace over these little forest glades, one area after another flares into light before itself becoming shadowed, thus causing a whole spectrum of very slightly crimson-warmed blues constantly un-rolling their fragile light and secret shadows through the wood. It is as if the dark engines of the earth are finally warming up, the generation of its inner fires smoking in drifts over these lush, subtly variegated carpets, for no plant conveys the seminal lushness of a May wood as do massed Bluebells. The leaves themselves squeak with juices, and the gradually in-

creasing density of blue mist which hazes the woodland floor
seems more a vaporous emanation of saps locked within the
earth than flowers. Their old Elizabethan name 'jacinth'
(derived from the Latin *hyacinthus*) is itself, onomatopœic, full
of the sound of juice. Bluebells thrive best under dappled
woodland shade, and derelict coppice with a few light-leaved
standards suits them best of all and are indicators of ancient
woodland sites and do not readily colonise new woodland.
They still thrive on many of our Atlantic cliff tops and on
islands such as Skomer, but these are more relict survivors
than colonisers. They reproduce both vegetatively from bulbs
produced in the leaf axils and also from the familiar black
seeds, although the latter is a slow process, for it takes three
years for a germinated seed to produce a flower-bearing bulb.

Bluebells bruise mortally with great ease, and there is an
old belief that whoever walked through Bluebells, believed to
be enchanted by the fairy-folk whose flower it was, would be
spirited away and cursed. Certainly to walk among them is a
kind of sacrilege; as to actually picking them, beware!

13 May

"'T is always morning somewhere, and above
The awakening continents; from shore to shore,
Somewhere the birds are singing evermore."
(From *The Poet's Tale*; *The Birds of Killingworth*, H.W.
Longfellow)

With these joyful words, Longfellow strongly communicates
the idea of dawn rolling ceaselessly round our planet and
unrolling a continuum of birdsong in its wake, day after day,
from east to west, everywhere birds waking up to sing. This is
such a powerful image that it emphasises the impossibility of
even imagining a dawn or a day without the accompaniment of
call or song, depending on the season, wherever one lives. The
French composer, Olivier Messiaen, a considerable ornitho-

logist with a passionate interest in birdsong, once wrote, "I doubt that anyone can find in any music, however inspired, melodies and rhythms that have the sovereign freedom of birdsong." Birdsong, moreover, has become recognised an indicator of our quality of lives – "Birdsong has been proved to reduce blood pressure. When we live in the centre of large urban areas we get more stressed and it's extremely good to have birdsong around us." Referring to the now well-documented phenomenon for some urban species – the Robin and the Great Tit, for example – to sing both louder and at higher frequencies in order to be heard against the context of urban noise levels, the author goes to say, "The impact of birdsong on humans is massive. It harms us as well as the birds if their songs become simpler, shriller and louder." (*The Sound Approach to Birding: A Guide to Understanding Bird Sound,* by Mark Constantine, Publ. The Sound Approach, Poole, 2006). Keats offers us an appallingly effective reverse of Longfellow's image of ongoing sunrise in the opening stanza of *La Belle Dame sans Merci*:

"The sedge is wither'd from the lake,
And no birds sing."

Those final weighty vowels of chimeless dissonance communicate instead a sense of utter despair and desolation, presenting a scene so appalling, so foreign to our common experience that the imagination can hardly grasp it. Such an environmental catastrophe, however, was forseen by the American writer Rachel Carson who, against formidably deafening opposition by the agro-chemical industries whose products were poisoning the land and decimating birds particularly, published the classic *Silent Spring* in 1962. The problems of rural toxic pollution persist, but some pro-environmental legislation, as a result of the furore caused by Rachel Carson's book, have ensured that, for the moment at least, birds continue to sing at dawn in Spring.

By mid-May all our birds, both resident and migrant, are fully occupied with their breeding programmes, the males greeting each morning with a full-blooded declaration of territorial ownership – that midspring phenomenon, the Dawn Chorus. This can be enjoyed on many levels – the pure magic and music of the hour is sufficient for many. It is also an opportunity to assess locally breeding birds either on a selected linear or a selected 'patch' basis, in which case familiarity with song and call notes now becomes an essential tool. Also essential is an early start.

Accordingly, 3am finds me on my way down to the gravelly point on the middle tarn where I am surrounded by my favourite 'patch' consisting of a variety of habitats offering the greatest variety of breeding birds – lake, bog, reed beds, carr, meadows, woodland, with the river always in the background. But after the superb May weather we've been enjoying recently, this morning is disappointing – a considerable drop in temperature and a corresponding change in weather conditions, with spats of rain blowing out of a brisk, cold west wind which probably also means that full song may start a little later. It's bitterly cold and I'm very glad of the extra clothes and coffee as I get settled under the shelter of the Ashes Point alders.

There's a succession of unseen splashes and calls as unsettled Mallards and Coot out on the water begin to rouse and all goes quiet until suddenly, like a clock wound up, at

3.18am – Snipe drums from over by Colwith – a rather unexpected 'voice';

3.35 – Tawny Owl calls from Fletcher;

Snipe drums from top-tarn meadow;

3.47 – Sandpipers – a 'tweedling' flight-call;

3.49 – Sedge Warbler – a few hesitant notes from the reedbed on the opposite shore;

3.54 – Chaffinch call notes;

Sedge Warbler starts full song.

3.57-4.15am – Onset of a long and very cold shower. Song suddenly stops, silencing both Sedge Warbler and the Colwith Snipe which has been drumming continuously. As light increases, the lake is revealed 'steaming' in a shifting, rather Gothic mist through which the rain hisses and drums on the water. Very slowly a pair of Mute Swans appears and disappears within the changing density of the mists like some presence from a Celtic myth, resolving into ghostly white shapes without detail.

4.18 – Colwith Snipe resumes drumming as the rain suddenly stops, revealing a griming of snow on the high fells. It's very cold!

4.20 – Sedge Warber resumes song, answered by another from the reeds about the Nab.

Goosander calls from Dead Sheep Bay.

Greylag calls from the bottom tarn.

Robin sings (on a perfect morning in May 1990 in the same place Robin started at 4.08am; in 1962 at 4.22am).

4.23 – Carrion Crow;

Snipe 'chippers' from over by the old boathouse on the top tarn. Greylags very noisy.

4.25 – Jackdaws;

Tawny Owl hoots again from Fletcher.

Cuckoo;

Blackbird (1962, 4.15; 1990, 4.16)

Song Thrush;

Reed Bunting;

4.27 – Redstart;

4.28 – Wren;

Willow Warbler (1962, 4.29; 1990, 4.20);

4.30 – Heron flies over to perch on one of the top tarn pines.

All these voices coming in to the belling of distant cattle, the almost continuous bleating of sheep and lambs from the meadows, the drumming of Snipe and the continuing activity of Greylags and Mallards, unseen, but heard, on the top tarn.

271

4.35am – Pheasant crows in meadows behind.

Sandpipers on the gravelly shore embark on an increasingly excitable pursuit display with much piping accompaniment, alternately raising and flicking their wings above their backs, displaying their pied underwing patterns as if signalling to each other. This, and their increasingly heightened vocal excitement, becomes too intense to be sustained for long, and they are soon off, 'tweedling' across to the far side of the lake.

4.37 – Mistle Thrush (1962, 4.25);

4.43 – Great Tit (1962, 4.29);

Canada Geese – two appearing through the mist from near the Nab.

Great Crested Grebe gains definition as it swims through the top tarn neck into the middle tarn.

4.45 – Blackcap;

 Blue Tit (1962, 4.45);

4.50 – Chaffinch song (1962, 4.50) – nearly an hour after its first calls.

(By this time the main period of full song is over, but still singing are Song Thrush, Blackbird, Robin, Chaffinch, Cuckoo, Willow Warbler, Blackcap, Wren, Woodpigeon and Sedge Warbler, with occasional bursts from the Fletcher Tawny Owl, all against a constant Carrion Crow background. Visibility clears again. The Sedge Warbler on the far side of the lake has been remarkable for his volume, persistence, variety of utterance in a very complex stream of notes.)

5.26 – Swallows and House Martins make their first insect-hawking forays out over the lake. Pied Wagtail comes down to the shillet margin.

5.30 – Buzzard mews in Fletcher – no early first light whistle this morning – a very late start!

6.00 – Pied Flycatcher audible near the river.

Dipper and Grey Wagtails at the river.

The onset of yet another stinging shower seems to depress further song for the moment, and I make my way home after a disappointing morning weather-wise, but quite pleased with the results of my three-hour vigil.

Comments:

At 7.30am a Roe doe and a young buck with his first head were standing on the shillets of Ashes Point where I had been not so long ago. Other birds moving about were House Sparrows, Starlings, Dunnock, Greenfinch, Siskin, Goldfinch, Nuthatch, Magpie, Swift, Garden Warbler, and Chiffchaff. Birds known to be in the area but neither seen nor heard this morning – Green Woodpecker, Great Spotted Woodpecker, Woodcock, Sparrowhawk, Kestrel, Jay, Marsh, Coal and Long-tailed Tits, Tree Creeper, Bullfinch. Summering wetland species lost over the years include Tufted Duck (in some numbers, for moulting), Coot, Moorhen, Curlew, Lapwing, with Little Grebe and Red-breasted Merganser become very irregular, and associated birds like Reed Bunting and Sedge Warbler considerably reduced in numbers, and Yellow Wagtail lost.

15 May

The break in the weather after the glorious conditions prevailing over the first half of May is disappointing. The brackens have benefitted from this combination of warmth and wet, and are growing rapidly. Their annual resurgence around the end of April, beginning of May, is certainly fascinating to watch – how after only a few days, from a tight-clenched fist and arched stem furred with dark, silky, purple hairs it unfurls and branches, seeming to feel its way into the upper air with mute, blind fingerings – more an alien, un-bidden presence than a plant regeneration, unpacking a dense, impenetrable, largely inhospitable forest over the lower fellsides – inhospitable because of the various toxic, insect-repellent chemicals within its fronds and therefore of little use to breeding birds. Nevertheless, one or two birds – Pipits and Stonechats, for example – do make use of the cover afforded by the brackens at their interface with other habitats.

The short, sheep-grazed turf of the Common – on grassy banks, beside the path and bordering the stream – is, however, a treasury of small plants, often overlooked, yet which in the days of mediaeval herbalism might have proved useful to the younger women of the village. The untidy tufts of Lady's Mantle with their tiny, yellow-green flowers, named for an ancient rural reverence for 'Our Lady the Virgin Mary' – a kind of homage, with 'mantle' referring to the appearance of the palmately lobed, young leaves before they open out – simulating the cloak in which Mary is traditionally depicted. Its speciality to young women, however, was, paradoxically, its use as a distilled infusion to be drunk as an aid to conception. Having conceived your baby – without the benefit of celestial intervention! – borne it to full term and been safely delivered of it, it must be fed. Among the least obvious of all the acid turf plants on the Common is the tiny Milkwort, its blues varying from a rich warm to very pale and which rejoices in the lovely generic name *Polygala*, from the Greek for 'much milk'. By the processes of sympathetic herbalism the milky secretion of its roots was recognised as an obvious specific for nursing mothers. Suppose though, that your baby then went on to suffer the griping pains of wind or indigestion, another trip up onto the Common could be made to pick the bright yellow, four-petalled Tormentil to ease what the Romans called 'tormina' – the colic or gripes – or, when older, a root preparation for easing toothache. But some of what grows wild on the Common was deemed not as beneficial to the local farmers as others were for young mums and their babes. Growing not so much out of the turf as out of the wet, rather acid flushes seeping into the little beck grow the pale, yellowy-green leaf rosettes of the Butterwort with its short-lived, white-mouthed, violet-like flower. This plant, like the Sundews, is carnivorous, its sticky, strap-like leaves rolling inwards upon any insect unlucky enough to alight. Yet, like the rather later flowering Lousewort, it was deemed guilty of causing liver-rot in sheep. The real problem, of course, lies not with the plants themselves but with the ground from which they grow – wet, acid and much favoured by one of the phases in the development of the liver-fluke which sheep naturally ingest with their pasturage.

The humid conditions have stimulated much insect activity and the Swifts flash low and fast over meadows and Common, air thrumming through visibly divided primaries. Preening at speed in full flight is a matter of towering up prior to a shallow downwards glide during which the primaries are pulled through the bill a couple of times in as many seconds! Depending on their flight direction, so the declining evening light strikes them. Against the light the wing's trailing edge seems to flash as if sharp-bladed, and flying down the light it illuminates their rumps to an almost pale grey-ochre. There's no screaming this evening – time only for concentrated foraging. Over the eastern boundary of the Common dozens of Swallows and two Swifts have gathered into a gradually rising, swirling column, attracting the attention of a Peregrine soaring over the ridge between Spedding Crag and Hunting Stile – probably the same Peregrine attracted to the Swallows foraging in the meadows three or four days ago. It joins the whirling, gyring Swallows as if playing with them, but they show no obvious response. Watched through binoculars, their non-stop circling – the Swallows flicker-winged, the Peregrine soaring with them – is almost hypnotic. The Peregrine suddenly breaks both pattern and rhythm, sweeping away and jinking back along its flight path causing the Swallows to sheer off and away, like children on the shore playing among the set rhythms of the little waves, suddenly disconcerted and fleeing before an unexpected big one. Again the Peregrine sweeps out of the group and back, and again, forming further rhythms and patterns, losing its edge of unpredictability and danger, and I wonder if this is an extended rhythm of familiarisation and whether the pattern will be broken a third and lethal time. Peregrines not infrequently 'play' before striking. But a sudden and unpredictable death is not the outcome of this exhibition, for the Peregrine surges vertically up through the throng of birds, soaring higher until it becomes a mere speck in the binoculars, hoisting away over Loughrigg and leaving the Swallows to their antics, until they, too, gradually disperse and the sky is left empty.

17 May

At last a really fine morning for a visit to Foulney. At 10.30am there's a cool south-westerly blowing over the causeway, and I'm hoping for a solitary day on the island, allowing the tide to cut me off until the ebb permits a return journey. This is a place I have known most of my life, a place where the sense of being with the wild, the elemental, is stronger than almost anywhere I know. It doesn't matter that Barrow shipyard is just round the corner – this narrow strip of ancient glacier-borne shingle and its terminal spit, Slitch Ridge, facing the everchanging structure and moods of the estuary, never fails as a bridge between the personal and the elemental, where sea and sky and light and land and their life forms blend and intermingle in a ceaseless pageant of change and wonder. Setting foot upon the causeway is an exhilarating adventure into the always unknown, evoking feelings and responses quite different from those experienced entering other habitats. Venturing into the inevitably restrictive perspectives of a plot of woodland, for example (thinking particularly of that small parcel of woodland near Baysbrown tarn where the ancient, mossy stones sleep time away), is akin to penetrating, for a while at least, a veil slung between an inside and an outside world, in which concepts of time unravel and meetings with wildlife, whether Jay, Roe buck, butterfly or a galaxy of Wood Anemones come either as fleeting imprints on a retina geared to looking through and beyond the columns and pillars holding apart earth and canopy, or as sharp, in-your-face encounters. Here, however, on this narrow strip of shingle, one endlessly faces the huge shimmer of changing light from sky onto the vast reflective surfaces of the estuary, simultaneously absorbing this magic as well as expanding out into it, connecting and healing.

The differences between the sides of this causeway are striking. To one side, the extensive salt marsh with its hidden channels looking superb now with its foreground of Pink Thrift and white compact clumps of Scurvy Grass receding into a vast spread of texture and colour – the subtle inter-minglings of grasses, Sea-purslane and Sea Lavender which will fill the marsh with colour later in the summer, while the causeway stones are vibrant with the brilliant orange splashes of the lichen *Xanthoria maritime*. On the other side, looking towards Piel Island and its rugged castle, a variety of different textures and colours – pools like little eyes of sky open to every change of light, lichened boulders, stretches of variegated green algae, shingle and shell-banks. A single Lesser Black-backed Gull stands motionless, like a carefully placed wood carving and a few solitary Oystercatchers stand at the edge of the mud, whilst from the distance, lost and found in the swirling, shifting wind, the mournful, drooping calls of Red-shank.

Once off the causeway, everything changes and multitudes of flowers spill from the short turf onto the shingle throughout spring and summer. A low pink carpet of Herb Robert forms a rich weave out of which white clusters of sweet-smelling cruciform flowers crown the cabbagey structures of Sea-kale, the massed pale lilac of Sea Rocket, dotted all around with small geraniums and sprouting Horned Poppies, sculptural sorrels and docks, Milfoil, Common Ladies' Mantle, various Hieraceae, glowing drifts of Thrift, swathes of White Sea Campion and brilliant cushions of Bird's Foot Trefoil. Much of the shingle and grassland is cordoned off by the seasonal warden to ensure optimum security for the birds which breed here, mainly now only a few Arctic and Little Terns, Oyster-catcher, Eider Duck and Ringed Plover, Meadow Pipits and the dozen or so pairs of rhapsodic Skylarks, but my memory goes back to when Mergansers, Redshank and Lapwing also nested here. Between the late 1950s, when I first came to know Foulney, and early 1970s it was host at one time or another to all our breeding terns, mainly Arctic and Common, with maxima of well over 200 pairs of Arctics and 500 pairs of Common Terns. Exceptionally high tides and predation by raptors, gulls, foxes and recurring plagues of rats have contributed to this sad decline, and the last Common Terns bred here in the mid-1990s. Now Foulney hosts the only Arctic Tern colony in Cumbria – a couple of dozen pairs at the most – and a very few Little Terns.

From a rough seat of two sea-washed logs on the 22 feet island summit one looks along the length of Slitch Ridge, its northern end covered with roosting female Eiders, their low skyline knobbly and dark against the brighter air, whilst the more south-facing Walney side is white with males. All around, absorbed into the expanding vastness of sea-light and mud-glint, is the ever-changing Bay where the tide is now creeping up towards its highest point. An Oystercatcher pokes about for shellfish down at the tideline. He finds a cockle and prises it open, dragging out the yellowy flesh, which also stains the tip of his bill yellow, vivid against the red. A solitary non-breeding Grey Plover stands motionless facing the tide, unaffected, indifferent, hunched as if always dealing with some personal inconvenience.

Further along a large late spring pack of Knot sweeps over the incoming tide displaying changing patterns of pale and

278

dark as they tilt from one side to another, the underparts flashing pale as the flock swings around. Some entertain a notion of landing, and they actually begin to raise their wings and lower their feet preparatory to alighting, only to find that the impulse of the flock to continue in flight is stronger than any individual will to land so that such 'landing' birds get swept along by the flock, as caught up as leaves in an autumn wind. This magic of flock behaviour among waders seen, particularly in the tight pack-formation of Knots (also, of course, in massed flocks of roosting Starlings), is now known to be a much studied form of behaviour named from the Greek for 'copying one's kind' – allelomimesis, or behavioural matching – and applicable to many creatures, from ants to humans. It describes a phenomenon in which each individual in a group imitates its neighbours' behaviour, falling almost automatically and instantly into the same pattern. Imagine the Mexican Wave performed at some sporting event, but flowing from one person to another at a far greater reaction speed than is humanly possible so that the ripple of action is almost in-stantaneous, like the flickering shuffle across a disturbed mass of African Bees, and there you see the phenomenon of massed wader flight. The same phenomenon has also been much studied with regard to the predator-evasion tactics of large schools of fish. It is seen in insect behaviour, where, for example, the more ants that follow a particular trail the more that trail becomes attractive to being followed, identical to the phenomena of mass human tourism or crowd behaviour at rallies or football matches. It is curiously satisfying that we share such a basic behavioural phenomenon with so humble, yet complex organisms as ants.

Behind the pack of Knots streams a typically twisting string of Dunlin, but it is the Arctic Terns that hold the attention. These deceptively delicate-looking birds arrive around mid-April after a 10,000-plus mile flight from the Ant-arctic pack ice at their furthest south right up to the Arctic circum-polar regions. In England their numbers have been declining for a number of years, and the typically favoured kind of shingle island, such as Foulney, is their only breeding base in Cumbria. Beating backwards and forwards over the shingle, out to sea and back, they reveal the remarkable economy of their flight-mode – long, deep, leisurely stroked beats, rhythmic and regular looking almost casual as if they could fly for ever – which they do, of course – 20,000 miles per year during the life of every individual! One pair is engaged in its fascinating courtship ritual which starts with the male strutting before his mate in a stiff, ritualised way. Both birds then ascend vertically on rapidly flickering wings changing position relative to each other as they rise, facing and screaming at each other, one bird rather above the other, and remaining at a tense apex until the tension breaks and they return to the shingle.

There is always almost too much here – the birds, the sea and changing light, the absorbance of elements into each other, the huge imaginative experience. Solitude is essential here, not only for hearing the true song of this place but also ultimately to divest oneself of the cerebral processes of ornithology. They remain the same birds whatever names we call them to satisfy our sense of organisation and place in the nature of things. In its essence this is just a wild place for plants and wild creatures and for submitting to the irresistible tug of an ancient reciprocation, call and answer.

20 May

The last two days have been cooler, with much rain and rain again this morning. The river still races under the bridge and it's midafternoon before the flooded meadows recede sufficiently to see if anything has happened to the Swans, whose nests are always vulnerable under these conditions. A few Swallows hawk the meadows, but of Swifts there's been no sign for a couple of days. The combination of warm and damp has brought into flower one of the little floral curiosities of the riverside footpath, a relatively recent introduction from North America, the attractive Pink Purslane, its common name describing the delicate porcelain-like appearance of its petals. Botanical authorities give its scientific name, strangely, as either *Claytonia* or *Montia siberica*. On the footpath it seems to like damp, shady positions, often growing among the toes of large trees and one of its local curiosities is that, although it is a perennial, it never appears in the same place two seasons running, so finding it every year always brings a pleasant surprise.

Several Black-headed Gulls revolve slowly on the swollen middle tarn, but there's no sign of the grebes. The Mute Swan pen swims up from the bottom tarn towards what was their nest but is now merely a half sunken, soggy heap of waterlogged rush leaves and stems. She seems unwilling to leave this sad pile and begins to pick up pieces of floating vegetation, passing them back along her side on to what was the nest rim and the buttressing support structure. She performs all the motions of nest-making and tending, picking stuff out from the water and passing it back along her side in ritualised movement. The cob comes to join her but remains some yards away, preening, as if totally unconcerned about the ritual being performed by his mate. It's interesting that, whereas both birds work together in the original nest-building, the cob actually collecting the nest material and passing it back to the pen for her to place, he may well not be programmed to work at a second structure, somehow 'knowing' that she's already sat on the original nest incubating her eggs to approaching full term. The pen adds structure whilst incubating and carries out repairs to the nest when she returns to brood after an absence for feeding. The cob sails away leaving her still working hard, pulling quantities of soggy vegetation from the surrounding water, rapidly rebuilding quite a sizeable structure.

Twenty minutes later she's made a considerable difference to the mound. Even when she's some yards removed she still performs the same ritualised movements of picking material from the water surface – the stretch, pick and pass back actions made when actually working on the structure itself. All this must surely be pure reflex stimulated by her proximity to the nest. If the eggs are still in the cup they'll be cold and dead, and she's doing what she's doing because it's programmed behaviour when near the nest and still bonded to it. She gradually moves away until it's as if she reaches some critical distance at which she becomes freed of this apparently programmed ritual. Perhaps, too, having reached this 'barrier' which seems to give her freedom, it will mark her last association with this failed nest? The cob is way down by the Nab cut into the bottom tarn, almost as if waiting for her to swim down the length of the lake to join him.

26 May

Having been away for four or five days, days of very mixed, wet weather, it was obvious that I'd missed nothing better and was returning to much of the same! However, the evening seems set fair and I head out for Fletcher. My way takes me past the top tarn where, to my astonishment, both Swans are yet again (nearly a week later!) present at their former nest site. It's fascinating how this pre-conditioned reflex works all along the line from gonadal readiness stimulated by increasing increments in spring light to brooding and rearing a nestful of youngsters. It is so strong that even a definite break in the sequence – in this case being flooded out whilst on eggs – determines a continuity of motivation and response which, although now, surely, getting weaker, remains powerful enough to draw these birds back to the site of a quite specific point in that sequence, although there is not the same obsessive, reflex ritual – on the part of the pen, particularly – that is re-building, as observed on the earlier occasion.

Many birds take advantage of the humid, insect-laden air, feeding young, some of which just having left the nest are still at the stage of more or less staying put where they were told. On a bit of muddy gravel near the lake shore three fledgling Pied Wagtails explore their immediate vicinity whilst waiting for their parents to return – which they do frequently – their full bills whiskered with insects. Every action of the youngsters seems dominated by the non-stop enthusiasm with which they wag their tails, whilst the remaining little tufts of down above their eyes emphasise their extreme youth and vulnerability. In a willow overhanging an old mossy wall, a party of four very streaked and spotty fledgling Redstarts waits patiently until galvanised into a noisy response by the arrival of the female with a beakful of caterpillars. My attention, however, is really taken by a Wren singing its full song as it flies over the tarn. It came as a real surprise the first time I observed this because such song, the full territorial output, is always, perhaps mistakenly, associated with utterance from one of a series of perches specifically designated by the bird for this purpose. The song elicited no response.

The greater part of Fletcher consists of oak, in this mellow evening light still retaining that yellowish clarity as if the whole wood were dusted by the shed pollen of its flowers. A Buzzard sails up over the skyline mobbed by a single Jackdaw. It isn't living as dangerously as it looks, slipping with great manoeuverability from beneath the snatching talons of the Buzzard and maintaining a raucous corvid mobbing call. The Buzzard soars, circling, not quite tolerating the animated tossing and diving attentions of the 'daw', the stately slowness of the one emphasising the manic activity of the other in a peculiar balance so that they appear to be not actually moving over the ground at any speed at all. Suddenly some critical point is reached and this noisy conflict ends abruptly. The Jackdaw breaks away back over the wood in a series of ritualised swooping 'steps'; the Buzzard continues soaring. It has the two central tail feathers and the inner primaries on each wing missing, suggesting that this might be the female of the local pair. She can begin her moult whilst sitting, whereas the hunting male needs all his unimpaired flight capacity to hunt for her whilst incubating and brooding small young as well as feeding them. They will be only about a week old now, but she'll be glad to stretch her wings after the long days and nights sheltering them from the heavy rains.

One's only true companion when out in the field, in my experience, is one's own shadow – it never talks, nor makes unwelcome noise and is a constant reminder that the utmost caution in movement is always essential. A shadow is one's mentor of stealth and silence, and a long morning or evening shadow can mean the difference between seeing and not seeing. It seems impossible to have everything together and at hand all at the same time – 'quarry', notebook, binoculars, camera, recorder, etc. Young birds and busy parents abound within the wood, particularly at those interfaces of clearing and tree which permit rather more diversity than under the closed canopy. I'm behind a wall watching the busy activity of a family of four young Mistle Thrushes which, although now well able to fly, seem quite content to walk and run about the clearing taking green caterpillars which appear to be their food of choice. Their parents come and go, still in protective attendance, though not feeding them. Suddenly the intimacy of this peaceful scene is shattered and the youngsters freeze, their unseen parents scolding furiously. They're hounding a Tawny Owl, moving it on gradually, a shadowy flickering through a thicket of hazels and birch poles. The owl, though harried, won't be hurried despite the persistence and determination of these zestful thrushes. Eventually the owl drops down the far side of the wall into the mottled litter of last autumn's dead leaves, relying on its cryptic fruit-cake colours to hide it away from the inconvenience of the mobbing birds and quite unaware of my crouching presence beyond the wall. It obviously worked, for although the thrushes continued to fuss and scold, they had lost the owl. A loose twig moved under my weight and, alerted to possible danger from my side of the wall, the owl elevated itself – there is no other word – in complete silence up to a hazel branch level with my eyes at a distance of a mere ten feet, and there it stayed and stared. The evening sunlight emphasised the rich creamy-whites on its breast, each feather delicately and darkly shafted, and staring from that great round head enormous eyes, deep purple rimmed pools, unafraid, indifferent. Those eyes draw one in, dark moongates inviting passage through and beyond into a totally 'other' consciousness and dimension, portals at the interface between the fading realities of daylight and thrush and the waxing realities of night and the utterly unclassifiable otherness of owl. Passing through those moongates for just a few seconds, the world re-adjusts and alters forever, I becoming visible to the owl as equally 'other' and alien. Thus it stared for a full fifteen seconds. It watched, unmoving, as I raised binoculars – a futile, foolish gesture! – after which it slipped silently, a brown shadow, to a more distant part of the wood where other small birds took up the challenge. It had allowed me not only to look but also to see, raise glasses, fiddle, all without moving – and I had my camera in my bag! Perhaps that was fortuitous, for all I would have acquired would be merely another photograph 'captured' through the barrier of yet another piece of glass, instead of by the lens of the greater truth of imagination.

It's later now, nearly 9pm, Venus clear and bright climbing above Lingmoor and the evening approaching what Henry Williamson called 'dimmity', a kind of glowing indigo grading up darker from the reflected sea-shine beyond the western hills. At the top of the wood there is quite a large clearing, part clear-felled, part cluttered with wind-blows and tangled bracken. A few silhouetted Long-Eared Bats flicker just above the trees between the frontier of wood and sky. Watching their aerial dexterity and their intersecting flight-lines gradually becomes almost hypnotic, until this semi-dreamlike state is jolted awake by a solitary roding Woodcock. Heard before seen, his typically erratic passage on slow, rhythmic wing strokes takes him just above tree height along one edge of the clearing on what must be a circuit of his territory. I wait, hoping to see him again on a second loop, but nothing happens. Some minutes later, however, there's a pair of Woodcocks, the male having 'picked up' the female for a joint flight on tremulous wings and uttering a strange kind of whistling. Woodcocks need a dry area in which to nest and an availability of soft, marshy ground for their crepuscular feeding – the meadows at the top of the watershed, towards which they are heading now, are ideal places.

28 May

9.15pm – It's a fine evening up here on the watershed, luminous almost beyond belief as the unseen western sea, only a dozen miles distant at the far end of Eskdale, gives back to the sky a quality of light which seems an accumulation of all that's been shed upon it during the day. Although dusk is gathering down in the valley, up here there is a radiance spread from the west and up into a beautifully graded darkening indigo. I've come up to the watershed to follow up the Woodcocks of a couple of days ago. It's always good to be fairly high as evening draws on, somewhere midway between the valley and the high peaks, for there's a special dimension to the silence seeping up like quiet smoke from meadow to mountain, an exhalation so that one can almost hear the high fells draw evening around them as they settle to sleep. A pair of Crows is still active in the wood behind me. One calls – the usual territorial bellow – whilst the other responds with a series of staccato 'call notes', rather like those sometimes uttered in flight. I can also hear snatches of what can only be called 'sub-song' in this context, strange creaky notes and a rapid percussive 'tocking'; the whole sequence is then repeated. What an extraordinary patterned sort of conversation, almost like a kind of vocal ritual – Crows are astonishing birds! When they stop, the aftermath of silence resonates around the marshy watershed until its ripples gradually subside to a new level of stillness.

I have missed the unobtrusive and, on this occasion, silent arrival of the Woodcocks at their feeding ground, but they've obviously not been down long and are still very restless and watchful before feeling secure enough to settle and feed. I find that an effective way of maximising visual efficiency in waning light is to hold the eyes open for as long as possible before blinking so that all the available light floods onto the retina. This gradual accommodation enables things – at first unseen – to begin to reveal themselves. Thus I gradually become aware of a small, white disembodied shape moving erratically up the flush of rushes towards the Woodcock. I move a foot fractionally to ease pins and needles; there's the merest whisper of grass rustle, and the white blob stops moving, and as I listen there's the strange sensation that something is also listening to me – an acute linked awareness in which the 'listener' moves in the sound shadow of your movement. Suddenly that disembodied pale shape floating up the drain resolves into a fox with a white-tipped tail stalking the Woodcock feeding around the marshy origins of the drain. The short tussocks of grass which form the dominant vegetation are the birds' only cover. The fox will have to creep up the drain and make a lightning pounce if he's to succeed in his Woodcock hunt. Despite the skill of his creeping, belly-to-ground stalk, the Woodcock, with their specialist all-round vision, catch the parting of the reeds at the top of the drain and are off before he has a chance to pounce. The successful strike-rate of any predator imposes a phlegmatic acceptance of failure. The fox stands a moment, shakes his fur and trots up towards the edge of Blackwood where a late Pheasant is still crowing.

30 May

A warm afternoon after some hours of rain. The quality of light, though, is slowly changing. It's not a clear light – there's a haze over the hills, a recessive milky fume, and even the nearer hillsides seem hazed over, a suggestion of 'atmosphere' softening edges and blending tones as if under some vaporous exhalation from the vast acres of green brackens now smothering the fell and tall enough in places to overhang the network of little footpaths and sheep trods which run all over the Common. Sure signs of late spring beginning its slow decline into summer are the first plumy heads of Cotton Sedge, blowing like little, white banners which will soon become a spectacular massed feature of all the marshy depressions on the Common. Its more descriptive, imaginative Gaelic name is *siodha monah*, or 'mountain silk', reflecting its bygone use for spinning and stuffing mattresses and pillows. The first pink-tinged Bog Pimpernels also indicate a coming change of season. Violets are numerous, but they must be approaching the end of their spring flowering – if conditions are right they may have a second, later bloom. The curiously named Jack-by-the-Hedge, or Garlic Mustard because of the smell given off by its leaves when bruised, stands up straight and tall anywhere where there's enough vegetation to give it backing, almost rivalling the brackens in its speed of growth.

Back in Rob Rash the canopy is closing rapidly and the Bluebells are almost over, but bright stars of Yellow Pimpernel wind through the darkening ground cover, and the easily missed hairy stems of Herb Bennet lift their delicate, yellow flowers into the upper shade to remind us yet again that the countryside and its wild herbs played a vital part in the relationship of medieval man to his environment. Its old title, *herba benedicta*, the blessed herb, indicates something of its use in an age when the Devil was known to be ever-present and anything which served to divert his intentions was indeed blessed. Hung by the door, its pungent clove-smelling roots

288

were a powerful weapon against the intrusion of evil, and a man who carried such a root with him was said to be immune to attack by any venomous beast. Out among the reeds in the wetter margins of the wood wave the tall bright banners of the wild iris, named after the brilliant Greek messenger of the gods whose personification as the rainbow connected earth with heaven. Although once known, because of its leaves, as the gladdon, from the Latin *gladiolus* – little sword – its common name, Flag, carries with it a brave flavour of the fourteenth century – for it was so-called at the time of the Battle of Otterburn in 1388. It's almost as if nature provides these bright accents as torches by which we may navigate both our once much more meaningful association with wild nature and the inexorably gathering shadows of approaching summer, for these flashes of bright colour are everywhere.

Among the clumps of soft rush and coarse grasses by the sitting stones glows yet another torch – Ragged Robin. Its generic name, *lychnis*, from the Greek, literally means 'lamp' because of the contrast between the brightness of its flower and its growing habitat. It was also said to have brought the light of love to those who carried it on their persons. The word 'ragged' describes perfectly the tattered appearance of its cleft petals, but the name 'Robin' is more obscure, perhaps relating to ancient folklore associations, among which are the legends of Robin Goodfellow, otherwise known as Puck, and immortalised by Shakespeare in *A Midsummer Night's Dream* as a mischievous nature spirit responsible for all kinds of trouble from curdling milk to harassing young maidens. It seems likely that the name Puck is a European derivative of that protective, but rather priapic Mediterranean nature divinity worshipped in Greece 1,400 years before Shakespeare, and whose very name reflects the universality of his following – Pan – that "Piper at the Gates of Dawn", yet again revealing an erstwhile integration of man with his natural environment. Ragged Robin's specific name, *flos-cuculi*, translates as 'cuckoo-flower', indicating both its and the Cuckoo's conspicuousness as spring winds down to the beginning of summer. This is a message reinforced on the river bank where just by the sitting stones is a spreading, sky-blue, white-eyed bed of Germander Speedwell – "Speed-well!", so called because of the readiness with which the petals fall off once picked, and thus associated with departure. It brings me to my own intended point of departure as the Cuckoo's voice begins to break and morning bird-song heralds in new generations, and the forwards procession of summer flowers in wood, field and hedgerow also traces back the history of our relationship with a living landscape.

It was never my intention to bring this account forward into summer for mainly practical reasons. Firstly, to have described the full calendar year would have produced a prohibitively unwieldy text; by keeping it within the bounds of my own favourite months, I hope that error may have been avoided. Second, the Lake District earns its living by mass tourism, and Elterwater and Great Langdale, because of the fine walking and magnificent landscape quality they offer, become a veritable honeypot from Easter onwards to the end of autumn. Environmental disturbance and destruction is an ever-increasing problem. An ever-shrinking habitat does not promote an ease of inconspicuousness and observation possible in other seasons. Many of the wanderings described utilise the comprehensive network of local public footpaths and such itineraries may easily be traced by reference to the text in conjunction with an OS map. There are, however, within the text, a few named places along my many years' discovering this place, as significant to me as were the named 'stations' along the imprisoned Bunyan's path to glory. Thus, via the Tanglewood, Ashes Point, the Gateway Oaks, various sitting stones and the Watershed, one arrives finally at those Delectable Pastures where I have sat for so many hours. None of these places will be found in any map! Also, over the years, and by the generosity of local landowners, I have had permission to wander freely over areas not generally available to public access; such explorations have yielded up precious, unfrequented places off the public path and I wish to keep them that way for their sake as well as mine. This becomes increasingly difficult in summer when there are eyes and feet everywhere!

The temptation is to view the great annual seasonal cycle as having symmetry – two active seasons in which things happen – the spring rise and the autumn fall – and two resting seasons – the withdrawal of winter and the somnolence of summer – but this is illusion. Summer, particularly, is a season in which boundaries become blurred and obfuscated – death with life, light with darkness. It is the one season in which things are neither beginning nor ending, save for the prodigality of new life and the extravagance of its little deaths. J.A. Baker's masterpiece, *The Peregrine*, says everything much more pithily, and there is a short paragraph I would adapt for the present purpose, "I have turned away from the musky opulence of the summer woods where so many birds are dying. Autumn begins my season…spring ends it, winter glitters between like the arch of Orion." It is a curious paradox that as the summer sun rises ever higher, ever brighter, whilst grasses are shedding their extravagant profusion of pollen, whilst flowers everywhere are ripening towards the culmination of seed, whilst every component of the landscape from lake to fell is bursting with new life, that same landscape becomes ever darker, the shadows deeper. The woodland canopy loses its spring loveliness of contrasting tender greens and delicacy of form, becoming more uniform, hardening off and prone to many diseases. Yes, young life is abundant after the productivity of spring, but whatever is young and born must find its way of avoiding a multitude of summer deaths lurking in the darkest shadows of the year, for these are full of restless spirits far less domesticated than those attending a nestful of eggs or young. Summer is the season for the terrible beauty of selection and death, for learning how to kill whether you are a Blue Tit or a Peregrine. Once the imperatives of territory, mating and rearing young, are over, the adult birds, too, lose their song, subsiding into a long silence, most of them until the following spring.

This is all the Great Dance, but I needed to end this adventure with an up-beat on a rising step and with the birds still in full song!

Epilogue

Since the publication in 1859 of Darwin's *On The Origin of Species*, some of the most vital conservation debates have centred around the question of where man properly fits into the natural scheme of things, a question perhaps more vital now than at any other time during the long history of man on this precious earth, for on our answers and subsequent actions depends the future. Incredibly, here in the twenty-first century it is still either unacceptable or distasteful to a great many people that as humans, as primates, classified as *Homo sapiens* and belonging to Phylum Chordata means that just as we share about 98% of our genetic material with Chimpanzees at one end of the scale, so do we also share in excess of 70% with such very primitive marine organisms as Sea Squirts at the other. Theoretically, within the biosphere we inhabit there exist no boundaries between the human and the non-human, yet within the imperatives of our almost exclusively homocentric lifestyle there would appear to be an ever-accelerating urgency to alienate ourselves from the implications of our phylogeny and from the embarrassment of dilemmas and responsibilities such a genetic legacy entails.

It takes our artists and poets to "see clearly into the heart of things". John Constable, that incomparable, wise genius of rural landscape and the life portrayed therein, always ensured that his figures – ploughmen, harvesters, boat-builders, drovers, shepherds and waggoners, children even – were depicted in total harmony with the nature and seasonal cycle they inhabited. Far from portraying an idyllic, romanticised vision of life, his work should be seen as an expression of an accurately observed reality. Constable once defined his figures not as compositional components but rather as "creatures in a landscape", thus by his very choice of words endowing them with a biological link with the natural world they serve. Within his apparently simple statement is, in fact, contained the whole span of geological time, the evolution of species and the emergence of man, the history of his imposed changes in land use and relationship with his natural environment. The further implication of Constable's statement is that the history of landscape and that of mankind are inextricably linked and, further, that any deterioration of landscape values inevitably reflects a corresponding degradation of human cultural values. We have allowed the despoliation of so much original wilderness and extinction of species, whilst deluding ourselves into believing that many of the clever technological advances, inventions and devices we admire so much as being essential to the organisation of our daily lives actually enhance our definition of 'reality' and sense of humanity. In reality, indeed, they offer us very little in terms of what it means to be but "creatures in a landscape".

The revolution in outdoor equipment and technology has played a major part in enabling ever more people an ever-increasing re-connection to the countryside in one form or another. However, the quality of management and planning for such mass-tourist assaults on our landscape and fragile eco-systems has yet to be evaluated in terms of long-term viability. The balance between the values of re-connection and the sustainability of the landscapes and eco-systems under pressure is everywhere fraught with huge problems and conflicting priorities. The conversion of such vulnerable and valuable areas into marketing brands and mass-tourist attractions contains the very real danger of obscuring our understanding of the realities and values inherent within them. What is certain is that we have lost much original wilderness; equally certain is that almost everywhere there is a touch of wilderness somewhere. The question remains how best to regain some sense of personally meaningful touch with what we understand as the 'wild', a reality forever eluding definition and intellectual comprehension, but which we recognise as embracing the butterfly on a bit of waste-ground bramble flower as much as the eagle soaring over Rannoch Moor. It is still possible to establish some kind of meaningful relationship with wildlife and its habitat as a medium for recovering something of that lost essential touch with the natural world by which we as humans are defined, so that we can re-affirm the correspondence of river with blood, rock with bone, flesh with the very cladding of the earth.

Becoming involved in Natural History interests of one kind or another is one way, developing an involvement in one or a variety of disciplines to whatever depths of expertise and sense of environmental responsibility suit the individual. But Natural History – i.e. knowing *about* nature, the disciplined, intellectual study of its multitudinous forms and their complex inter-relationships inhabiting the wild – and *knowing* nature – those moments of gnosis gained via intense, revelatory connections with what Wordsworth calls "unknown modes of being", and Lawrence simply as "otherness" – are not necessarily synonymous. At the end of the day, if all that remains to us is life in the mind – "our brains sucking all the blood out of our hearts", to slightly misquote Yeats – then we will have cut the connections that bind us more subtly to our ancestral organic origins, foregoing that essential imaginative leap of truly awakened perception which, perhaps takes artists like Constable, or, more recently, perhaps, those extraordinary visionary Pembrokeshire paintings by Graham Sutherland, works in which the simplest organic elements form the components of what Edward Sackville-West calls "his non-scenic vision of landscape," and Sutherland himself once commented on the totality of his felt intimacy with the various organic landscape components with which he was engaged; or writers such as Hardy, Lawrence or Hughes to articulate for us – our Virgils in the dark thickets of denial and non-understanding – Coleridge wrote, "The Imagination I consider to be the power and prime agent in all human perception". However much we classify, count and evaluate it is surprisingly difficult to travel beyond species identification and its ancillary disciplines to a more visceral recognition of that 'otherness' which is the essential non-human characteristic of the wild, whether this be represented by a blade of grass or a Humpback Whale, a process rendered all the more difficult because of the paradox of making this imaginative leap whilst simultaneously acknowledging our essential phylogenetic relationships, but I would suggest that long hours of solitude in the field are a first and essential ingredient.

This book has been an attempt to weld together various personal aspects of, and adventures in, natural history study with poetry, music, the arts, mythology, folklore together forming a series of portals, interfaces – call them what you will – so that what begins as an observation of something in the 'wild', becomes something bigger, other, more meaningful to us as "creatures in a landscape", more than the sum of its constituent parts, with a heightened consciousness of what the wild means and what is our part in it, and offering the potential for a much enriched sense of personal completion.

Windermere, 2013

Acknowledgements

The firm belief that Acknowledgements should be both concise and much better and more logically placed at the end of the text together with the Bibliography (thus causing no un-necessary or distracting intervention between Title, Contents and Text) in no way detracts from their importance or sincerity.

The short extracts from
1) *The Rest Is Noise, Listening to the Twentieth Century* © Ross, A., 2008
2) *The Lake District* ©Pennington, W. and Pearsall, W.H. 1972
3) *The Peregrine* © Baker, J.A., 1967
are reprinted by kind permission of Harper Collins, Publishers Ltd. Thanks also to Faber and Faber for kind permission to quote from
i) *The Waste Land*
ii) *Ash Wednesday* and *Dry Salvages* (from *Four Quartets*)
All from *Collected Poems, 1909-1962*, Eliot, T.S.
Also to Faber and Faber for kind permission to quote extracts from the following poems from *Collected Poems*, Ted Hughes; ©The Estate of Ted Hughes, 2003.
i) from *Hawk Roosting* (*Lupercal*-1960) and
ii) from *Buzzard*, and *Bullfinch* (*A Primer of Birds*, 1981)

Many thanks also for kind permission to quote from *The Sound Approach to Birding – A Guide to Understanding Bird Sound* © Mark Constantine, The Sound Approach, Poole, 2006.

I would like to offer grateful thanks to Drs. Nicola and Hugh Loxdale at Brambleby Books for their editorial skills, patience and encouragement – I hope this end product justifies their initial enthusiasm!

Finally, to my wife, Audrey, who would absolutely hate it if I expressed much more than my most heartfelt gratitude and appreciation for her patience, encouragement and belief.

Bibliography

Acworth, B. (1946) *The Cuckoo and Other Bird Mysteries*, Eyre & Spottiswoode, London.

Attenborough, D. / BBC (2009) *The Life of Birds*, BBC, London

Baker, J.A. (1967) *The Peregrine*, Collins, London

Brown, L. (1976) *British Birds of Prey*, New Naturalist Series, Collins, London

Brown, L and Amadon, D. (1968) *Eagles, Hawks and Falcons of the World*, (2 Vols) Hamlyn, for Country Life Books, London

Browning, G.H. (1952) *The Naming of Wild Flowers*, Williams and Norgate, London.

Buntin, T.F. (1993) *Life in Langdale*, T.F. Buntin

Couzens, D. (2006) *The Secret Lives of British Birds*, Christopher Helm, London

Coward, T.A. (1950) *The Birds of the British Isles*, Warne, London.

Delacour, J. and Scott, P. (1954) *Waterfowl of the World*, (4 Vols) Hamlyn, for Country Life Books, London

Fisher, J. and Lockley, R.M. (1954) *Sea-Bird*, New Naturalist Series, Collins, London

Greenoak, F. (1979) *All the Birds of the Air*, Andre Deutsch, London

Grey, V. (1926) *Falloden Papers*, Constable, London

Grey, V. (1927) *The Charm of Birds*, Hodder and Stoughton, London

Guirand, F. (Ed.), Graves, R. (1959) *Introduction to Larousse Encyclopedia of Mythology*, Hamlyn, London.

Hudson, W.H. (1910) *A Shepherd's Life*, Reprint by Macdonald Futura, London

Hutchison, M (1985) *Cumbrian Birds: A Review of Status and Distribution 1964-1984*, Frank Peters, Kendal.

Jeffries, R. (1878) *The Gamekeeper at Home*, Reprint by Oxford Books, 1948

Jeffries, R. (1879) *The Amateur Poacher*, Reprint by Oxford Books, 1948

Lack, D.L. (1946) *The Life of the Robin*, Reprint by Pelican Books, London, 1953

Lack, D.L. (1956) *Swifts in a Tower*, Methuen, London

Macpherson, H.A. (1892) *A Vertebrate Fauna of Lakeland*, David Douglas, Edinburgh (Reprint by P.B. Minet, Buckinghamshire, 1972)

McClintock, D. and Fitter, R.S.R. (1955) *Collins Pocket Guide to Wild Flowers*, Collins, London

Madge, S. and Burn, H. (1988) *Wildfowl, an Identification Guide to the Ducks, Geese and Swans of the World*, Christopher Helm, London

Page, C.N. (1988) *Ferns*, New Naturalist Series, Collins, London

Pearsall, W.H. and Pennington, W. (1973) *The Lake District*, New Naturalist Series, Collins, London

Peterson, R., Mountfort, G. and Hollom, P.A.D. (1965) *A Field Guide to the Birds of Britain and Europe*, Collins, London

Rickards, G. (1997) *Jean Sibelius*, Phaidon, London

Ross, A. (2008) *The Rest is Noise – Listening to the Twentieth Century*, Harper Collins, London

Simms, E. (1983) *A Natural History of British Birds*, Dent, London

Stokoe, R. (1962) *The Birds of the Lake Counties.* Transactions of the Carlisle Natural History Society, Volume 10.

Society Ed. Stott, M., Callion, J., Kinley, I., Raven, C. and Roberts, J. (2002) *The Breeding Birds of Cumbria A tetrad atlas 1997-2001*, Cumbria Bird Club

Thorburn, A. (1925) *British Birds*, Longmans Green and Co

Waterhouse, M. (1996) *A Wandering Voice: A Diary of Birdsong*, Bellew Publishing Co Ltd., London

White, G. (1789) *A Natural History of Selborne*, Reprint by Penguin Books, London, 1977

Wilson, J. (1974) *The Birds of Morecambe Bay.* Dalesman Books, Clapham, Yorkshire.

Other books by Brambleby Books

Arrivals and Rivals – A duel for the winning bird
Adrian Riley
ISBN 9780954334796

UK500: Birding in the fast lane
James Hanlon
ISBN 9780954334789

Winging it – Birding for Low-flyers
Andrew Fallan
ISBN 9780955392856

The Ruffled Edge – Notes from a Nature Warden
Pete Howard
ISBN 9781908241061

Birduder 344 – A life list ordinary
Rob Sawyer
ISBN 9781908241092

British and Irish Butterflies
Adrian Riley
ISBN 9780955392801

Bird Words – Poetic images of wild birds
Hugh D. Loxdale
ISBN 9780954334734

Scilly Birding – Joining the madding crowd
Simon Davey
ISBN 9781908241177

www.bramblebybooks.co.uk

304